HOLISTIC GUIDE TO
HEALTH AND SELF-AWARENESS

HOLISTIC GUIDE TO HEALTH AND SELF-AWARENESS

Jacqueline Blackett SRN, PhD.

Copyright © Jacqueline Blackett 2007

First published in 2004
Second Edition - Published 2007 by Jacqueline Blackett

British Library Cataloguing-in-Publication data
A catalogue record for this book is available from the British Library
ISBN 978-0-9556106
Printed by Chandlers Print, Bexhill-on-Sea

FOREWORD

Jacqueline Blackett's authoritative medical work is more than simply an extremely accessible exploration of health issues. It includes a far reaching discussion of important faith issues, popular culture and black identity to produce a holistic motivational guide to self-help for all 'races'.

Blackett makes a powerful case for more diverse health provision through complementary therapies and responsiveness to patient requests and needs. The medical profession is not to be presumed to be king.

The book draws on extensive research that is illustrated and developed by Blackett's personal experience as a nurse, carer, complementary practitioner and patient. Existing conventions and trends are challenged using bursts of comic material.

'Man, know thyself' is the driver of Blackett's thesis, asserting the importance of self-identity. However, the book also seeks a re-examination of, and pride in, black identity. It emphasises the importance of our personal and social history and journeys in our present well-being and acts as a rallying cry to community self awareness and belief as a resource to personal health, fulfilment and self-respect. As a society we are requested to pay greater attention to protecting the natural world for the benefit of all and to achieve particular health benefits.

Our mental state is key to our physical health. There is a strong moral code underpinning Blackett's arguments that reflects a view of rights and responsibilities, including the role of the parent in educating the child. The challenge is most forceful when focused on the role of the black male in the family and the benefits of two-parent households. We are asked to develop self-love to challenge historical myths of inferiority, but to be reflective of our progress and our failings and to tackle our weaknesses.

Blackett has outlined the building blocks of a healthy life system; our beauty, health and strength come from within and from balance in the natural world. This is a book that draws on identity and humanity to challenge us to adopt a better and more knowing path to health. You will probably not agree with everything that you read, but you will undoubtedly be stimulated by the arguments presented to you.

Richard Tomlins
Professor of Race, Diversity and Housing
De Montfort University

TESTIMONIALS

Speaking as a Librarian, with many years of experience helping people find information on health and medical conditions, I welcome Jacqueline Blackett's book and I am sure it will be a useful addition to the range of health books available.

I know that the author is a determined and thorough person who has put all her heart and dedication into producing a book that will help people prevent, as well as deal with, common diseases and conditions. I wish her well and hope that the book succeeds in its aims.

Fiona Marriott
Principal Librarian, Luton Libraries

A well written book making reference to every aspect of healing which is beneficial for Christians and non-Christians alike. The author speaks of spirituality which provides her with a quality of understanding and empathy that she needs in order to help others.

Brother Andrew
World Healing Crusade

I find this work exceedingly uplifting. Not only does the author painstakingly explain her subject matter, every aspect of her work makes ample sense and is powerfully convincing. This book is a ray of sunshine to everyone, including elderly people like me.

My only regret is that this revolutionary work was not accessible years ago to bring about changes to the lives of mankind.

Doreen Sharp
Caddington, Beds

It was a privilege to have Jacqueline Wendy Blackett as a postgraduate student in our University. Her outstanding knowledge of Health Care in the present context of our society has eminently placed her in a position to author the *Guide to Health and Self Awareness*. The topics are current and obviously would be a great delight to read.

Prof. Anton Jayasuriya
The Open International University for Complementary Medicines

Dr Blackett's book *Holistic Guide to Health and Self Awareness* touches amongst other things Aids, diabetes, high blood pressure, sickle cell, obesity, way of life, counselling and death.

This is a book that will appeal to everyone. It is a 'must read' for anyone with a desire to improve their way of life

Dr Edward E Adams M.B.B.S, L.R.C.P, M.R.C.S

ACKNOWLEDGEMENTS

'ALL WRITING IS A FORM OF PRAYER.' (John Keats).

This book is dedicated to the memory of my dearest departed parents, Conrite and Sheila Halley.

I would also like to express my gratitude to my devoted husband Victor, for his continuous support for me in all my endeavours.

Special thanks to my clients for consenting to be included in this book and to all those who have endorsed my work.

I would also like to thank all those who wholeheartedly offered me support with this project, especially Jerry Waysome, my tolerant computer technician; Maureen Scarlett, Leyton Holgate and Dr Daniel Thompson for critiquing my work on Sickle Cell Disorder; Professor David Barrett of the University of Luton for his advice on the presentation of my work; my 'spiritual mentor' and friend Brother Andrew, of The World Healing Crusade in Blackpool, for his support and for suggesting that I include the chapter on Nutrition. A special thank you to Phillip Day for permitting me to use some of his work in the chapter on Nutrition and the inclusion of 'unnecessary deaths' mentioned in the chapter on Herbal Medicine; Dr Peter Atherton for the chapter on Aloe Vera and Gary Wilson, a dedicated Jehovah's Witness.

I would like to express my profound gratitude to Professor Anton Jayasuriya, Dean of the Open University in Sri Lanka, for his kind gesture of support for this book. I am truly enriched by the depth of scholastic enlightenment from him.

I would like to express my gratitude to Paul Turner, printer at Stonecastle Graphics in England; Ebony Magazine in Chicago and Iyanla Vanzant's 'Inner Visions Worldwide Network' in USA for their kind advice regarding the publication of my work. I was particularly touched by this encouraging message from Alex, Iyanla's executive assistant: 'Don't give up five minutes before the miracle! Have Faith!'

To my 'angelic' friend Margot, wife of Gordon Herbert, a former Assistant High Commissioner of Australia, for her extraordinary hospitability in 'adopting' and granting me (a total stranger) the 'liberty' of staying with her and her family in their seemingly 'palatial' home throughout my studies in Sri Lanka. Margot epitomizes what is commonly perceived as Godliness. May she be richly blessed.

I would like to express my gratitude to the staff at Serendipity for their confidence and optimism in my work.

Thank you to the following people for their encouragement and good wishes: His Excellency Laleshwar K. N. Singh, High Commissioner of Guyana; Lennox Adams and the staff at the Marsh Farm Library.

Lastly, but most importantly, I would like to give praise to God, for giving me courage, strength and determination to accomplish this task.

CONTENTS

INTRODUCTION

This book is a simplistic approach to the identification and treatment of a considerable number of health related problems. However, although I have targeted the black population, many of these problems are applicable to all races.

As a practitioner of complementary medicine in the United Kingdom, I felt obliged to highlight and address some health-related issues.

The idea of writing a book has 'plagued' me for several years, and whether it was a spiritual intuitive conception, or a timely induced motivation, I felt obligated to undertake this challenge after much discussion with my husband and some of my patients, all of whom encouraged and supported me.

During the years of my involvement in nursing and complementary medicine, I have nursed and privately treated thousands of patients. However, I am of the opinion that a vast proportion of those patients would have promoted and maintained a reasonable standard of health if self-help information were more accessible.

I also feel somewhat sympathetic towards overworked doctors whose service is constantly on demand, sometimes for non-urgent 'problems'. Like most of us, some of those doctors have families. They too would like to spend adequate time with their families and loved ones, instead of constantly visiting patients complaining of simple or non-life threatening problems. This leads to insurmountable stress on members of the medical fraternity.

Whilst conducting my research for this project, a consultant physician told me that he was becoming alarmed at the high percentage of black females who were overweight and also suffering from high blood pressure. He stated that from his observation of this particular group of patients, they were the most reluctant to participate in trial programmes set up to encourage weight loss. He further remarked that the reason for non-participation was probably due to the fact that it is customary for women to be 'big' in certain cultures.

However, I personally believe that it is more sensible to be conscious of one's health than to adhere to a cultural tradition that is unhealthy and climatically unsuitable in the West.

In light of the fact that Christianity commands the largest number of followers of religion in the world, consequentially making the Bible the most read book, the inclusion of scriptural references is meant to have a reminding or `play back' effect on people. It is also intended to play a directional part in our quest for health and fulfilment in life, not to prove that I am holier than others. In addition, several of the other main religions of the world have based their concepts on a similar moral code to that of Christianity.

Therefore, as a believer and follower of the teachings of Christ (to my level of maintenance), I believe that my decision to include some Biblical excerpts to substantiate some of the issues in this book is reasonably justifiable.

Today we are witnessing a resurgence of diseases which were once under control. During the 1970s, I administered powerful medication to patients suffering from tuberculosis and a decade later TB was greatly reduced. However, to our astonishment, there are now reports of a rising increase in the number of people suffering from the disease. This is because the responsible organism has become resistant to the spectrum of antibiotics used to fight it. There are also new diseases presenting themselves on the environmental attack and scientists are feverishly working to identify and treat these organisms.

However, although humanity has made astonishing advancement in science and technology, our intellectual development is out of balance with our spiritual and emotional growth. We need to adopt a holistic approach if we are to succeed in minimizing disease, because in reality the spiritual, physical, mental and emotional ordinance of our being do not exist separately; they are part of an integrated inseparable whole. Disease in any unit of that link (i.e. spirit, body, mind and soul) is likely to be manifested in the others.

This book also includes certain relevant aspects of philosophy, psychology, politics and religion, thereby substantiating their positive or negative influences on our health. It also addresses the need for self-awareness. Without self-knowledge, we are destined to be psychologically and spiritually 'lost'.

Finally, this book is not a panacea. It is a selection of self-help theories, treatment and techniques in the prevention of certain conditions. It is therefore advisable to contact your doctor for expert help when faced with serious or doubtful problems.

Jacqueline Blackett SRN, PhD

PART 1

CHAPTER 1

The Causes of Disease

Western Perception

In his forecast of life in the future, the prophet Isaiah assures us:

'And the inhabitant shall not say I am sick.' (Isaiah 33:24). However, until such time as foretold by the good prophet, we must concern ourselves with living healthily, identifying the causes of diseases, and addressing our illnesses by accessing a range of appropriate treatments.

The attainment and maintenance of good health is essential in the prevention of disease. No matter how wealthy we may be, if we are unhealthy our ability to enjoy the wealth that we have amassed will be somewhat limited. Although wealth is important to living comfortably and accessing medical treatment, it does not afford much joy during sickness.

It is therefore imperative for us to attend to our health to the best of our ability. No individual can be expected to be 'super fit' and one hundred per cent healthy until old age; however we can try to make an effort in maintaining a reasonable quality of health.

When there is disease the general health is disturbed. The World Health Organization defined health as 'a state of physical, mental and social well being'. The prefix 'dis' in disease means part or parts of the whole body not being at ease. Therefore, there is discord, tension or conflict within the bodily structure.

Western perception of diagnosing disease is based on finding the cause; this often involves isolation of the organism responsible for causing the disease.

The following is a brief summarization of some of the conditions that can affect different parts of the body:

Organs & Parts of the Body	Diseases/ Medical Conditions
Brain	Meningitis, abscesses, tumours, haemorrhage, Parkinson's disease, psychiatric disorders, Alzheimer's disease, tumours.
Head	Headaches; these may be due to stress, eye problems or migraine. They can also result from symptoms of disease in the brain such as meningitis or tumours.
Eye	Conjunctivitis (pink eyes), cataract, glaucoma, discharge, blindness.
Ears	Infection, earache, discharge, disruption of balance, tinnitus.
Nose	Discharge, bleeding, frequent sneezing due to allergy, inability to smell (anosnia).
Mouth	Halitosis (bad breath), blisters, and ulcers.
Teeth	Ache, decay resulting in bad breath, infection, bleeding.
Tongue	Inflammation (glossitis), heavily coated: this can result from retention of food in the stomach and intestines and certain diseases.
Alimentary or Food Tract	Reflux of food, indigestion, obstruction, ulcers, pain, vomiting, bleeding, diarrhoea or constipation, cancer.
Breast	Mastitis (inflammation), cysts, abscess and cancer.
Lungs	Asthma, bronchitis, TB, pneumonia. Breathlessness resulting from the above.
Heart	Birth defects, enlargement due to disease, angina, irregular heart beat, heart disease, blood clot (thrombosis).
Blood	Anaemia, leukaemia, sickle cell disorder, haemorrhage, clotting.
Liver	Inflammation (hepatitis), jaundice.
Gall Bladder	Gall stones, inflammation (cholecystitis), tumours.
Pancreas	Inflammation (pancreatitis), tumours, diabetes.
Skin	Eczema, psoriasis, shingles, dry or sweaty skin.
Hands and fingers	Arthritis, circulatory problems, clubbing of fingers.
Legs, feet and toes	Arthritis, bow legs, club-foot.
Muscles	Inflammation, myalgia (pain), wasting (myopathy).
Bones	Osteoarthritis, brittlebone, softening, inflammation, cancer.
Joints	Rheumatoid arthritis, too much or too little fluid.
Nerves	Neuralgia (pain), neuritis (inflammation), neuroma (tumour connected with a nerve).
Spinal Discs	Curvature, slipped disc, inflammation, meningitis, crumbling of the discs.
Uterus/Womb	Endometriosis, fibroids, retroverted uterus, cancer.
Testicles	Enlargement, torsion (twisting), hernia, hydrocele (fluid), cancer.
Prostate gland	Enlargement (non-cancerous) and cancer.

There are several causes of diseases according to Western perception. The following are some of the causes identified:

Genetic diseases and congenital abnormalities

Today many cases of inherited diseases have a reasonable chance of life expectancy. Improvement in the quality of the lives of patients who formerly experienced severe suffering, which was often relieved by merciful death, must be mainly attributed to the advancement in knowledge. This includes improvement in diet, genetic counselling, antenatal diagnosis and better living conditions. All of these coincide with the advent of 'Western' or modern medicine and the popular rebirth of complementary (and alternative) medicine, including acupuncture and herbal medicine.

The origin of Western medicine is not as recent as it is made out to be. The Greek physician Hippocrates is accredited as the father of medicine, but as scholars of history would attest, the Egyptian multi-genius Imhotep, who lived around 2890 BC, is the originator of medicine. According to the *Encyclopaedia Britannica*, 'Practitioner Sir William Olser considered him [Imhotep] the first figure of physicians to stand out clearly from the mist of antiquity.'

It is a well-known fact that ancient Egypt was the cradle of civilization. When the Greek general Alexander the Great invaded Egypt, thousands of books were stolen from the Egyptian Mystery system and taken to Greece. As J. A. Rogers stated in his book, *World's Great Men of Colour*, 'When Egyptian civilization crossed the Mediterranean to become the foundation of Greek culture, the teachings of Imhotep were also absorbed there. But as the Greeks were wont to assert that they were the originators of everything, Imhotep was forgotten for thousands of years and Hippocrates, a legendary figure who lived 2000 years after him became known as the father of medicine.'

Some conditions associated with defective genes passed on by ancestors are:

Huntington's chorea. The cause of this disease is unknown. It is a condition in which there are uncontrollable movements and insanity. Each child of an affected parent has a 50–50 chance of developing it.

Cystic fibrosis. This is one of the most common and serious diseases in white people. It affects the mucus secreting glands of the lungs, the pancreas, the mouth, the gastro-intestinal tract and the sweat glands of the skin. Symptoms include failure to gain weight despite a good appetite, frequent bouts of bronchitis and foul smelling slimy stools.

Phenylketonuria (protein deficiency). This is one of the less common, but very serious, forms of mental deficiency. It is due to the inability of the infant to metabolize the amino acid phenylalamine. Phenylketouria can be diagnosed at birth by urine testing or by testing a drop of blood (the Guthrie test). If the affected infant is given a diet low in phenylalamine, there is a good chance of normality.

Haemophilia. This is an inherited disease in which there is prolonged bleeding even after minor injury. This is due to deficiency of Factor VIII, the anti haemophiliac factor, which is essential for blood clotting. This condition requires frequent blood transfusion to enhance blood clotting. The gene responsible for haemophilia is carried by females and 50% of their sons will be affected whilst 50% of their daughters will be carriers. The sons of haemophiliac men are unaffected, but all the daughters carry the trait.

Sickle cell disorder. A chronic inherited blood disorder. (Refer to chapter 2.)

Some other congenital diseases in this category are the so-called diseases of modern society i.e. diabetes mellitus, hypertension and coronary artery disease. It is therefore no wonder that incidence of these conditions is rife amongst members of the same family. Some psychiatric disorders such as schizophrenia and in some cases manic-depressive psychosis also fall under this classification.

Immune deficiency

From conception we are protected against the invasion of harmful organisms. The placenta plays a very important role in providing the developing foetus in the womb with nourishment and immunity. It also serves as a protective barrier against infection reaching the unborn infant.

After birth, breast-feeding strengthens the infant's immunity against diseases. However although it is evident that breast-feeding mothers who pursue a healthy diet are likely to provide an invaluable source of first line nutrition, mothers who choose to provide their babies with bottled milk can be assured that this is adequately enriched with vital nutrition.

Routine immunity against certain diseases is also given to babies, infants and children, either orally (by mouth) or by injection in the form of vaccination. However despite natural and artificial protection, the immune system is not guaranteed total protection against disease.

Some of the prevailing factors responsible for inadequate immune protection against disease are:

- Weak constitution – This may be an inherited factor or the result of malnourishment. People who fall into this category are those with frequent colds, flu, sore throats and other infections.

- Environmental or climatical – Our survival is partially dependent on our adaptability to the environment. We need certain requirements, including the correct amount of oxygen in the air, healthy food and clean water in order to survive.

Temperature control mechanism

Our internal body temperature is kept even by maintaining a balance between the heat produced and the heat lost within the body.

Situated in the brain is a mechanism that is responsible for controlling the heat of the body. This mechanism regulates the body's temperature to cope with prevailing climatic conditions, which is why we sweat and our colour becomes brighter when we are too hot. We shiver, we have goose pimples and we become paler when we are too cold. This is an ingenious way by which the body can adjust to the temperature it requires in order to function adequately. However if we experience extreme variations in weather patterns, in the same way as vegetation is damaged, the human body is also liable to be affected.

I once owned a personal stereo that automatically reversed at the end of one side of the tape and then started to play from the beginning of the other side. I often used the stereo for jogging and mediation. To my utter delight, someone gave me a tape of the late *Otis Redding (who to me is unquestionably one of the greatest soul singers of all time). I flicked the reverse button so often to replay one of my favourite songs, 'Change Gonna Come' (also sung by Sam Cook, another great artist), during my daily jogging sessions, that the reverse button became defective.

A similar principle is applied to our bodies. If the heat regulating system in the brain adjusts the body's temperature to suit the presenting weather conditions too often, it is liable to be damaged, thus it will not operate satisfactorily.

*As in the majority of Otis's works, to me 'Change Gonna Come' is an exceptionally thoughtful rendition of life and love in the world today. To me, it is also a classic ballad for waltzing – hence my attraction to this style of musical composition.

Anyone, especially people of Caribbean and South American origin, would agree with the fact that just as Jamaicans are the grand masters of reggae, Cubans the greatest in the merengue, Brazilians the greatest in samba and Trinidadians the best in steel band, Guyanese are often portrayed as the perfectionists in waltzing. Several people, including some of my European acquaintances, have commented that Guyanese people appear to be excellent demonstrators of the art of waltzing.

Environmental Rape – an obvious cause of climatical changes.

It is unquestionable that man's destruction of the rain forests is one of the foremost contributors to the progressive changes in the environment.

According to *Awake* 1998:

'A reliable analysis on climatic changes came from the Intergovernmental Panel on Climate Change (I.P.C.C). This report was based on the expertise of more than 2,500 climatologists, economists and risk-analysis specialists from 80 countries.

In their 1995 report, the I.P.C.C. concluded that the earth's climate is becoming warmer. The report stated that during the next century, if the situation remains unchanged, it is possible that the temperature could increase by as much as 6.3 degrees Fahrenheit.'

The following are foreseeable for the coming century:

(a) Regional extremes in weather. In some areas, droughts could be longer; in others rainfall could be heavier.

(b) Decrease in health. Disease and death could soar. According to the World Health Organization, global warming could expand the range of insect-borne tropical diseases such as malaria and dengue. (During this decade, there have been reports of sporadic outbreaks of dengue fever in some developing countries. This infection is transmitted to man by the *Aedes aegypti* mosquito.)

There is also a risk of reduced fresh water supplies owing to changes in regional rainfall. Snowfall could cause an increase in water-borne and food-borne diseases and also multiply the amount of parasites on earth. Seasonal changes would consequentially incur a global effect. It is only through education and a united effort that we can change attitudes and hopefully halt the violating of the rain forests.

As Senegalese ecologist Baba Dioum warned: 'In the end we will conserve only what we love; we will love only what we understand; and we will understand only what we are taught.' Source: *Awake*, 8 May 1998.

Infection

This is the condition arising when harmful organisms invade the body. Effects of infection on the body include the following symptoms:

The Nervous System: Headache, tiredness, feeling unwell, insomnia despite feeling drowsy, shivering, delirium and convulsion in some cases.

The Circulatory System: Pale, muddy or yellowish complexion, rapid pulse, irregular heartbeat, cold hands and feet.

The Respiratory System: Rapid breathing, breathlessness, cough and feeling of congestion in the chest.

The Alimentary System: Loss of appetite, frequent intake of liquid (as a result of fever or thirst), dry mouth, furry tongue, nausea and vomiting.

The Excretory System: Sweating or hot dry skin, reduced urination, which is usually brightly coloured, diarrhoea or constipation.

The Muscular System: Aches and general weakness in the muscles.

It is very important to drink large amounts of fluids in order to prevent dehydration. An adequate amount of fluid is beneficial in helping the body's immune system to fight invading organisms.

Some of the main pathways for infections are:

1. Inhalation. This is usually in the form of droplets originating from the back of the throat and in the mouth. These are expelled through talking, sneezing and breathing thereby contaminating others in close proximity. One example of this nature is the common cold and MRSA (multiple resistant staphylococcus aureaus). This virus is usually contracted in hospitals.

Severe Acute Respiratory Syndrome (SARS) is one of the new diseases. It originated in Guangdong Province in China in November 2002. It has since been reported in several countries and has unfortunately claimed a number of lives.

2. Faecal/oral spread. Infection of this nature is spread by eating food and drinking water contaminated by the faeces of a (human) carrier of the infection, as in the case of typhoid. Infection from this source is occasionally the result of low standards in personal hygiene by kitchen workers.

3. Mammals. Animals may spread disease by direct contact with man. Rabies is one of the most dangerous diseases spread by infected animals.

Rabies: This disease, caused by a deadly virus which infects the tissues of the central nervous system and the salivary glands, is one of the most distressing illnesses one will ever encounter. It is a highly infectious disease contracted from a bite by affected animals such as dogs, wolves, foxes, vampire bats and skunks.

According to Black's *Medical Dictionary* 'only one person in every four bitten by a rabid dog contracts rabies, whilst the bites of rabid wolves and cats almost invariable produce the disease'.

Patients develop symptoms within days or weeks of being bitten. There is fever, anxiety, irritability and fear. There is difficulty in eating and, despite thirst, there is an abnormal terrifying fear of water. The mere sight of water sometimes causes spasms in the muscles of the mouth and the throat, hence the alternative name for the disease 'hydrophobia': which is a fear of water.

Later there may be difficulty in breathing, delusions, hallucinations, insane behaviour, spitting and biting. There are times, however, when the patients seem quite lucid and they converse quite rationally. Death from rabies can occur within a week to nine days of contracting the disease. However, owing to recent improved medical interventions, many patients make a satisfactory recovery.

4. Insects. Those responsible for causing infection are primarily the blood-sucking species. The principal infections in this category are malaria, yellow fever and dengue, all caused by mosquitoes.

5. Antenatal transmission. This is infection contracted by the unborn baby in the womb of an infected expectant mother. This was a rare occurrence seen only in such cases as gonorrhoea and syphilis, but since the advent of HIV/AIDS this mode of infection is more commonplace.

6. Transmission by medical and nursing procedures. This form of infection is mainly due to inadequately conducted medical and surgical procedures, contamination of transfusion products and poor sanitation in hospitals. (See chapter on HIV/AIDS.)

7. Soil. Tetanus (lockjaw) is one example of this form of infection. Tetanus is contracted in a wound in which there are the remains of some foreign body such as rust from nails, a splinter of wood or a portion of a bullet. It can also occur in cases of insignificant cuts or abrasions from dirty instruments. The disease is manifested by lengthy painful spasms of voluntary muscles throughout the body.

8. Formites. These are articles such as furniture, bed-clothing, crockery, toys, books, carpets and toilets, which can be receptacles of infection when brought into close contact with a person suffering from an infectious disease such as tuberculosis. Unless they are disinfected, these articles are likely to retain the infectious substance and spread the disease.

9. Sexual contact. If appropriate protective measures are not followed, both heterosexuals and homosexuals can transmit infection during sexual intercourse.

Sexually transmitted infectious diseases

'To the stupid one the carrying on of loose conduct is like a sport.' Proverbs 10:23). This Biblical prophecy has evidently become a truism, particularly since the sexual revolution of the 1960s.

Spread of sexually transmitted diseases

The most obvious contributing factors to the spread of sexually transmitted diseases are promiscuity, drugs, low self-esteem, peer pressure and paedophilia.

If consenting adults are prepared to be adventurous with inappropriate behaviour, then the choice is theirs. There are, however, 'sexual predators' who are prepared to destroy societies by luring and procuring vulnerable innocent children into paedophilia and prostitution. Unless concerted efforts are made by society to halt the baneful tentacles of this immoral practice against children, this evil pursuit will have dangerous repercussion on the future of victims.

A brief discussion of some common sexually transmitted diseases:

Gonorrhea (the clap). This is one of the more common sexual infections. This disease frequently affects the mucous membranes of the urethra, vagina, rectum, throat and eyes. It is caused by the gonococcus or *Neisseria gonorrhoea* bacterium.

Those who are already infected pass on the disease to others. It is mainly passed on through vaginal, anal or oral sex. However, according to Black's *Medical Dictionary*, it can also be passed on through 'French' kissing, and occasionally through 'the discharge on sponges, towels or clothing as well as by actual contact'.

Signs and symptoms of gonorrhoea:

- During the acute stage, men may experience white or yellowish discharge from the tip of the penis, which may be enough at times to stain the underpants.

- There may be scalding pain or discomfort during urinating and the urine is cloudy.

- Yellowish threads of pus may be seen in the urine.

- There is usually itching or discharge from the anus.

- Sore throat.

Most women may have no indications of the disease until the infection has reached the cervix (the neck of the womb). Others may notice pain or discomfort in urinating and an increase in vaginal discharge, which may also become thin and watery, yellow or greenish.

Chlamydia. Apart from HIV/ AIDS, Chlamydia appears to be one of the most rampant sexually transmitted diseases in the UK. The condition is due to infection with a particular type of micro-organism known as chlamydia trachomatis.

The signs and symptoms are similar to those of gonorrhoea, although less severe. In men there may be a discharge from the penis, whilst the infection may be symptomless in women; however it can lead to salpingitis, which is inflammation of the fallopian tubes. That is why it is good practice to test female partners of infected men.

Children born to infected mothers are often infected in the eyes during birth, producing an inflammatory condition known as opthalmia neonatorum. The lungs of the child may also be infected, resulting in pneumonia.

Anogenital herpes simplex. The Herpes Simplex virus is responsible for causing this condition, which has the appearance of cold sores. The virus is spread during sexual intercourse and kissing. Some symptoms of the Herpes

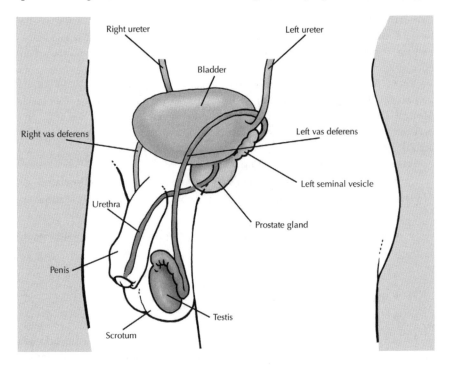

Male sexual organs

Simplex virus include itching and tingling in the genital or the anal area and recurrent crops of small fluid-filled blisters. These burst and leave small painful sores.

With the first infection, they may take two to four weeks to heal properly. There may be fever and flu-like symptoms. The anus of an infected homosexual man is usually affected. Women who are affected with the disease are at risk of infecting their babies at birth.

Hepatitis. There are different types of hepatitis, which is inflammation of the liver cells. On entry to the body, each form attacks the liver, thus causing inflammation and destruction of liver cells. Some of the causes of hepatitis are drugs, chemicals and viral infection.

Hepatitis B is considered the easiest blood borne hepatitis to contract. It is found in high concentration in all body fluids of an infected person. These fluids include blood, urine, saliva, sweat, semen, and breast milk. It can be transmitted through sexual contact, injection, through using contaminated needles or other

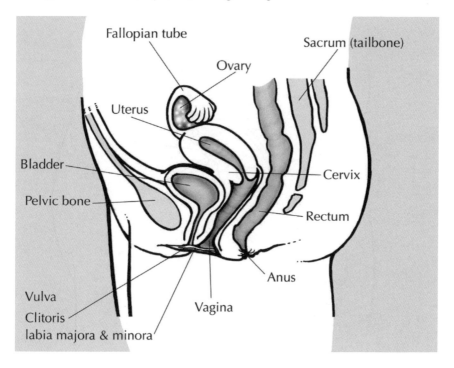

Female sexual organs

skin piercing implements such as tattooing and acupuncture, through infection with contaminated blood as in transfusion, by splashing contaminated fluids into the eyes or mouth, and from mother to baby during pregnancy and breast-feeding.

In over 50% of cases of Hepatitis B, there are no symptoms and the duration of the infection is short. In the remainder of cases there are general aches and pain, loss of appetite, stomach upsets. Some people may develop jaundice. The signs of jaundice include a yellowish colour of the skin and the white of the eyes, dark urine and pale stools.

Recovery can take up to 6 months. A minority of cases may progress to chronic active hepatitis or cirrhosis of the liver.

HIV/AIDS

This disease has so far proven to be the most destructive health crisis ever experienced in the history of humanity.

Some people through lack of information or wrong information assume that if someone is diagnosed with HIV, that person has AIDS. Infection with the HIV virus does not mean that the individual has or will necessarily progress to full blown AIDS.

When was HIV/AIDS discovered?

In 1981 homosexual men in Los Angeles and New York were found to have unusual symptoms of lung infection (pneumocystis carinii pneumonia) and skin tumours called Kaposi's sarcoma. Tests showed that the level of the CD4 cells were extremely low in those patients. Later, it was discovered that people in the United States of America, Western Europe and Africa presented with similar symptoms.

What is HIV?

HIV is the abbreviation for Human Immunodeficiency Virus. The virus attacks and suppresses CD4 or T cells, a type of white blood cell responsible for preparing the immune system to fight infections entering the body. If these crucial white blood cells (lymphocytes) are reduced, the immune system is incapable of protecting the body from disease. HIV infects CD4 and then uses them to make new copies of itself; these new HIVs go on to infect more cells in the body.

What is AIDS?

AIDS is the abbreviation for Acquired Immune Deficiency Syndrome. It results from being infected with HIV. AIDS is the climax or last stage of the HIV infection. However, not everyone infected with the HIV virus will reach that stage. Some people can develop AIDS within a short period of being infected with HIV, whilst others can carry the virus for decades without developing AIDS. However, weakened immunity predisposes people to other infections such as frequent colds and flu, pneumonia, tuberculosis, cancer and meningitis. These conditions, described by some doctors as 'the late stage' or advanced HIV, are indicative of AIDS.

Research conducted in France and the USA during 1983 confirmed that HIV was the causative infectious agent for the disease AIDS.

Who are exposed to HIV/AIDS?

- Anyone participating in unprotected anal sex. Some heterosexuals practise anal sex as a means of birth control. Although the virus affects several categories of people, homosexuals are believed to be one of the high-risk groups affected by this epidemic.

  In his book, *The Truth About AIDS*, Dr Patrick Dixon wrote: 'Anal intercourse has always been known to carry a certain health risk: hepatitis B virus is spread easily by this route and many active homosexuals appear to have chronic low-grade infections of various kinds that may then lower their resistance to HIV.'

- Anyone participating in unprotected sex.

- People infected during unsafe medical procedures such as vaccinations.

- Intravenous drug users such as heroin addicts. This results from using unsterilized needles.

- Heterosexual women whose partners are in the risk groups

- Unborn babies and infants of HIV infected mothers.

- Haemophiliacs can become infected during blood transfusion.

- Other recipients of blood transfusion such as sufferers of sickle cell anaemia, those with other forms of anaemia, people undergoing routine operations, emergency surgical procedures such as accidents resulting in excessive loss of blood, and maternity cases.

Signs and Symptoms of AIDS

Although not everyone infected with the HIV virus would experience any symptoms during the early stage of infection, some develop a flu-like illness lasting for several weeks. The most common symptoms during the initial stage are sore throat, fever, joint and muscle pain and swelling of the glands in the neck.

Some people infected with HIV do not automatically present any evidence of the disease if they are well nourished, in reasonable health, or on antiretroviral drugs (the present treatment for AIDS). Those infected with the virus carry on life as normal for months or years. Then gradually, like poison, the disease takes its toll on the body's weakened immune system, especially in the case of those unfortunate sufferers who are unable to access antiretroviral drugs. Some manifestations of the disease at this stage are:

- Tiredness.

- Minor infections leading to more serious ones, such as oral thrush, meningitis, tuberculosis and pneumonia.

- Chronic unexplained diarrhoea.

- Weight loss becomes more pronounced giving the patient a gaunt appearance. This is why before diagnosis was confirmed, AIDS was known as 'the slim' in Africa.

- Severe pain and high temperature.

- Death. However treatment including antiviral therapy can increase the quality of life, thereby prolonging life.

Despite the pandemic loss of incalculable lives from AIDS, including innocent ones such as infants, children, teenagers, blood recipients and people accidentally infected, some people seem to be least concerned by the virulence of the diseases. Promiscuity remains undaunted by the devastation of this modern day sexually induced plague.

Every conceivable excuse and argument is contrived to justify the unsavoury behaviour of some of today's generation. However as Voltaire remarked: *'Men can argue, but nature acts.'* Yesterday's prophetic words by that reputable Frenchman, are today's sad reality. Unless attitudes are modified, we will not be able to control teenage pregnancies, sexually transmitted diseases including HIV/AIDS and consequently including early death.

Condoms. One of the means of minimizing the risk of contracting the disease is the use of condoms. It is a well-known fact that condoms are not 100% guaranteed. Some are pervious, as is evident in cases where women became pregnant despite their partners wearing 'rubbers'. There is also a marked increase in venereal disease despite the use of condoms by some of those affected.

Not only are condoms likely to have holes in the same way as other appliances made of rubber, they can also be improperly worn sometimes and they can easily slide off. The most realistic safeguard from sexually transmitted diseases is a monogamous relationship and abstinence instead of the use of sex as a form of recreational pastime. Although condoms may afford some degree of protection from sexually transmitted diseases and pregnancies, they cannot provide emotional protection.

None the less, it is advisable to advocate the use of condoms, even if two have to be worn at the same time. People are simply playing Russian roulette with their lives by continuing to participate in unprotected sex. This is not a problem confined to one part of the world; it is pandemic. We must note well – HIV/AIDS virus is no respecter of persons; nor does it discriminate. It is an opportunistic, powerful and 'wicked' virus. Therefore, like the old devil, it would host itself whenever the opportunity arises.

When I was a young child growing up in my native Guyana, if there was any fieldwork to be done in an area infested by mosquitoes, adults would advise the children to stay away. However, the brave adults would undertake the work. Some even applied mosquito repellent to their skin as deterrent from the horrendous bites from these bloodsucking parasites.

It was inappropriate for children to be in those mosquito-infested areas. Not only did children experience more discomfort from the bites, they were also susceptible to more reaction than adults, who had developed immunity because of longstanding exposure to the mosquitoes.

Children as young as twelve and thirteen are offered contraception in schools in England, as a precaution against pregnancies and sexually transmitted diseases. However, they also need to be told that condoms do not provide protection from the other issues associated with premature sexual relationships, such as abandonment and a broken heart.

This quotation by John Barrymore should be a warning to teenagers: *'Sex is not taxed, but it can be taxing.'*

Children should not be encouraged to participate or experiment in sex. This is likely to disrupt the natural progression from childhood to maturity. Consequentially this unnatural 'metamorphosis' may lead to trauma later in life.

Ideally in a society that staunchly encourages and maintains moral and spiritual virtues, children would not have the need to be lectured on condoms at an age when they should be blowing up balloons, or playing with dolls or balls. However, realistically society is not what we would like it to be; therefore at times we have no option but to divert from lecturing on abstinence and teach protection from sexually transmitted disease and pregnancy.

In order to disengage children (both female and male) from contemplating sexual experimentation, they should be encouraged to explore and implement a positive direction in life such as advocated in chapters 12, 14 & 15.

HIV in the UK. A NAM report on 24 November 2003 stated: 'Almost 50,000 have been infected with HIV, according to a report published in advance of World AIDS Day by the UK Health Promotion Agency (HPA).'

NAT, one of the charities actively involved in the war on HIV in the UK, also observed: 'HIV impacts greatest on marginalized groups such as gay men, drug users and Africans living in the UK. NAT seeks to *highlight* the policy changes required to address the social factors which drive the epidemic.'

HIV in Africa. In 2001, according to NAM, another UK based charity:

In seven of eleven studies conducted across Sub-Saharan Africa, more than one in five women under 25 were found to be HIV-positive. Rates of infection in young African women are far higher than those found in young men. Among women under 25 the rate was 3 times higher than in men under 25.

'Young women are much more likely to have sex with or be coerced into sex by older men with more sexual experience. It is these men who place young women at a higher risk of HIV infection. Women are less likely to be able to negotiate safer sex because of the power imbalance between genders. Additionally, women are more likely to be infected during vaginal intercourse. More positive, there is evidence from a number of countries that if children, and especially girls, can delay the age at which they first have sex, they are much less likely to be HIV positive.'

Although HIV/AIDS is a global issue, no other continent has felt the brunt of its destructive rage against mankind more than Africa. Of the 42 million people living with the virus a staggering 28.1 million are in Sub-Saharan Africa. The number of people dying from war, a commonplace occurrence in Africa, is now secondary to those dying from HIV/AIDS. During 1998, an estimated 2 million people died as a result of HIV/AIDS in Sub-Saharan Africa, whilst 200,000 (ten times fewer) died as a result of war.

Sickness and death in such proportions as a result of the HIV/AIDS epidemic is likely to incur catastrophic affects on society. This epidemic is no respecter of people, age or status. It claims the lives of parents, grandparents, aunts and uncles who are responsible for raising and nurturing the children; farmers who provide the food; teachers who educate and guide the children towards a successful future; health carers who help in the prevention and treatment of disease and police who enforce the law and guide the young. Deaths in such proportion are likely to destabilize the national economy. How much more destabilization can Africa withstand?

There are currently over 11 million orphans in Africa resulting from AIDS. With little or no adult supervision and imminent starvation, these unfortunate children are likely to resort to any available means, including robbery, as a means of survival.

Some of the reasons for the escalation of AIDS in Africa

The origin and spread of HIV/AIDS remains a contentious issue. An international team of scientists claimed that only 30% of HIV cases in Africa were sexually transmitted. 'The claim, directly challenging the belief that 90% of cases were sexually transmitted, implies that the African Aids pandemic is largely the result of unsafe medical practices and mismanaged vaccination campaigns.' (*The Times*, 20 February 2003)

Documented evidence has reported that health care is poor, particularly in some rural areas in Africa. African women now residing in the UK have reported that they have observed that needles were rarely changed at mass immunizations in schools and clinics in Africa.

Owing to shortage of skilled doctors and other healthcare professionals and the lack of NHS resources, there has been a noticeable increase in the number of iatrogenic diseases (diseases induced unintentionally by physicians and health care workers) in Britain. It is therefore understandable that an impoverished continent such as Africa is likely to present more than average statistical evidence of healthcare errors, resulting in high rates of morbidity and mortality.

Although it can be argued that sexual activity in Africans is not different from that of people living in other AIDS related areas, ignorant primeval customs, such as fathers offering their young teenage daughters to visiting military personnel, is undoubtedly one of the contributory causes to the high percentage of AIDS in Africa.

During the 60s, an ex-boyfriend who was a Royal Air Force serviceman told me of his experience of this disgusting practice.

The serviceman was stationed in a former British airbase in the Middle East (originally known as North East Africa). Being of Black-Caribbean origin, he was soon befriended by some of the native African men. On one of his days off he was invited by a senior local gentleman to spend the day with him and his family. As the serviceman prepared to make his way back to his base during the evening, he was invited by his host to spend the night at his residence.

As the night progressed, there was a gentle tap on the door of the bedroom allocated to the serviceman; when he opened the door, the teenage daughter of his host shyly told him that her father had sent her to keep him company during the night. The airman told me that he promptly sent the child away and at the first sign of daybreak he left for his base after reprimanding his host severely.

On another occasion, a White Yorkshire born British Air Force flight sergeant who was attached to an Air Force in East Africa told my husband and several others of a similar experience. One of his African colleagues in the Air Force suddenly became ill and the British flight sergeant went to visit him in a remote part of the country. As the village was a long distant from the airbase, he was invited to spend the night at his colleague's home. During the night a teenager entered his room telling him. 'They've sent me to keep your company.' In the past, there have been other isolated reports of this nature involving military personnel.

It is the fundamental human right of every child (no matter how financially deprived) to be loved, respected and protected by its parents, carers and community. This includes the right to be shielded from the indignity and consequential detriment of immoral sexual abuse.

A NAM report in 2001 stated: 'The prevalence of HIV among military personnel is often higher than in the population as a whole, following the long established pattern of sexually transmitted disease. This has serious implications for the role of the military within societies as well as internationally, in peace keeping operations.'

One way of triumphing in the fight against HIV/AIDS, is enlisting the support of religion and other respectable community organizations as demonstrated by Uganda under the leadership of President Yoweri Museveni. As a result of the moralistic stance of Uganda, the rate of HIV/AIDS dropped from 14% during the 1990s to only 8% in 2001. There is evidence that Zambia and Senegal are now emulating the trend set by Uganda.

HIV in North America. At the end of 2001, there were 940,000 people in the USA and Canada living with HIV.

HIV in The Caribbean. An estimated 420,000 people in the Caribbean were living with HIV/AIDS at the end of 2001. This is around 2% of the adult population, and is believed to be higher than in any region outside Africa. Haiti has the highest incidence of the disease in Caribbean, with an estimated 5.17% of the adult population (210,000) living with HIV/AIDS.

Treatment

Antiretroviral Therapy: This therapy is also called HAART (Highly Active Anti-Retroviral Therapy). It is a combination of three or more drugs used to control the level of the virus in the blood and boost the immunity. As mentioned before, HIV attacks CD4 or T cells to reproduce hundreds of copies of itself.

Although antiretroviral drugs have been researched for several years, combination therapy has only been used since about 1997. It does not cure the disease, but each of the drugs used in combination therapy acts on the virus at different stages of its life cycle, thereby lowering its reproduction in the body to small amounts.

Diet: One of the less cost effective methods (compared to antiretroviral drugs regimen) in maintaining health, thus preventing the HIV virus from developing into full blown AIDS, is to eat a varied healthy diet. Good nutrition is an essential ingredient in assisting the weaken immune system to fight infections induced by the virus.

Complementary Therapies

Acupuncture: An internet article extracted on 14/3/2003 by Medicine net.com on the topic of antiretroviral therapy stated:

> 'It is thought that treatment during the primary infection may be an opportunity to help the body's natural defence system work against HIV. Thus, patients may gain an improved control of their infection while on therapy, and perhaps even after therapy is stopped. For the present, unfortunately, patients who initiate treatment during primary infection will need to remain on some form of antiviral therapy indefinitely. Studies are underway to determine if there are circumstances in which therapy can be safely discontinued without resulting in an increase in viral load.'

One of the most powerful attributes of acupuncture is its immune enhancing effects on the body (refer to chapter 4). This natural therapy used in conjunction with other therapies (including antiretroviral) will evidently play a crucial role in the treatment of this disease.

If acupuncture were to be part of the initial recommended treatment regimen for HIV, it might well contribute towards the reduction of several symptoms of this disease and also the unpleasant side effects associated with antiretroviral therapy. Acupuncture also elevates the levels of endorphins circulating in the body thereby providing natural pain control. It also alleviates depression.

Herbal therapy: Similarly to acupuncture, herbs afford natural treatment in containing the HIV virus. This form of treatment would be invaluable to people living in areas where it is difficult to access antiretroviral treatment owing to unavailability of the drugs or financial restraints.

Spiritual Enhancement: Religion can be a positive accessory in combating disease. Although people tend to feel despondent when faced with ill health, those of a religious persuasion often experience some degree of spiritually induced respite in coping with illness.

Mind Control: Through the powerful influence of thoughts, we all have the choice of becoming either victims or victors of our own destiny. The ability of the human mind is far beyond our capability of cognitive perception. The mind can create wonders through positive thinking and meditation. It is therefore imperative for anyone experiencing sickness to maintain a positive mental attitude.

Until such time as an effective drug regimen is manufactured to cure this fatal epidemic, described by Nelson Mandela as 'the war against humanity', education, morality and commonsense must be deployed as armaments in our struggle to survive this battle of the decade. We must contribute altruistically in this fight for the survival of mankind, or this pandemic crisis will have a devastating effect on humanity. Judging from the evidence so far, the effect of HIV/AIDS upon mankind could replicate that of the Black Death, which wiped out one third of the population in Europe during the fourteenth century.

Multi-national pharmaceuticals must consider reducing the price of antiviral drugs, thus making them more affordable to poor countries. This would help to ameliorate the suffering of other human beings, who owing to demographic demarcation and poverty experience disparity in accessing appropriate treatment. It is foolhardy for wealthy reputable pharmaceuticals to argue over the fact that their patented drugs should not be copied and sold cheaply to patients in poor countries. We all have an invaluable role to play in fighting this disease. It is immoral for wealth and power to hinder our mission in assisting our fellow humans.

Nutritionally related disorders

I have coined the acronym WOE to describe three of the greatest contributors of nutritional related diseases. WOE represents W*ar*, O*verpopulation and Environmental* catastrophes such as droughts, floods, hurricanes and earthquakes. WOE often leads to famine and economic and social problems, culminating in migration and in some instances death. It is often children, the poor, seniors and the sick who endure most of the suffering associated with malnutrition.

One of the main contributory causes for economic problems is the vast amount of debt owed to the World Bank and the International Monetary Fund by developing countries. The continuous interest repaid leads to poverty.

Another cause of financial burden is blatant covetousness on the part of some world leaders. As is well observed, following the independence of some former colonies during the late 60s and 70s, some heads of Government misappropriated the wealth of those countries. Therefore whilst they, their families and their 'crowd' enjoyed a sumptuous lifestyle, the less fortunate suffered.

A third, but very important, contributory cause for economic depression in some developing countries is the debt incurred by some of those countries by the purchasing of weapons from wealthy industrialized Western countries, to engage in warfare against their own countrymen or their neighbours. In some instances, the feuding neighbours are of the same tribe. Observers can easily note that those who encouraged those wars by readily supplying arms do so for their own financial gratification, yet those embroiled in senseless combat appeared to be impervious to this fact.

As is often observed, whilst countries are interlocked in war, the inhabitants are deprived of basic food, medicine and other vital requirements. This is because the seemingly senseless act of war often leads to financial constraint, embargo from other countries and disease such as malnutrition due to inaccessibility of food and medicine.

The following excerpt was obtained from *Medical and Health Britannica* 1991 in a chapter under the caption: 'Nowhere a Promised Land: The Plight of the World's Refugees', by Doctors Michael J. Tool and Ronald J. Waldman. Page 131 states.

'When deprived of food, humans develop protein energy malnutrition (PEM), or starvation. Malnourished individuals often show signs of weight loss, weakness, apathy, and depression. Symptoms may progress to cachexia (general physical wasting), diarrhoea, anorexia (loss of appetite), immobility, and finally death. Oedema (severe bloating caused by fluid retention) is rarely seen in association with total starvation but is commonly seen with semi-starvation.'

Tool and Waldman continued:

'While the predominant form of PEM affecting young children is marasmus (wasting only), there are circumstances that can produce kwashiorkor (wasting plus oedema), such was seen so commonly in Biafra in 1969 among young children, whose major energy source was cassava, a starchy food that provides virtually no protein.'

As a descendant of the developing world, I am particularly concerned about diseases resulting from malnutrition, as it is undoubtedly one of the leading contributors to sickness and death in poor nations.

I am relieved that the term 'developing nations' is now popularly replacing 'the third world countries'. To my way of thinking, the term 'third world' is a misnomer. The impact of systematic exploitation by slavery and colonization of some of those countries under that classification may have incurred a psychological inferior image of them, not only in the eyes of the assailants, but by the 'beaten down' inhabitants of those countries also. Nonetheless, God created one universe, therefore I acknowledge every country, no matter how large and financially affluent or small and impoverished, as a part of God's original construct. I am therefore reluctant to acknowledge a numerical tag to describe any part of the world.

There is also a psychological danger in the concept of numerical listing of countries, wherein people from countries labelled as 'third world' are liable to feel somewhat inferior to those preceding them in numerical order. Likewise, people from countries higher in rating are likely to develop a psychological feeling of superiority over those ranked lower. We must be cautious of the power of language.

Nutritional diseases are classified as follows:

1. Under-nutrition. This is a situation where there is not enough energy value in food. Intense under-nutrition in children results in marasmus (a progressive wasting disease). When under-nutrition hits epidemic proportions there is famine and in some instances death.

2. Malnutrition. This is a deficiency of specific nutrients in the diet thus causing diseases such as rickets, scurvy and kwashiorkor. It is used generically to describe conditions related to underfeeding. Protein deficiency, which affects millions of children especially in Asia and Africa, is the most important disease in this category.

3. Qualitative over-nutrition. This condition occurs when there is too much concentration of a particular food, which may be either an essential form of bodily nourishment such as vitamins and iron or a non-essential one such as saturated fats. One example of over-nutrition is siderosis, a chronic fibrosis of the lungs and liver occurring in people working with iron. This condition is common in African men who cook and brew beer in iron pots.

High cholesterol caused by the intake of fatty foods is another example of over-nutrition. This predisposes to hypertension, which may progress to coronary heart disease if not managed. (Refer to chapter 2.)

4.Obesity This is a condition of being overweight with an excess of fat stored in the body. (Refer to chapter 2.)

Emotional trauma

At some stage in our lives, we are each likely to experience physical, psychological or emotional trauma. However whilst a physical injury may heal with little or no complication, emotional trauma can lead to diverse diseases, if the initial problem is not addressed appropriately for the benefit of the individual.

There is no general recommendation for addressing emotional perplexities; each case merits an individual formula. This is why I often question the rationale of physicians doping people who fall into this category with medication intended to induce the mind into coping with the situation.

A pill cannot reverse the impact of an emotional catastrophe; it merely suppresses the natural process of addressing that problem rationally. However, it may be offered (cautiously) to deal with symptoms of the problem if the situation is indicative of such intervention. Some symptoms of emotional trauma include insomnia, depression and anxiety states. Medication may be used as a secondary aid in ameliorating these associated problems.

An increasingly popular method of addressing complex problems is by spiritual enlightenment, as in religion and meditation, although religion appears to be the most popular method employed. Several people have stated that it was their religious belief which had helped them cope with problems.

'The Lord Jesus Christ said I will not leave you comfortless.' (John 14:18).

'The Lord's hand is not shortened that it cannot save; neither His ear heavy that it cannot hear.' (Isaiah 59:1).

Although a grim reminder of finality (although only in the physical sense), emotional trauma incurred through death is often perceived as more acceptable and easier to cope with than the trauma of abandonment or rejection.

It is a well-known fact that during the early years, a substantial number of young immigrants to the United Kingdom, including several female nurses, experienced several varieties of emotional and psychological turmoil as a result of leaving their families and communities and integrating into a new culture. Some of those pioneers were institutionalized in mental hospitals at the behest of 'men in white coats' (psychiatrists), magnifying their personal egos with what may have appeared to them as post- Freudian prodigies.

Diagnoses were often conducted in a manner that seemed blatantly arrogant and ignorant of knowledge of ethnic minorities. It is also reasonable to assume that some of those early psychiatrists were more interested in their professional standing than in the welfare of some of their patients. Some appeared to be devoid of human sensitivity and compassion. They made grave diagnostic errors, as is now revealed by the medical fraternity. This blunder in misunderstanding people was not confined to an individual race; other patients were susceptible to misdiagnoses.

Several of those unfortunate members of the ethnic minority 'banged up' in mental institutions were no 'madder' than distressed children separated from their parents in a large shopping complex. What was needed to remedy their predicament was not incarceration into institutions for the insane. They longed for others to recognize and accept them as an equal part of the human race, to listen to them and understand their concerns. They longed to explain the pain of separation from their families.

Doctors are not infallible. In order for them (and other health practitioners) 'to get it right', they must be prepared to listen. If adequate time is spent on listening to patients and the information gleaned is used in diagnosing and treatment of patients, results would be inclined to be somewhat more satisfactory. It is arrogant to believe that because someone is a professional, he or she has the formula to every conceivable problem related to his or her specific field.

Example. Shortly before my marriage, I developed a minor infection in my left ovary. Whilst working one night on a busy surgical ward in a hospital in Berkshire, England, the pain was so severe that I was rushed to the emergency department during the early hours of the following day.

I told the registrar that my illness was probably due to an infection and that my doctor was aware of my condition. I had visited my general practitioner the previous day and he had examined me and prescribed antibiotics, but I had not had the chance to obtain them.

Although I had stated the situation as best as I could, added to the fact that I was an experienced nurse, the registrar disagreed with my suggestion of an infection. With an unfriendly facial expression, he proceeded to subject me to a rather painful examination. After he had finished examining me, he turned to the nurse and told her to prepare me for an emergency operation, because he believed that both of my ovaries were 'severely diseased'. And yet I had only complained of pain in the left side of my pelvic cavity. I also observed that he did not speak to me. In my presence he was informing the nurse, my colleague, of his decision to take control of my body by operating.

Whilst the registrar went to prepare for my operation, the nurse dressed me in the traditional white open-back operation gown. Then as she left to prepare my pre-operative medication with another nurse, I thought to myself I would be an absolute idiot if I agree to surrender my body to this man, who was either tired or a very miserable individual. 'If this man finds that my ovaries are normal, with his attitude, there is no way he would accept that he was wrong in his diagnosis. Good heavens! He is likely to rip out my ovaries and quickly dispose of them before question are asked.' That thought affected me like a terrible nightmare.

Despite my pain, I hurriedly eased myself off the couch, assembled my belongings, and then briskly made my way out of the unit via the back door. That area was located at the rear end of the nurses' home where I resided. I found myself climbing a fence over five feet tall, whilst still wearing my operation gown, and walking in an area of tall grass and trees to make my get-away to my room. My colleagues commended me for my courageousness in walking out; nonetheless they thought that the undignified manner of my escape was hilarious.

As soon as I got to the nurses' home, I telephoned my fiancé. After I had explained the situation to him, he exclaimed, 'What!' Then he instructed me to lock myself in my room and await his arrival.

Although this was a serious issue, I could not restrain myself from giggling when he sternly advised me not to let anyone into my room until he arrived to take me away. I thought that he must have had a fleeting mental vision of a horror movie, in which the hospital authorities would devise a plot to kidnap me. He might have imagined them strapping me down onto a trolley then wheeling me off (kicking and screaming) to the operating theatre to dissect a fundamental part of my womanhood.

I obtained the prescribed antibiotics soon after walking out of the emergency department and within a few days, I was better. I have never had any recurrence of the problem and I have had children after my marriage.

I thank God that I had the presence of mind to walk away from that operation and I often wonder what might have been the outcome if I had not had the courage to do so. The outcome might have been satisfactory; nonetheless, that does not alter the fact that surgery in that case was quite unwarranted.

There are times when doctors have to make drastic decisions in order to save lives. But there are also moments when with the utmost certainty of the situation, patients have the right to take control of their lives or the outcome may be regrettable.

I am often amazed at the eagerness of certain elements of society (professionals and lay people alike) to label behaviour differing from their concept of 'normality' as abnormal. This often raises debatable questions regarding the description of 'sanity'.

A sane person should understand and accept the fact that personality is an individual attribute. Everyone should not be expected to display a common pattern of behaviour which is perceived as 'normal' and therefore acceptable. Wouldn't life be terribly boring if everyone behaved in the same manner?

When an infant is learning to speak, at times he/she finds it difficult to form and pronounce words. Although mentally the child is aware of what it wants to say, formation of words may be difficult. We do not dismiss the child as stupid or lazy. Instead we assist the child by using phonetics (speech-sounds corresponding to pronunciation) or we guess what the child is trying to say and assist it. Why do we not adopt a similar attitude towards adults by assisting them with their emotional problems instead of judging them wrongfully, thereby sinking them deeper into an emotional abyss?

Abandonment. I was part of the statistics of love abandonment soon after my arrival in the United Kingdom, following a seven-year innocent friendship that commenced at the giggly age of 15. After my initial reaction of shock, disbelief and self-denial of an obvious foreseeable catastrophe, I entered a state of profound grief. Several factors were contributory to my reaction to abandonment.

Firstly, I have always been very childlike and to this day my behaviour reveals startling tendencies of childishness that are often unconsciously displayed. Even in my early twenties, I was but a mere child, trapped in an adult's body. Therefore I was not mentally prepared to handle emotional problems of that magnitude.

However, I will not relinquish my childlike tendencies for the simple reason that without them, I would not be operating in my true self. I am of the opinion that clinging to childlike dispositions during adulthood is one of the bastions of self-preservation from some of the pressures of an 'over mature' world. Owing to its innocence and purity of mind, a childlike persona can access the shelter and security that is psychologically reflective of a person's imaginary safe 'little world'. This is a useful antidote to the problems of a turbulent world.

Some people are inclined to attribute a childlike predisposition to psychological childhood deprivation. One acquaintance, who is deeply preoccupied with psychology, told me that due to the fact that I was an older child, who had been placed in the position of assisting my parents to rear my younger brothers and sisters, I was probably deprived of a natural childhood. Therefore, by her reasoning, my childish tendencies are a belated grasp at my lost former years!

I had often related to her that although my parents were not wealthy, my childhood days are foremost in my memory of happy times. Yet she did not consider the fact that perhaps my childhood meant so much to me that it is now an integral part of my adult life that I am desperate to preserve.

I told her that it was complete nonsense to suggest that I had been robbed of a natural childhood. It was traditional during my youth for children in developing countries to assist their parents. We felt a great sense of privilege in playing 'mummy', therefore, why should something that had given us great pleasure have an adverse reaction on us?

It is this nature of negative evaluation of behaviour that is partly responsible for the mounting scepticism levelled at psychoanalysis. At times, it appears that the foremost intention of those involved in the profiling of human behaviour is to set out to interpret every presenting pattern of behaviour in a negative light (perhaps with the wilful intention of coercing people into having unnecessary therapy). This act is likely to inflate the professional ego of the therapist as well as boosting their financial assets.

Abraham Maslow referred to the assessment of man's basic nature when he observed: 'the human being does seem to have instinct remnants and that clinical and other evidence suggest that those weak instinctoid tendencies are good, desirable and worth saving.' (*The Theory and Practice of Counselling Psychology* by Richard Nelson-Jones, page 19).

The other reason for my reaction to abandonment was the fact that I came from a large close family of eight and I had never travelled overseas away from them before. The impact of my dilemma would have been less traumatic had I been abandoned whilst in the confines of my caring and understandable family and friends back home. Although there was sure to be the odd index finger gesticulating menacingly to that familiar proverbial 'I told you so!', I would have coped much better.

> *'But the God of all grace, who hath called us unto his eternal glory by Christ Jesus, after that ye have suffered a while, make you perfect, stablish, strengthen, settle you.'*
> (1 Peter 5:10).

During that period in my life, I found myself on the brink of an emotional collapse. Despite my emotional torment, however, I was fortunate to avoid meeting those 'men in white coats' because of my resilience. I believe that my spiritual and physical strength is a dominant constituent of inherited ancestral gene. The origin of this attribute is the slaves, my ancestors.

Tragedies Trigger Tutelary (guarding) Tendencies.

I discovered that I had a substantial amount of spiritual strength to protect me from falling completely into the abyss of emotional catastrophe. That strength might have remained stagnated had I not been forced through sheer necessity to explore and utilize it.

Those experiencing loss of any nature must have the required time that is necessary for them to grieve before appropriate healing can effectively commence. There is no set time limit for the duration of grief. We are all individuals with our in-built mechanism of grief endurance level. Some of us mourn briefly, while others take longer. However, the healing process may be hampered because of several contributing factors. Some of the common ones are: insensitivity reaction, insufficient period of recovery, and inappropriate recourse.

Insensitive Reaction

It is a well-known fact that some white British people tend to cross to the other side of the road in order to avoid others mourning the death of their loved ones or broken romances. This behaviour is condemned by some as cold, selfish or cowardly, but I would be more accepting of being shunned by people than withstanding some of the other reactions.

How many times have we not experienced or overheard people making insensitive remarks to those who are hurt such as, 'Surely you could have done better'?

That was the person's choice, therefore statements of that nature are hardly likely to lift the spirit of the 'sufferer'. It is more likely to plunge him/her in a deeper state of discouragement, because his/her choice of companionship has been ridiculed. The victims may perceive themselves as worthless individuals who are destined to make bad choices.

Some people would be inclined to ignore such depressing comments, but when one is emotionally and mentally weakened, any negative insinuation, even if made in good faith, is likely to exacerbate instead of ameliorate the situation.

Ill advice from others if followed can also add to further problems in the lives of those bereft with loss. However we must remember that in some cases, the non-professional advisers who try to assist by advising the victims, are merely addressing the problem in a manner in which they themselves would have handled it. Some people do not consider the victim's personality before offering advice.

Case History. Lea (fictitious name), a brilliant academic from Asia, came to the United Kingdom to pursue a career in nursing during the early seventies. On her days off she would often engage in private nursing to supplement her income. She forwarded most of her income to her fiancé back in her country to assist him financially with preparations for their future. I accompanied her on a few occasions to the bank when she conducted some of those transactions. It was decided that after a few years she would return to her country to marry the young man.

Having not received any communication from her fiancé for a considerable period, and fearing that he might have been ill and probably hospitalized, Lea became very concerned. She contacted her sister and requested her assistance in investigating the matter. Soon after, Lea received the most devastating news by telephone from her sister in Asia.

Lea's hysterical sister informed her that not only had her intended husband built a house on another location in their country with the money she had sent him, he had also married another woman.

Poor Lea walked around dazedly, whilst some of her compatriots held on to each other and wept. As soon as the news was out, her room was packed to capacity because we were a close knit group of nurses and Lea was a very polite and respectable person.

Although I was quite angered by the news, I was worried and concerned for Lea's health. I remember cuddling her and asking her to speak. She began to tremble, and to my relief she held on to me tightly and uttered in a weak voice, 'My God, what am I going to do?' At that point a middle aged senior nurse who was standing outside Lea's room shouted, 'What do you mean by saying what are you going to do, you silly girl? Go and find yourself a nice young man. Don't let any man have the satisfaction of feeling that he is the Alpha and Omega in your life.'

Some people may accept statements of that nature as positive and encouraging gestures, but in some circumstances they can be interpreted as highly inappropriate and offensive.

According to my perception of humanity, the foremost basic need of humans is the gift of love (to give and to receive). Therefore, if we are devoid of love, or if it was supposedly given then taken away from us, we are then likely to experience grief.

My observation of human behaviour has shown that we do not all form relationships with the same objective in mind. I firmly believe that if a relationship is of genuine spiritual and emotional construction, it is unlikely to crumble easily. If that relationship is dismantled, then some people would not find it easy to build any subsequent relationship.

Furthermore if people hastily propel others into retaliatory relationships, their interpretation of love cannot be truly representative of the meaning of the word.

Lea was traumatized by her experience. Not surprisingly, she was apprehensive to enter any future relationship. Several years later, I was told by one of her friends and compatriots that she became ill and despite several tests, the cause of her illness remained a mystery to doctors here in England.

My informant also stated that one of Lea's younger brothers took the situation so badly that he armed himself with a meat cleaver and went in search of the gentleman who was responsible for his sister's torment. Fortunately, his concerned relations alerted the police, who arrested and cautioned him before he had the chance of avenging Lea.

Fellow Feelings (Compassion). Parents, especially mothers, must teach their sons from an early age to respect members of the opposite sex. We must teach them to have integrity. Let them realize that no one is beholden to another person, but equally, no one should wilfully mislead another.

Let us mothers not place the maternal arms of protection on our female descendants, whilst we nonchalantly observe the destruction of the daughters of our sisters.

In our void of fellow feeling we are likely to be repaid accordingly. Some people are of the opinion that this inevitable reaction to our action is the doing of 'a just God', whilst others believe that it is an act of Nemesis – the Goddess of Retribution.

However, the role of mothers to teenage and adult children is simply advisory. Therefore, although some parents may recommend that their sons' conduct be honourable towards females, they have no direct influence towards their behaviour.

Insufficient Period of Recovery

It is unwise for people to enter a subsequent relationship soon after overcoming a broken one. If we fracture a limb, we rest it until healing is well established. If we continue to use that limb, we are likely to experience pain and there is also the possibility of delayed healing; this may also cause the fracture to develop complications such as infection or mal-alignment of bones during healing. These are some of the manifestations of complications to physical injuries. It is believed that emotional 'wounds' are much more difficult to heal than physical ones, therefore time is a crucial factor in overcoming emotional problems.

I am always baffled when I hear or read of people going from one relationship to the next. How many times have we not heard or read: 'This time I have found the love of my life', or 'I love him / her with all my heart.' Yet no sooner is that relationship terminated than these people move on to find someone else, giving us yet another public affirmation of the perfect relationship. I often wonder about the identity of those skilful surgeons who manage to mend those broken hearts so quickly.

Inappropriate Recourse. Some people affected by emotional problems seek solace by turning to alcohol or drugs for 'comfort'. This is not a sensible thing to do. These substances inhibit the mind from making rational decisions regarding survival after the crisis. Alcohol and drugs are also two of the most potent precursors to a problematic life.

Closure

In order to move on with life, there must be a closure to an emotional chapter. Most disappointments in life occur as a protective mechanism for us, although at the time of occurrence our somewhat confused minds are devoid of rational ability to comprehend the situation that has befallen us in a positive light. Nonetheless, no matter how painful our experience, we must not harbour hatred and malice; if we truly loved, then there would hardly be space for hatred in our hearts. Negative emotions would only destroy or obscure our capability to move on and love again. That would be unfair to genuine and deserving prospective partners.

We have no insight into the minds of the people who disappoint others. We are not aware of the mental anguish that they themselves may be experiencing (due to no fault of their own in some instances). We do not know the psychological level in which they are operating as humans. Therefore, our immediate concern (after hauling ourselves up from the floor and dusting ourselves down) is to redirect our lives in a positive manner. Bearing in mind that *love* is one of the foremost gifts from God, if we are fortunate to be blessed with it, we must assert ourselves appropriately, and only when the time is right must we share that precious gift with another worthy person, if we so desire.

The following is my formula in overcoming the pain of rejection and discovering a satisfied and fulfilled life.

SAVED

Search for your true self, then treasure and protect that precious gift.

Analyse and accept the situation. It may well be a blessing in disguise.

Vindicate yourself – do not attribute blame on yourself if you are the innocent party.

Exorcise the anguish – Let it gently depart. Mentally reflect these words of counsel from Malcolm X: *'Don't look back and don't cry.'* Educate yourself from your experience and evaluate your life with renewed passion.

Discover a beautiful calm: a peace that heralds freedom to enjoy the life that you deserve; a life filled with your perceived expectation of LOVE. Accept it as your precious gift.

Changes in lifestyle

There are a number of factors under this category that are contributory to diseases. The following are some important considerations:

1. Changes in living conditions and eating habits
2. Changes in schooling
3. Unreasonable or unfamiliar working conditions
4. Retirement

1. Changes in living conditions and eating habits

I arrived in the United Kingdom during early spring in 1969 to pursue a career in nursing. As I stepped out from the warm confines of the aircraft, an unfriendly chilly breeze greeted my face. My nervous system automatically responded to this difference in climate by prompting me to take flight.

As I stood at the bottom of the aircraft I glanced back at its welcoming open doors. I was suddenly tempted to make a quick dash back into the plane.

A Trinidadian businessman, who had been seated next to me during the flight, was standing behind me. Probably sensing my thoughts, he placed a fatherly arm around my shoulders. 'Now, now,' he said, 'you strike me as a very brave and sensible girl, you are not going to let something as menial as the cold weather put you off, are you?'

After those encouraging words I took a deep breath, giggled at my cowardice, then walked off with the gentleman still resting his arm around my shoulder. I was grateful for his presence, but that did not stop me from thinking, 'It's all right for you, mate, you have been travelling between the Caribbean and England for years, and anyway you are white skinned (he was of Portuguese descent). You are not likely to feel the cold to the same intensity as me, a black-skinned initiate to this country, who always had the sunshine beaming down torrents of heat on me.'

A few days after my entrance into nursing, I became ill with a severe bout of diarrhoea. My symptoms were merely a combination of psychological and emotional discord, manifested in a physical manner. This was because I had to cope with a different climate and integrate into a new community (a completely different way of life). Also, I had never flown before; suddenly there I was, thousands of miles away from my family and friends; furthermore also my diet was different from that which my system was accustomed to.

I have used my experience to explain how changes in living conditions and eating habits can induce the organs of the body to become ill. Our bodily reaction is the result of mental impulses operating through the central nervous systems. It is therefore obvious that the mind plays a crucial role in our general health.

There are several other situations in which our health can be affected by changes in living conditions such as:

Extreme climatic changes. If an inhabitant of the Arctic Circle goes to live in the Sahara Desert, he is unlikely to adapt immediately to the extreme changes, so his health is likely to suffer, especially if he is not adequately dressed. Likewise the same situation would occur if an inhabitant from the Sahara went to the Arctic Circle.

Lengthy hospitalization. Patients who are hospitalized for a number of years find it difficult to cope after discharge. After their discharge some are soon re-hospitalized with symptoms that are sometimes unrelated to their initial problem.

Example. During the early 1970s, when I was a student nurse, I was privileged to meet several patients who were farmers from Wales and the West Country of England. Until recent years when the majority of the coal mines were closed down, many Welshmen worked in the coalmines, therefore they suffered from a variety of lung related conditions and many were admitted to the West Country hospital where I was employed, which specialized in chest diseases.

One particular gentleman was a patient on a ward for nine years. Although he was middle aged and had a loving and supportive family, he seemed to wield a degree of psychological control on his condition so that he would not be discharged. It seemed that owing to his lengthy hospitalizations, he found it almost impossible to believed that he could survive anywhere except on that particular ward, which he mentally visualized as his home.

Although he was a very quiet man, he exerted control over the setting of the ward, even where other patients should sit, and if someone happened to occupy 'his chair', he would complain or sulk. He insisted that windows remained closed for fear of catching a cold, even during the hot summer months.

The gentleman would shuffle around arranging the ward according to his preference, but as soon as he was offered a walk in the hospital grounds, his legs would literally start shaking uncontrollably or he would complain of feeling faint.

His symptoms appeared so genuine that we often had to abandon the idea of taking him for walks fearing that he was going to collapse and probably die on us. As soon as he was taken back to the ward, his phantom symptoms would immediately disappear and he would be his old self again.

One day a determined senior staff nurse persuaded him to venture outside in a wheelchair; she was so adamant to take him out that she literally lifted the trembling chap from his bed into the wheelchair all on her own. A few minutes later they returned to the ward and he looked very pale and terribly ill. He was sneezing a lot and between sneezes, he complained that he had caught a cold because he was taken outside. It was only then that I fully understood why that unfortunate man had spent so long in hospital. He died shortly after his discharge.

2. Changes in schooling

Children are usually petrified of changes that will separate them from their parents. Some children will react negatively when commencing school because they are apprehensive of being taken away from the safe confines of a loving and sometimes doting family, even though the time away from home is often only five or six hours.

Parents are also known to react emotionally, when their children commence school. When our last child started nursery school, I missed her so terribly that on several occasions, I had to restrain myself from returning to the school to fetch her back home after leaving her. I know of other mothers who have had similar experiences and some have actually taken their children back home. If adults react so emotionally at periods of brief separation from their children, is it not understandable that children too would be affected by temporary separation?

In order to integrate with other little strangers, children are often reliant on a back-up team to instil self-confidence and bravery into their minds. A familiar means of encouragement is usually in the form of siblings, neighbours and friends attending the same school. It is good practice for the child to start associating with a few children to gain confidence and then gradually familiarize with others.

Once the child begins to associate with schoolfriends, bonding commences. It is therefore understandable that when a child is removed from one school where friendship and trust has been established, then transferred to another school where he/she is a total stranger, it is more hurtful to them than others can ever imagine.

I often wonder whether some of us parents are aware of the damage we incur on our children's health when we constantly change our living environments. This means that the children are frequently changing schools and friends, the consequence of which may be psychological and emotional disturbance, often accompanied by physical manifestations of disease.

There are instances when changes in living conditions and schools are solely compatible with the parents' materialistic aspirations, whilst the children's interests are devoid of serious consideration.

The following are some conditions experienced by children who are affected by frequent change of schools:

Asthmatic attacks, bedwetting, diarrhoea and vomiting, headaches, loss of weight due to insufficient eating or obesity due to comfort eating, panic attacks and abdominal pain and other unexplained aches and pain. These children have little or no confidence and are therefore targeted by bullies.

3. Unreasonable or unfamiliar working conditions

Occasionally a new working environment may cause some degree of tension and continuous tension is likely to be injurious to health. Some people are forced by financial necessity to conform to changes in the workplace. If one is aware of the requirements of those changes, then there is less stress in coping. However, people sometimes indicate that because they were not given any induction to acquaint themselves with a new employment, they found it difficult to work efficiently.

Many of us are well aware of the fact that some scheming employers deliberately place employees whom they would like to dismiss in a difficult working situation. The unfortunate employee is likely to feel incompetent and would therefore be forced to learn the job speedily or be prepared for dismissal. There is going to be a certain degree of psychological damage incurred by this public display of humiliation. Unfamiliarity is a medium for fear and resentment.

Example. In 1996, I started to exercise frequently at a local gym. Although I had never squatted with weights before, within days of training I was squatting with 120 pounds. That amount was increased the following week to 200 pounds, which was the maximum on that particular apparatus. I squatted with that amount of weight 10 times each on three attempts in the space of seven minutes. I could hardly believe what I had embarked upon. My excitement at that extraordinary feat was equivalent to a child who had discovered a new game that it was mastering and enjoying.

My husband, a keen body builder since the age of 16 years, still exercises regularly to maintain fitness. He, my son (who was also a body builder), and others in the gym were astounded at my performance with the weights.

A few of the men attending the gym told my husband that they were surprised to see a woman lifting that amount of weight because they had never seen men lifting that much in our gym before. I felt pleased that I had struck a convincing blow in demonstrating the strength of the supposedly weaker sex.

I developed a psychological bonding with the squatting equipment and on every occasion that I visited the gym I would use it. My husband insinuated that

I was becoming too obsessed with squatting and that I was not investing enough time on other disciplines.

I agreed with my husband's observation, but I was convinced that I was powerless to change the situation unless I went to another gym where there were no squatters. I was not prepared to do that, because the gym was within walking distance from my home, and it is located in the recreation centre where I held my acupuncture clinic. I decided that the only alternative was for me to employ a personal trainer who should be able to discipline me and assist me in cutting down from over-using the squatter.

I chose an excellent trainer who was based at the recreation centre in question. Sasha Clark was the winner of the 1989 Junior Mr Great Britain Bodybuilding Championship and the following year he competed in the World Championships. Sasha was also very surprised at my squatting capability. I explained my obsession with the apparatus to him. He devised a schedule of activities for me to work on and he suggested that I should only use the squatter once in three visits.

On the first visit with Sasha, I complied with my schedule. However on the second visit, I lingered in the gym until he had left, then I followed him out of the building. After he drove off, I immediately sprinted back to the squatter and promptly started using it. My world of fitness collapsed soon afterwards, when I entered the gym to find that the squatter was amongst a few pieces of equipment demolished to make space for more sophisticated ones.

As I gazed in total disbelief at what I perceived as a collection of silly, diminutive uninteresting playthings, I started to shake slightly and my stomach was seized by a peculiar gripping sensation, then I felt nauseated. I now realize the plight of addicts deprived of drugs.

After gaining my composure, I went to the manager's office to inquire the reason for the alterations. I further asked why he had not consulted clients of the gym before implementing alteration. I also objected vociferously to the removal of the squatting equipment. I even inquired whether it could be retrieved so that I could purchase it, but unfortunately it had already been discarded. I felt depressed at that news.

After returning to the gym, I made a nervous attempt to use the new appliances, but I could not simmer down my emotions enough to concentrate on exercising. After a few minutes of attempting to use several pieces of equipment, I left vowing never to return. After constant persuasion, I returned on a few occasions, but unable to enjoy the routines, I soon discontinued.

My problem was due to over familiarization with the old and unfamiliarity with the new equipment. Also, no one was available to introduce the new pieces of equipment to me on my initial encounter with them. It is understandable for people to be apprehensive of changes, especially if they are already operating satisfactorily and efficiently. No one would readily give up a well-known routine for one that is unknown.

My experience at the gym is used to demonstrate an example of unfamiliarity on the part of employees. I had the choice of staying or walking away from my situation and I chose to walk away. Exercising and demonstrating my skills at weightlifting were important to my health, fitness and personal enjoyment; nonetheless I am not dependent on those qualities for financial stability. Unlike my situation, people faced with unusual situations in the work place have no choice but cope to the best of their ability, because they are dependent on a job in order to manage financially. The effort in coping can lead to insurmountable levels of stress and ill health on some people.

Important observation: *The Almighty has a mysterious way of substantiating the truth, no matter if it takes decades.*

I am of the opinion that many foreigners, including nurses, who developed emotional and psychological problems during the 60s and 70s, were also casualties of homesickness and unreasonable working conditions.

In 1998 it was reported in a local newspaper (*Luton on Sunday*) that some of the nurses recruited from Australia and New Zealand to the United Kingdom, returned to their countries of origin. It had been observed that those nurses, whose fares had been paid by hospitals recruiting them to England, spent as little as one day before returning to their countries.

The nurses and the Union cited unsatisfactory conditions as the reason for their departure. However the spokesperson for one of the hospitals involved refuted that claim, stating that the nurses were young, so they missed their families.

Ironically, this information was reported in a local newspaper exactly one month after I had written about the black emigrants who were misdiagnosed as mad, simply because no one seemed to understand their problems.

Britain, the colonial power, did not create job opportunities in the British West Indies and British Guiana (now called Guyana) for the natives of those countries. However during the period following the Second World War when there was a critical general shortage of workers, people from the colonies were invited to come and work to rebuild Britain. Those colonial immigrants were recruited to work in various places including London Transport, British Railways and hospitals. This was primarily the reason why the then health secretary Enoch Powell recruited Caribbean nurses to Britain.

During that period, immigrants from the colonies were grateful for the opportunity of employment. They either borrowed their fares from family and friends or it was loaned by their respective governments. They had to make sure that they honoured the agreement to work and repaid those loans.

It was impossible for those Caribbean immigrants in question to cut and run; therefore, they opted to stay even if that exposed them to the risk of 'burning'. Never mind the fact that the work was hard, they managed it well. Some patients often remarked, 'You black nurses are ever such hard workers.'

During my period in nursing, I often observed that several white student nurses abandoned nursing a few weeks after the induction period, claiming that it was too demanding. Those completing their training were promoted to nursing sisters soon after passing their examination, whilst the hardworking black nurses who had managed to pass the same examination (in some instances several years prior), were often passed over for promotion. They had to work under the charge of less experienced white colleagues.

Some people were of the opinion that the white British nurses were entitled to senior positions because Britain was their country.

In recent years I have noted a marked increase in the number of European tourists who were so captivated by the beauty of the Caribbean that they decided to reside there. Several of those immigrants to the Caribbean have gained employment especially in the hotel industry and it is obvious that some (particularly the Scandinavians) experience difficulty conversing in English (the language spoken in the countries in question). Nevertheless, the majority that I have met were offered supervisory positions over the indigenous workers. Some of the local employees have stated that although they had worked for several years at the same hotels, they were not offered promotion.

Indifferent treatment levelled at black people, including nurses and other employees, in Britain and other countries is gravely unjust. It is often easily recognizable. Those who are victims of this inequity are liable to be mentally and emotionally affected by the public demonstration of what must be perceived as incompetence in executing their appropriate responsibility.

One would have hoped that nursing, a profession created on the basis of care and compassion for the sick, would have steered clear of the idea of donning a puritanical mask, meanwhile covertly promoting racism. Racism is so institutionalized into the infrastructure of British society that it is impossible to eradicate it.

Racism can be compared to an advanced type of cancer. The primary growth may be excised, but if the cancer is not arrested in time, there is a possibility of metastasis whereby the disease spreads to other parts of the body. Some of the recourses to a palliative life for patients are chemotherapy (chemical treatment) and radiotherapy (radio-active treatment), painkillers, complementary medicine and appropriate diet.

Similarly, some of the course of action in addressing racism is by addressing various issues including education in diversity, accepting the cultures of other nationalities and respect for each other. Like cancer, if we ignore the signs – what we see occurring, and the symptoms – what the perpetrators of racism express either verbally or by their 'attitude', the problem is likely to deteriorate instead of improve and others are likely to be affected by its harmful progression.

The consequence of overwork. Some damages incurred to health through working excessively are irreversible even if work is reduced. Some of the consequences of working under difficult conditions are the following: stress related conditions including frequent headaches, peptic ulcers (ulcers of the stomach and duodenum) and frequent absenteeism from work.

If someone who is accustomed to working in an office is employed as a farmer, he is likely to have health related problems, because he is not accustomed to that degree of manual and mechanical arduous occupation. Likewise if a manual labourer such as a farmer takes a sedentary job such as typing, he is likely to become ill owing to the insufficient amount of physical exercise he is accustomed to.

NB: Notably high incidences of heart related problems are reported to be prominent amongst sedentary workers owing to lack of physical exercise and also to the levels of stress, which is often common in those occupations. It is therefore advisable for office workers to take adequate amounts of exercise and pay attention to diet by avoiding foods high in fat.

4. Retirement

Retirement should herald the second phase in life (not the end). It should be a time to continue working, if so desired, at a comfortably relaxed pace. It is also a time when work is more meaningful and enjoyable because one is then working according to the dictates of an understanding and reasonable boss – oneself.

It is a sad reality that sickness and death amongst retired people is alarmingly high. Some of the reasons for this increase in incidence of disease after retirement are unfortunately attribut   actors involving health, education and the welfare of older people.

I have carved the acronym *PITIFUL* to describe some of the contributing causes of post retirement related illnesses; it represents: Psychological, Isolation, Turbulent retirement activities, Idleness, Frustration and Uncertainty, and Lackadaisical behaviour.

Psychological. Some people experience a vacuum in life after retirement. It is understandable for those who have spent most of their lives working, to experience a sense of loss when they retire. One woman told me that her retirement was somewhat similar to bereavement. This situation if left unattended can progress to depression.

One concerned daughter of a retired man told me that since her father's retirement all he did was mope around his home feeling sorry for himself. She went on to add: 'I wish my Dad would pull himself together.' I am often bewildered by this 'pull yourself together' formula, which is somewhat over-prescribed by well meaning lay people and to some extent professionals who should know better. It is a well-known fact that just as individuals suffering from hormonal imbalance cannot instantaneously rectify that problem, likewise anxious or depressed individuals cannot automatically pull themselves together.

Another aspect of psychologically induced disease is a result of the negative imagery of the ageing process adapted by some individuals. Some people are of the opinion that once they reach retirement, their sojourn on earth is approaching the end. They therefore start to make preparation for their funeral; they then proceed to find a comfortable chair in which they intend to sit feebly anticipating the arrival of death.

Meanwhile the mind operating through the brain receives and acknowledges the message continuously relayed to it by the individual. Death is therefore likely to ensue.

The Mind is the master key to bodily performances. It has the choice of letting in, or locking out health or disease. We have the choice of influencing the direction of that key.

Isolation. Isolation is a common way of life in the West and although incidence is much lower in recent years, it is a contributory factory to loneliness, depression, alcoholism and accidents among the old and infirm. It is also inter-connected with a considerable number of suicide attempts (a cry for help) and suicide fatalities. The causes of isolation in the West can be attributed to several contributing factors; some of the commonest ones include the way of life in Western countries:

a) Climatic: The unfavourable winter months are some of the main causes of isolation in Europe. During this period, people are more inclined to remain within the confines of their homes rather than travel in the cold to visit friends and acquaintances.

In adverse weather conditions such as heavy snow, severe frost and freezing fog, people are advised to remain at home. These are the periods when the lonely are more isolated. It would be a good gesture if the able-bodied members of society could find time to offer friendship and assistance to those who are in need. Acts of goodwill would provide happiness and peace of mind to those who are lonely and distressed.

Another contributory reason for isolation during the winter months may be due to the busy lifestyle of people living in the West. The shortened periods of daylight during winter afford little time for visits.

b) Relocation: A large proportion of people decide to spend their retirement years in an area which is suitable for them. People sometimes leave their existing homes to retire in smaller and quieter areas.

It must be taken into account that some of those people have lived most of their lives in one area; therefore it is understandable that they would miss long-standing friends, families and acquaintances. Some have reported experiencing a feeling of isolation within their new communities.

c) Migration: A significant number of Afro-Caribbean immigrants (some of whom I am acquainted with) came to the United Kingdom with the expectation of returning to their native countries after a certain period. For various reasons, it has been observed that a growing number of those immigrants found it difficult to cope after returning to their country of origin.

Those people have spent most of their lives in the West, therefore some find it difficult to re-adapt to living conditions in their homelands, some of which have understandably changed drastically in recent years. It has also been reported that there is a certain degree of resentment by some local inhabitants, which makes it somewhat difficult for the returnees to enjoy life. Some of the returnees are also likely to languish for relations and friends back in the West, so there is likely to be some degree of unhappiness.

These factors undoubtedly lead to illness within this group and several have returned to the West. However it seems that a considerable proportion of the number of people returning to their native countries are happily readjusted.

Whatever the determining factor for those returning to the West, it is a very daunting prospect for people to be travelling backwards and forwards in search of a reasonable quality of contentment whereby they can spend the remainder of their lives. This exhaustive meandering is likely to result in distress, which may further progress to general ill health. Stress can be interpreted as **S**ystemic **T**rauma **R**esulting from **E**motional **S**train to **S**elf.

d) Racial, cultural, religious, and language barriers: These are also some of the prime targets for isolation in the West, although in today's multi-cultural society, the first two barriers are not as ponderous on society as they were during the earlier years of migration. Religion on the other hand is undoubtedly the least problematic of this quartet.

Language barrier. It is difficult to communicate with people if there is a language barrier. Not only is it difficult and somewhat frustrating for the person trying to converse, it is equally hard for those trying to understand what the speaker is trying to say. Difficulty in communication is a common problem experienced by some senior non-English speaking patients in British hospitals.

When I was actively involved in nursing, I made it my priority to learn a few words of some languages. I would ask other foreign speaking patients or their relations to teach me a few important words that would assist me in my communication with the patients concerned. When patients heard me using terms in their language, they seemed pleasantly surprised. It was as if it had a therapeutic affect on them.

Once a senior Polish woman who could not speak English was admitted to my ward. Whether it was sheer frustration due to her inability to communicate, fear of hospitalization or discomfort from her illness, she was constantly tearful. A couple hours after her admission, I asked the nurse caring for the lady whether she would permit me to see if I could pacify her. My colleague agreed with my request.

Up charged the imperfect linguist to the distressed patient's rescue. '*Dzien dobry* [pronounced gin dobry] *Mamuska*,' which when translated into English means, 'Good morning, mother.' The patient gasped and held her breath. Then she grabbed hold of me and kissed me about half a dozen times on each cheek consecutively. She then started to speak very fast in Polish to me, without pausing for my response. I dashed to telephone the Polish maid who was working in the nurses' home, to ask her to get over as fast as she could to the ward to interpret.

On her arrival, the maid and the patient began speaking to each other quite excitedly; the sparkle in that patient's eyes was a wonderful sight. That day I experienced more job satisfaction in observing that patient's happiness as a result of verbal communication than I could have achieved by dispensing tablets to ease her pain or to sedate her.

I firmly believe that verbal communication is contributory to recovery, even in cases when patients appear unresponsive, as in instances of unconsciousness.

Hospitalization is often a petrifying experience to many people. That fear is likely to intensify for those who are senior and are isolated because of a language barrier. This can result in nervousness, which in turn can result in incorrect information on the part of the patient. Therefore, when providing pertinent information regarding the nature of illness, it is important for people to know how to communicate effectively; if not, they must have an interpreter.

Example Several years ago, one of my neighbours told me that her mother had died shortly after entering hospital. She told me that although her mother worked very hard to raise her children single-handedly, she could not recall her having any serious illness before. Her husband died accidentally when the fourth child was only a few months old.

Apparently the doctors told the children that their mother continually complained of pain in her stomach, so various tests were carried out on her abdomen but no sign of disease was detected. After her death the post-mortem examination revealed that her illness was confined to her chest and not her stomach as she had indicated. It appeared that she, like a number of senior people I have met, referred to her chest as her stomach.

The doctor who attended to that unfortunate woman told the children that their mother might have been saved if only she had been precise in explaining the location of her pain. That particular incident was gravely distressing to me, because as a general nurse, I felt that it should not have occurred.

During my period in nursing, it was customary for doctors to ask patients to point to the area of pain or discomfort whilst examination was being conducted. That procedure was particularly common when dealing with children, the senior, foreign speaking patients and those who appeared slightly disorientated. This procedure is replicated in hospitals throughout the United Kingdom. It is more an act of common sense than an institutionalized custom and as such it is undoubtedly incorporated in hospitals universally. And yet this unfortunate case occurred in the United Kingdom, where medical management is indisputably amongst the best in the world.

That unfortunate occurrence does not constitute medical negligence. I do not believe that fault should be attributed either to the unfortunate patient or the doctor involved in her case. That senior patient could have been somewhat confused or she might not have had elementary knowledge of anatomy. Anatomy was not generally implemented within the curriculum of most schools during the period of her schooling, which was calculated to be around the beginning of the twentieth century.

The doctor concerned may have believed that the patient was somewhat knowledgeable in anatomy; therefore he overlooked the idea of extracting further information regarding the location of her pain. It must also be borne in mind that doctors in England are grossly overworked. They see and treat a considerable number of patients; therefore there is the possibility of human error in diagnosing and treatment of diseases. Nonetheless, to avoid similar occurrences, patients must have basic knowledge of anatomy, and doctors should ask more questions and be more observant.

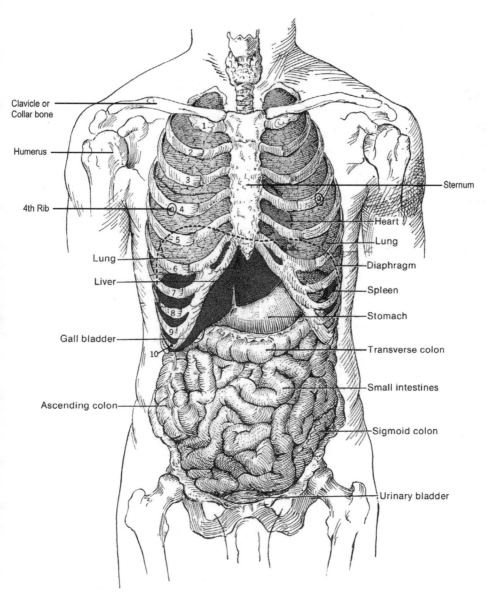

Clavicle or
Collar bone

Humerus

4th Rib

Lung

Liver

Gall bladder

Ascending colon

Sternum

Heart

Lung

Diaphragm

Spleen

Stomach

Transverse colon

Small intestines

Sigmoid colon

Urinary bladder

Anterior View

Human Anatomy

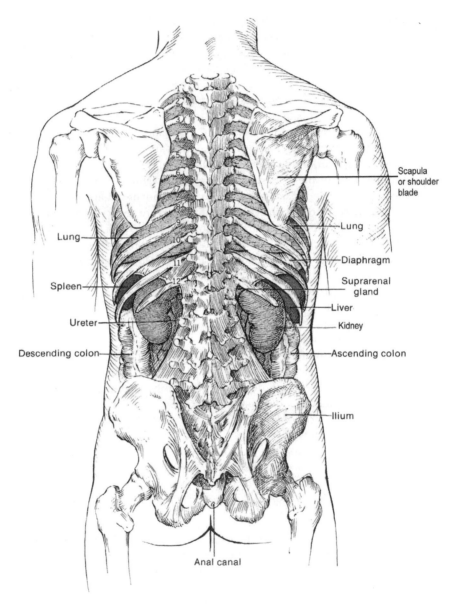

Posterior View

Human Anatomy

Turbulent Retirement Activities. After retirement, some people decide to engage in strenuous and complicated labour. This results in physical exhaustion, leading to diseases which may progress to death in some instances. Examples of such cases are well known in the immigrant community. After retirement some decide to return to their native countries (as mentioned above), which is admirable, while a noticeable number become actively involved in the construction of their 'dream homes'.

This is a dangerous custom that needs to be addressed. Some have never actively engaged in manual labour before. Occupations such as nursing, office duties, transport work and others of similar category bear no parallel to the physical demands of the construction industry. Several of those brave people become ill whilst trying to achieve their goal at an advanced age.

This is a sad situation, because those individuals are generally dedicated and aspiring folks, who like any retired person are entitled to live in a manner whereby they should enjoy the remainder of life according to their desire. Theirs is a highly personal achievement and they should be admired for their ambitious endeavour.

However it is not advisable for those who are not accustomed to performing heavy physical work to actively participate without adequate preparation. Even younger people who participate in routine exercises are cautioned to start gradually and to be careful.

It would be helpful to have a medical check-up before involvement in such proposed ventures. However even if prospective labourers are given satisfactory health reports, it does not necessarily guarantee that they are safeguarded from illness. Commonsense and caution are two useful guiding factors against incidences of labour-related illness.

Idleness

Go to the ant, thou sluggard; consider her ways and be wise: Which have no guide, no overseer, or ruler, provideth her meat in the summer, and gather her food in the harvest. How long wilt thou sleep, O sluggard? When wilt thou arise out of sleep? (Proverbs 6: 6–9).

Some people are prepared to sit leisurely day after day enjoying retirement, simply because they seem to assume that retirement is a time to relax.

One senior woman told me that her retired husband would not lift a finger to assist her with the household chores. He would constantly remark that he had worked hard all his life to support his family; therefore it was now his turn to rest.

Whether such behaviour is the result of continuous pampering by doting partners, domineering tendencies or laziness, it is an unwise situation, which may later incur an unhealthy consequence.

It is good practice for retired people to be reasonably active in order to keep healthy. Simple exercise such as walking for half an hour to one hour daily would be beneficial to the body.

Frustration due to uncertainty. Through uncertainty some retired people are simply frustrated after they have reached the end of their working life. Some of those people were remarkably dedicated to their work. It is commonly observed that this category of people live for their work.

I believe that most of the frustration and boredom experienced by retired people is a result of insecurity in the management of life from the point of departure from work. Society in general habitually imposes what it perceives to be the positive aspects of living; anything falling short of its domain is excluded from the preparatory agenda for happiness and contentment in life.

From childhood, parents and teachers habitually condition children to mentally adapt to situations and to strive to achieve in order to gain meaningful employment and financial stability for the future. This **steering** throughout our lives takes the form of:

Schooling from an early age, followed by

Training, when we are groomed for

Examinations, after which we proceed to seek

Employment and if we are the

Right candidate for the job, we are

Inducted into our expected role. After we familiarize ourselves, we then

Navigate our course in life. We decide whether we are contented with our assumed occupation; if so, we remain in the job and some of us may even seek promotion. If we are not contented we seek alternative work. After we have achieved our personal employment

Goal, we believe that we are a success, because we are mentally conditioned to think that way.

After achieving our goal, we often delude ourselves by thinking that all is well. Then when we are faced with the issue of retirement some of us suddenly become lost. This is when the unprepared face a life of uncertainty, simply because lessons on the management of retirement were not implemented in the curriculum to prepare us for survival after employment. Once we fulfil the employers' expectations and we reach retirement, they expect us to take charge of our life from that point on.

Lackadaisical Attitude. It is no wonder that some people who are unprepared in dealing with retirement spend the remainder of their lives in a perpetual listless manner.

If there were no mental stimulation and little meaning to life, some people would simply totter around in a stupefied state. They would probably feel that although they might have achieved success both professionally and financially, there was still a vacuum in their lives after retirement.

Personal comment. Society should adapt a more caring and protective attitude towards retired people. It must be acknowledged that these people have contributed to the achievement, advancement and conservation of the industrial revolution. Therefore it is fitting that these pioneers should be respected.

Employers should be encouraged to operate a voluntary advice scheme whereby pre-retirement employees could be educated about retirement related issues. This would also give them an opportunity to discuss any fear or misconception pertaining to retirement.

It would also be a useful gesture if established groups of this nature network with others in various areas, thereby creating an organization where pre-retirement employees could meet and establish friendship with others.

Ageing

Ageing is a natural process, however our systems function less efficiently as we advance in age. No matter how well we look after our bodies, we cannot escape this perfectly natural metamorphic change which all life forms and vegetation are destined to encounter.

Disease contracted during old age is not necessarily due to degenerative changes. Physical, chemical and psychological changes in seniors may cause the following problems:

Skeletal. This is a result of the natural process of wear and tear, also some degree of loss in bone density as in the case of osteoarthritis.

Lungs. Due to decreased elasticity in the lung tissues, breathing becomes slower and the capacity of the lungs becomes decreased.

The prostate gland. This structure lies at the neck of the bladder in men. In later life it is prone to enlargement, thereby causing obstruction of urine from the bladder. It is also a common site for cancer in men.

The urinary bladder. Incontinence of the bladder usually occurs as a result of disease of the bladder, or injury or disease of the spinal cord. However inability to control urination can occur to seniors if there is weakening of the muscular ring responsible for keeping the bladder closed. Incontinence can also occur in cases of constipation as the impacted bowels exert undue pressure on the bladder.

Cardio-vascular. The tissue of the heart becomes thicker, there are changes in the arteries in the heart, and the blood pressure is affected. There is also the possibility of cerebro-vascular-accidents (strokes).

The central nervous system. This may result in the following:
- Deterioration in memory. This is partly due to lack of mental stimulation. See chapter 13
- Reduced control of bladder and bowel movements
- Increased tendency to sleep
- Impairment of hearing and sight
- Parkinson's disease, motor neurone and Alzheimer's disease.

Other organs of the body that are likely to be affected by ageing include the oesophagus or food gullet, the stomach, the bowels, the liver, the kidneys and the spleen.

Hormonal Deficiency of androgen in men results in impotence, and deficiency in oestrogen in women results in frigidity. There are also menopausal problems commonly called 'the change of life'.

Mental and Emotional. Self-neglect, depression and anxiety states, alcoholism, hallucination, paranoid psychosis, dementia and acute confusion.

The Ageing Process

Several contributing factors are responsible for the delay in the signs of ageing which is apparently noticeable in some people. Some of the principal factors are racial and hereditary traits, exercise, a positive mental attitude, adequate rest, dietary influence, abstinence or controlled use of potentially harmful habits such as alcohol and tobacco.

However we should not concern ourselves unduly about our physical appearance. We should focus on our general health and contentment. If we are contented within, then we should not be concerned if others perceive us as looking too old for our calendar age.

It is wrong for any one to insinuate that another person looks old. Poverty, stress, ill health and other unavoidable factors can cause people to age prematurely.

Those intent on appraising the physical exterior are sometimes mentally inept at scrutinizing the interior. They themselves are sadly deprived of internal insight and peace of mind, therefore they would not realize that the most important and genuine attributes in people radiate from within the self. If we have inner peace, we should have self-love, appreciation and respect for others, despite their age.

Seldom have I encountered a spectacle more dishonourable to nature than that of an unhappy human trying to camouflage the signs of ageing (a perfectly natural process) through such a drastic procedure as the scalpel of the cosmetic surgeon. This act may at times conceal the signs of ageing without distorting the appearance, but it cannot conceal the symptoms of old age as the body is beset by naturally impending changes.

There are some justifications for cosmetic surgery, such as congenital deformities and other medical conditions. However, when vain gratification takes precedence in overriding nature, one cannot help but wonder how far is mortal man prepared to do combat with the inevitable course of nature.

'Education is the best formula for old age.' (Aristotle). In order to promote the chances of maintaining, or in some instances improving the quality of life, seniors should be educated on a number of important health related issues. With education, people would be accessible to vital information on the management of health.

Not only would education reduce the burden on medical and other caring organizations, it is also a useful exercise in the prevention of memory loss. Everyone, including senior people, must be taught the following simple procedures:

- First aid techniques and meditation.
- Some complementary techniques such as acupressure.
- How and when to use certain herbal remedies.
- Detecting the symptoms of some illnesses.
- How and when to take prescribed medication and when to discard it.
- When to contact the doctor.

Education instils confidence in people, whilst ignorance (lack of knowledge) instils fear. One is often inclined to imagine the worst scenario when one is unwell if there is lack of knowledge regarding that illness. Fear is a medium for psychological maladies. The fearful person is likely to suffer from psychosomatic (mind and body) related diseases. These are disorders caused or made worse by psychological factors.

Examples of some psychosomatic disorders are asthma, certain types of eczemas, and headache.

CHAPTER 2

Some common diseases in black people

Diabetes mellitus

Diabetes is one of the conditions with a high incidence in black and Asian people. It has been know to affect several generations of the same family and for that matter, there seems to be strong evidence in the claim that it is a genetic disorder.

Glucose, which provides our body with energy, is obtained from starchy or sugary foods such as bread, potatoes, rice, pasta, cassava, yam, dasheen, plantain, bananas, sugar cane (which has an exceedingly high glucose energy level), cakes and biscuits. Therefore a substandard lifestyle, including poor diet, frequently resulting from social deprivation, consequently resulting in poverty, appears to be another contributory factor in the high incidence of diabetes amongst the black and Asian population, who are traditionally raised on such diets.

One of the properties in cassava is cyanide. Although cyanide, which is a form of salt known as hydrocyanic or prussic acid, is not heavily concentrated in cassava, it is poisonous and several instances of cassava related poisoning occur. Cyanide can affect the function of the pancreas, thereby causing diabetes.

In Britain many black and Asian people (like other foreigners) consume a fair amount of their traditional diet. A fatty diet coupled with lack of exercise is a predisposing factor to obesity and an ideal recipe for diabetes. Obesity stands a 85–90% acquired risk to type 2 diabetes.

Diabetes is controllable if adequate instructions given to sufferers are followed. Public awareness of the symptoms of diabetes is also of vital importance in the recognition of a diabetic coma. This would result in prompt action, thereby hastening recovery and probably saving lives.

There have been instances where diabetics showing some of the symptoms of low blood glucose levels such as mental confusion and lack of coordination were assumed to be drunk or misbehaving. If appropriate steps are not taken to rectify this imbalance in the blood sugar level with a glucose derivative such as a sweet drink or even a piece of chocolate, the situation may progress to a coma.

The tendency of concealing illness is baseless and it can have dangerous

53

repercussions. This habit tends to be endemic in some black cultures and I personally find it difficult to comprehend. There are certain personal issues that we are entitled to be secretive about. However, why conceal sickness when the possibility may arise when we may be in need of prompt and appropriate assistance? How are people supposed to know what are our needs during a health crisis if they are unaware of our specific problems?

Even a health enthusiast cannot guarantee a life of complete well being; therefore no one should be ashamed or secretive about health related problems.

If it is the reaction of others that worries us, we need not let this be a hindrance from revealing our illness because as long as there is life, we are all susceptible to diverse diseases.

What is diabetes mellitus?

Diabetes mellitus is a condition in which the body is unable to use up glucose for its nutritional needs. This over accumulation of sugar is due to insufficient or lack of insulin, the hormone produced in the pancreas. As sugar builds up, the body can no longer cope with the excess level and a variety of symptoms appear.

The disease is classified into two main categories

1. Type 1 or insulin dependent diabetes

This type of diabetes often affects people from infancy to 30 years of age, but it can occur at any age. It appears quite rapidly owing to severe lack of insulin by the insulin producing cells in the pancreas. This type of diabetes requires insulin injections throughout life.

2. Type 2 or non-insulin dependent diabetes

This type of diabetes mainly affects overweight people, middle-aged people, older people and those with a family history of the disease. People at high risk of suffering from diabetes are unaware of the risk they run. Occasionally, this group of diabetics is diagnosed because of symptoms linked to the disease. Symptoms include extreme tiredness, blurred vision, increased thirst, impotence in men, genital itching and thrush.

The causes of other less common types of diabetes mellitus

Gestational diabetes affects some pregnant women. This condition often disappears after delivery, but pregnant women who experience it stand a higher risk of developing the disease in later life.

Maturity Onset of Diabetes of the Young (MODY) is a rare form of inherited diabetes. Although insulin secretion is impaired in MODY, the action of insulin is normal or just slightly defective.

Pancreatic conditions, such as surgery to the pancreas and pancreatitis.

Hormonal conditions, such as Acromegaly, a condition in which there is over-production of growth hormone by the pituitary; and Cushing's disease, also causing over-production of the pituitary gland. Both these diseases result from tumour or other disorders of the pituitary glands.

Some medicines taken in large doses, such as diuretics (taken to rid the body of excess fluid) and steroids.

During 2002, it was estimated that a staggering 1.4 million new cases of diabetes mellitus were diagnosed in Britain every year, Type 1 accounting for approximately 5–10% of cases and Type 2, the commonest form of the disease, accounting for 85–95% of cases. However there also remain up to a million undiagnosed cases. Without adequate treatment, these people are at risk of developing complications such as coronary heart disease, strokes, gangrene of the limbs leading to amputation, kidney failure and blindness.

Some symptoms of diabetes

Sugar in the urine, excessive thirst, frequent urination, hunger, unexplained weight loss, tiredness, irritability, blurred vision, tingling of hands and feet, dry and itching skin, low sex drive, infection and boils.

However in some instances there are no symptoms until a routine urine test is carried out on admission to hospital (frequently for problems unrelated to diabetes) or for insurance purposes. Diabetes can also be detected in instances where there are symptoms such as circulatory problems, heart problems, poor vision due to retinal changes or cataracts and kidney problems. These may be complications of the disease.

Incidence of diabetes is more common in overweight people; it is also prevalent in middle aged and older people, though it may occur at any age and children make up a large percentage of sufferers.

Treatment

There are three methods of treating diabetes; this is determined according to the degree of the disease. Mild diabetics are usually controlled by diet alone. Nonetheless, it is important to realize that all cases of diabetes are serious. People may have the idea that their condition is mild; therefore it is all right to treat the situation lightly by ignoring advice. This dangerous habit could lead to serious complications. Diabetics who are reasonably manageable are treated with anti-diabetic drugs, whilst cases that are uncontrollable with diet and tablets are treated with insulin.

Education and Management

Management of this disorder is principally dependent on the cooperation of patients. Health professionals may advise, however, that if success is to be achieved and maintained, it is up to the individual to manage the condition in an organized self-disciplined manner. Doctors, specialist nurses and dieticians can offer advice regarding treatment and diet.

It is important to have some form of 'diabetes' identification, such as a bracelet or a necklace; this can ensure prompt and appropriate action by the public in the event of an emergency. In case a diabetic is in urgent need of assistance, members of the family, friends, associates or members of the public should be able to appropriate the necessary first aid procedures for this condition.

The sufferer should carry out regular urine and blood tests, in order to check the level of glucose in the body.

They should be aware of the symptoms of hypoglycaemia, commonly described as a 'hypo'. This occurs when the blood sugar is below normal (4 mmol/l). Symptoms include headache, bad tempered behaviour, palpitation (fluttering in the chest), hot or cool feelings, sweating, tingling in the tongue, lips, hands or feet, blurred vision, difficulty in concentration and mental confusion.

One gentleman told me that his normally placid wife who had diabetes suddenly started to behave in an irritable manner towards him one day. He said he left the home to get some peace. On his return, he found her slumped at the bottom of the stairs. She had had a hypo, but her husband was not aware of the symptoms.

Hypoglycaemia may occur as a result of the following:

(a) *Food intake* – Insufficient or not enough eaten on time.

(b) *Insulin* – Too much.

(c) *Infection* – This causes weakened resistance.

(d) *Exercise* – Too much causes extreme tiredness.

(e) *Medication* – Some anti-diabetic drugs taken by mouth.

Hypoglycaemic attacks (hypos) need prompt treatment by taking three dextrose tablets; this is equivalent to 10 g of glucose. If you do not have any dextrose, simply take two teaspoons of sugar (three lumps), sweets, chocolate or a sweet drink.

ALWAYS REMEMBER TO CARRY SOME TYPE OF THE ABOVE MENTIONED SWEETS WITH YOU AT ALL TIMES. ALSO, KEEP SOME BY YOUR BED IN CASE YOU HAVE AN ATTACK DURING THE NIGHT.

If you experience a hypo, try to find out the reason for its occurrence, then try to avoid recurrence. If you cannot find the cause for your hypo, it is advisable to decrease your insulin slightly, but if you continue to have frequent hypoglycaemic symptoms despite attempts to prevent them, you must consult your doctor at the earliest opportunity.

General Advice For Diabetics

Patients must be advised about the affects of diabetes on the body.

- It is not sensible for them to continue taking sugar or large portions of fat based meals.
- Try to control your weight. The diet regimen for diabetics is reasonable and it can result in moderate weight loss. Eat small portion of meals regularly.
- Some tissue changes may occur. The main tissues affected are the eyes, nerves, kidneys, heart and blood vessels. It is therefore important to stop smoking.
- Have frequent medical check-ups on the eyes by seeing an optician, and on the feet by visiting a chiropodist. Look after your feet; keep them clean, warm and moistened. The feet are vulnerable to damage because the pain receptors are not very sensitive in diabetics, therefore they can be easily injured without the person realizing it.
- In order to prevent infection, seek prompt medical attention for any cuts, bruises, wounds or sores. Healing is slow in diabetics and infections can have serious effects on the body.
- Pay frequent and strict attention to your teeth, gums and mouth.
- Visit your doctor as soon as you feel unwell.
- Have regular exercise. I firmly believe that a suitably established exercise routine is one of the most reliable methods of keeping fit and healthy and managing some health problems.

Example: Several years ago, a diabetic was told that he had to be hospitalised after a routine check-up. He ignored the request. His blood sugar became unstable and it trebled the normal range. This situation had definitely not incurred as a result of any mismanagement on the part of the patient, who amazingly continued to exercise and remained reasonably well despite the whole ordeal.

By exercising, the individual developed a natural tolerance level to cope with the dangerously high blood glucose level circulating in the body. In a letter sent to me by the consultant in charge of the patient, the following comment was made, 'Exercise is good for diabetics; it lessens insulin requirements.'

Other useful suggestions Meditation; acupuncture; Aloe Vera (Bitter Aloe) – this is very helpful in stabilizing blood sugar level; garlic minimizes the chances of yeast infections caused by high sugar levels in the circulating blood; zinc boosts the body's resistance against infection.

Note: Do not take too many self help remedies or medication bought from the chemist without seeking approval from a doctor, a pharmacist, a qualified medical herbalist or a nurse, as some of these treatments may cause the blood sugar level to be unstabilized.

Hypertension (High Blood Pressure)

Blood pressure is the tension of blood on the arteries as it is pumped out of the heart. It also depends on the thickness and hardness of the walls of the blood vessels and the amount of blood pumped out of the heart at each beat.

The pressure of blood in the circulation is an essential factor in assessing the fitness of the heart and blood vessels. Depending on activity, blood pressure can vary from moment to moment and day to day. In a healthy person, the pressure can be raised with physical exertion and fall at rest.

The blood pressure of a healthy young adult should read 120 systolic pressure over 80 diastolic pressure. Persisitant blood pressure higher than 140/90, even at rest, is an indication of high blood pressure. However since two healthy people of the same age may have slight difference in blood pressure, these figures are only used as a guideline.

The lower or second reading is the most important. It is an indication of the minimum pressure of the blood within the walls of the blood vessels taking blood from the heart to the body.

Symptoms of Hypertension

There are no noticeable symptoms in some people with high blood pressure; however, acute or sudden rise in blood pressure may cause headache, dizziness, palpitations, low energy, exhaustion and sleeplessness (insomnia).

The complications of chronic or long-standing high blood pressure include enlarged heart, heart failure, myocardial infarction (destruction of part of the myocardium or heart muscle, due to blockage of blood supply to the heart). Other complications of chronic hypertension include haemorrhaging in the brain and stroke, two potentially life threatening conditions.

Some causes of high blood pressure

1. Narrowing of the aorta (the large blood vessel opening out of the left ventricle of the heart which distributes blood to the whole of the body).

2. Kidney problems.

3. Stress

4. Hereditary. High blood pressure sometimes affects members of the same family. It has been assumed that owing to a genetic link, black and South Asian people are more prone to hypertension.

5. Over-weight.

6. Salt consumption. Hypertension is believed to occur in some people whose systems cannot excrete salt easily. It has been argued that there is lack of biological evidence to explain the basis for this hypothesis. However it is a well-observed fact in hospitals that salt restriction in patients with high blood pressure contributes to stabilizing the condition.

7. Food rich in animal fat.

8. Smoking and alcohol consumption.

9. Thickening of blood as in a condition known as polycythaemia in which there is an abnormal increase in the haemoglobin, the compound responsible for producing the red colouring in blood.

Complications can arise when the blood pressure remains high for a long time; this situation is described as chronic. There is also the possibility of complication when the blood pressure becomes abnormally high.

The following are some of the common complications in hypertension:

- Cardiovascular problems. These are the most frequent complications of high blood pressure; they include heart attack, cerebral bleeding due to a ruptured artery and cerebral vascular accidents, commonly known as strokes.

- Problems associated with the kidneys and the eyes.

Signs and symptoms of heart attack

- Pain or discomfort in the middle of the sternum (breastbone). This may feel like a band tightening around the chest, uncomfortable pressure in the chest, pain or a feeling of fullness in the chest. This unpleasant sensation may last a few minutes or it may disappear then return.

- Pain or discomfort in the centre of the chest may be accompanied by an ache or discomfort in one or both arms, the back, the neck or the jaw.

- Shortness of breath. This often accompanies pain or discomfort in the chest, but there are instances when it precedes the distressing feelings in the chest.

- Sweating

- Nausea

- Vomiting

- Dizziness or lightheadedness.

NB: Those experiencing chest discomfort with or without any of the other signs and symptoms associated with heart attack must seek medical attention immediately.

Signs and symptoms of strokes

- Sudden unexplained severe headache.

- Mental confusion including difficulty in speech, especially if the left side of the brain that houses the speech centre (in the majority of people) is responsible for the stroke. The speech centre is located in the left side of the brain in right-handed people and in the right side of the brain in left-handed people. Therefore, speech would be affected accordingly in people. However, this depends on the severity of the stroke.

- Difficulty in understanding others.

- Numbness or paralysis of the face, arm and leg on the opposite side of the body to the site of the accident in the brain. Therefore if the left lobe of the brain were responsible for the stroke, the right side of the body would be affected.

- Loss of balance, inability to walk at all / or walk properly.

- Loss of vision in one or both eyes depending on the severity of the illness.

Management and treatment of hypertension

- Try to change your life style regarding smoking, alcohol and unhealthy diet.

- Exercise moderately (have your doctor's permission before commencing).

- Eliminate or at least reduce salt from your diet. Eat plenty of green leafy vegetables, onions, garlic and fresh fruits. Since salt attracts water, it is reasonable to assume that reduction in salt intake is justifiable in the management of high blood pressure.

- Avoid fried food especially those cooked in 'cholesterol littered' coconut oil and animal fats. Also avoid coffee and strong tea.

- Be involved in relaxation and meditation techniques to enhance your general health.

- If you can tolerate pets, consider having one. They can be an asset to our health as I have stated in the chapter on pets.

- Recently some doctors are reluctant to prescribe drugs for the treatment of hypertension. These are only prescribed as the last course of action. Instead of medical intervention, they are more inclined to suggest techniques such as exercise, meditation and complementary therapies as the first line approach in controlling the disorder. Patients are also educated about the disease. However it is argued that there are cases, especially in situations where people with high blood pressure also suffer with diabetes, where early aggressive lowering of the blood pressure is of crucial importance in saving lives.

- Comply with the medical treatment as prescribed by your doctor. However if you experience unpleasant side effects such as feeling unwell, nausea, vomiting and dizziness inform your doctor, because the medication recommended may not be suitable for you. Doctors are not likely to have any indication that drugs prescribed are unsuitable for individual patients unless patients comply with the necessary check-up appointments and also inform their doctors of possible adverse reactions.

If medical treatment is needed, anti-hypertensive drugs may be prescribed at the discretion of the doctor. Diuretics – the drugs used to increase urination

– may also be prescribed to assist in the excretion of salt and water from the kidneys.

Complementary treatment:

- Meditation
- Herbal remedies such as garlic and Aloe Vera
- Acupuncture.

NB: Some people with high blood pressure are known to have refused to take prescribed medication. This is a dangerous practice that should not be encouraged, as people are likely to develop complications such as heart problems and strokes.

The Importance of Exercise in the Prevention and Management of Hypertension.

I have written a chapter on exercise, but I will briefly explore the justification of physical exercise in the fight against hypertension. Owing to lack of information, some people with high blood pressure are of the opinion that exercise is likely to worsen the condition. This is a fallacy. Reasonable physical exercise is likely to control this disease. However, it is important to consult your doctor for his/her personal opinion before commencing exercise.

The heart is a muscular pump and one of its functions is to distribute blood throughout the body. Exercise is undoubtedly beneficial to health and there is a growing school of thought that exercise is beneficial in the prevention and management of high blood pressure. It can contribute to a reversal to normality in cases of raised blood pressure.

Exercise boosts the body's production of endorphins, the feel-good factor, thereby reducing stress, a contributory factor in some cases of high blood pressure.

Exercise increases the amount of oxygen in the body. It is also influential in the dilatation of the blood vessels; therefore it increases the supply of blood transported by the blood vessels to the heart. This causes the heart to pump blood with more ease; therefore high blood pressure is likely to be reduced with exercise.

Exercise is also contributory to weight loss. It is also helpful in the reduction of the bad cholesterol in the blood, known as LDL (low density lipoprotein). Whilst LDL is decreased during exercise, HDL (high density lipoprotein), which is the good cholesterol, is increased. This phenomenon minimizes heart disease.

Low Blood Pressure (hypotension)

This condition is not experienced as frequently as high blood pressure and it rarely indicates a serious health concern. Teenagers with no apparent medical history of disease sometimes experience symptoms of low blood pressure.

Rapid changes in posture such as from sitting down to standing up or from lying down to sitting up can also cause the blood to rush down from the brain, thereby resulting in a sudden fall in pressure. This may last for a few seconds, but the blood pressure soon returns to normal.

Other minor causes of lowering of the blood pressure include prolonged vigorous coughing and straining to empty the bowels as in cases of constipation, or the bladder owing to blockage.

The main symptoms of low blood pressure are feelings of giddiness, fainting or actual loss of consciousness due to temporary reduction of blood to the brain.

Hypotension is found in some patients with an illness known as adrenal insufficiency. This is a condition in which the adrenal glands, which lie on top of each kidney, are destroyed. It is also sometimes found in some people with abnormally low salt intake and those on vasodilators (drugs used in widening the blood vessels) to reduce high blood pressure.

One situation when abnormally low blood pressure is a matter for concern is after extreme and sudden loss of body fluids, such as during surgery, after severe injuries resulting in bleeding or after prolonged bouts of vomiting.

Heavy loss of body fluids causes shock; with shock there is a drastic fall in blood pressure and the risk of damage to the kidneys.

Obesity

As we enter a new millennium, there still remains a noticeable degree of ignorance and prejudice regarding this sensitive and often distressing condition. Therefore, it is a pertinent subject for discussion.

What is obesity?

Obesity is defined as a condition in which there is excessive fat stored in the body. Its classification is widely accepted as Body Mass Index (BMI) greater than 30. BMI is calculated by weight in kilograms divided by height x 2 in metres.

Therefore the BMI calculation of an individual weighing 90 kg (14st), with an height of 1.5m (5ft) would be estimated as follows: 90 divided by 1.5x2 =30.

BMI (W/Hx2)	Grade of obesity
Less than 25	normal
25–30	pre obese
30-35	class I obese
35–40	class II obese
40–60	class III obese

There are several schools of thought in describing this condition. There is no readily defined basis of BMI for which the World Health Organization criterion is universally agreed. Evidence from Asia suggested that unwanted effects of excess body weight starts at Body Mass Index over 23 (BMI>23). Some people are of the opinion that because bone structure, physical endurance and stamina vary in individuals, it is inconclusive to determine the percentage of excess weight of an individual.

It is stated in Davidson's *Principles and Practice of Medicine* that 'In affluent countries obesity is more common in the lower socio-economical groups. In developing countries it can occur only in the prosperous elite.' However, it is worth mentioning that as a direct result of poverty, obesity is also common amongst poorer people in developing nations where the principal affordable diet is starchy and also high in fat.

Causes of obesity

1. Familial. Inheritance of a particular gene, which is influential in minimizing energy output. Like diabetes and high blood pressure, obesity is also common in black people. These disorders appear to affect generations of the same family to a degree. It is therefore not surprising that some authorities on these diseases strongly suggest that black people are genetically linked to them.

According to the Association for the Study of Obesity in the UK, 'Analysis of the prevalence of obesity in the USA has indicated marked ethnic differences in the development of obesity, with Black and Hispanic groups at much greater risk than White Americans.' The Assoication further stated, 'Asian immigrants to the UK have more central fat than Caucasians and across Europe, Mediterranean women have more central fat than Northern European women. These differences may be the consequence of genetic, cultural or socio-economic factors or more likely, some combination of all three.' (The Association for the Study of Obesity).

2. Consumption of the principal affordable carbohydrate and high fat meals. Obesity appears to be diet related.

3. Energy intake greater than energy output over a lengthy period, or occupational changes leading to lack of exercise, as in the case of those leaving an active physical working environment for a sedentary occupation.

4. Inappropriate diet during infancy. Children who are overfed or given an unhealthy diet are at risk of becoming obese throughout their lives. It is not easy for these children to abandon a habit introduced to them since infancy because it is part of early conditioning; therefore this becomes an integral part of their way of life.

5. Endocrine, such as in situations where there is under activity of the thyroid gland, the pituitary gland and the gonad.

6. Drug-induced. This is experienced in cases where certain medications are taken for lengthy periods. These drugs include hormones such as the contraceptive pill primarily used for protection against pregnancy; hormone replacement therapy, which is taken to combat symptoms of the menopause; steroids used to suppress the symptoms of diseases and antidepressants.

7. Anxiety state resulting in comfort eating.

Complications of obesity

Increase in weight can lead to complications such as high blood pressure, heart disease, strokes, diabetes mellitus (sugar diabetes), disorders of the gallbladder, increased risk to arthritis, back problems, hernia, gout, irregularities in menstruation and ovulation problems in women (leading to difficulty in conception), flat foot, constipation, urinary incontinence, breathing problems, snoring, tiredness, increased risk of complications during surgery and higher incidences of sickness and death.

There is also increased incidence of fatty tissue related cancer and difficulty in discovering lumps in the breast because of the high percentage of body fat.

Prevention of Obesity

There are an estimated three million obese children in the UK in 2003. Education is one of the most reliable methods of avoiding obesity. If parents were educated about the dangers of overfeeding or comfort feeding infants, there would be a decline in the incidence of childhood related obesity. Even during infancy, some children can manipulate parents. If the comforting breast is popped out to appease the infant each time it cries, the child can have a field day playing 'pop-the-treat' with mummy whenever it choses.

People sometimes believe that they are being exceedingly loving and caring by offering extra portions of food to children. Over a lengthy period, this seemingly kind gesture can lead to obesity and other associated health related problems, such as high blood pressure, heart disease and strokes, not to mention depression resulting from bullying that unfortunate children are likely to be subjected to.

I have observed mothers overfeeding their children and when questioned about the justification for their apparently doting gesture, some would state that because they were raised in financially deprived households, they did not have much, including food, therefore they are determined that their children can eat as much as they want.

On one occasion after enduring yet another earful of that ridiculous excuse, I retorted, 'The poverty that you had to endure did not kill you. It made you a psychologically strong and resilient individual, but if you continue to stuff your children with food each time they request it, not only will you be raising a weak spoilt brood, you may also unintentionally contribute to their premature demise.'

Adults must also be aware of the dangers of overweight. It is important to avoid foods that contribute to excess weight, eat a sensible nutritious diet and exercise.

Genetic occurrence, cultural acceptance and cultural competence in coping with obesity

I was astonished when an overweight individual told me that her doctor jokingly advised her to do something about her weight because 'fat people are unattractive'. That is the sort of negative labelling from supposed highly respected professionals which inadvertently instigates and propagates prejudice towards the psychologically vulnerable, including obese people.

Although it ought to be emphasized that for our health and wellbeing, we must not be complacent about the problems associated with excess weight, while numerous people desperately try to accomplish and maintain their precise physical stature, it is often an arduous task. As in any case of disappointment, failure to accomplish weight loss often has a psychological effect on people. This is further compounded by ridiculous and insensitive remarks regarding the public's perception of them.

In order to cope with the extremely cold climate, Eskimos have a thick layer of fatty tissue under the skin, which makes them appear 'chubby'. This is a naturally occurring compensatory act of nature in minimizing energy loss, thus affording protection from the cold. Thereby Eskimos are protected from freezing to death. Would we therefore suggest that because those people do not have a lean appearance, they are unattractive? Should we not acknowledge that they look the way they do in order to survive?

In some societies, people are inclined to be overweight. This tendency is culturally acceptable within their communities. However, those societies are primarily from developing countries and several are in the tropics, so they are likely to gain some health benefits from the hot climate and their way of life.

Unlike people in the affluent West, many people in developing countries are unable to afford personal transportation; some cannot afford the fares for public transportation. Some people are so accustomed to walking that it appears to be a habitual excursion for them, and they frequently walk a considerable distance in the heat. Physical exercise from walking, manual work and sweating as a result of exercise and the heat from the sun are all of vital importance in the expenditure of calories and also extremely contributory to a healthy life.

It is constantly drummed into the minds of Westerners that to be wafer thin epitomizes beauty and attractiveness (especially in females). This message is wreaking insurmountable repercussion on the young females of today as cases of anorexia nervosa, bulimia and other slimming related disorders have escalated proportionally in recent years. It has been reported that children as young as ten years of age are victims of slimming related disorders.

As financial conditions are often hazardous, it is not usual for people in the developing world to indulge in so called 'comfort eating', one of the contributing factors for obesity. Some find it a struggle to muster up one main meal, let alone to acquire supplies to binge for comfort. There is also a communally spirited solidarity, so loneliness, anxiety and stress, which seem to be some of the contributory reasons for comfort eating, are minimal in developing nations.

Bearing the above discussion in mind, it is therefore unwise for black people residing in the West to imitate the 'don't care' attitude of overweight people in developing countries. Those people are often much sturdier and more resilient to weight induced illnesses than their counterparts in the West. It is difficult for some to lose weight even when they try desperately hard. They appear to be competent in coping with their weight. I have known several overweight people in the Caribbean who have lived to a ripe old age.

Lack of exercise

It is implied that some cases of obesity are directly linked to lack of exercise due to laziness, embarrassment, a carefree attitude to health or ignorance of health risks. I am in agreement with each of those given reasons as contributory factors to the disease. However, considering some of the predisposing factors to obesity such as genetics, endocrine disorders and stress, it is not easy to determine whether lack of exercise is a contributory factor to obesity or whether obesity is the reason for insufficient exercise.

Although it is advisable for everyone to be attentive to the problem of weight gain, which can escalate to obesity, this information must be taken much more seriously in the West. There is a disparity in life style between people in the developing countries and those in the West. Those in the West are greatly influenced by an affluent life style which is not compatible with physical activities. This leads to ill health.

Some barriers to health in the West are: travelling by car even for short journeys; the use of sophisticated equipment to carry out simple manual household chores such as cleaning, washing and cutting the lawn. Even activities such as watching television predispose to weight gain and therefore health risks due to physical inactivity. This has worsened with the advance of technology in recent years.

Modern technology heralds serious health-related consequences for mankind. It provides the perfect missile to hurl us into a state of physical inertia. People in the West are now living in a 'lazy' era whereby simply pushing a button substitutes for natural manual duties, even for the simplest of chores.

When we habitually succumb to the wonders of modern living, including watching television, we unconsciously sign a warrant for bad health. Once we have located a suitable seat, we can remain comfortably glued to the television screen for hours. This is because by simply touching a magical button on the remote control by our side, we can access a variety of programmes of our choice. We illusively believe that we are enjoying a life fit for a king or queen.

Moreover, through hours of supposed relaxation, the only physical exercise one is likely to get is the movement of one digit, the index finger, as it operates in robot-like response to impulses from our 'television hypnotized brain'.

Oh! One hand and the facial muscles might also experience a little exercise as the hand dips into a packet of calorie-infested potato crisps or sweets. With robot-like mimicry, the welcoming mouth is targeted with the unhealthy feast in a bid to ameliorate imaginary hunger (most likely induced by sheer boredom from watching too many hours of television).

Treatment of Obesity
Due to the fact that obesity can lead to a range of complications in health it must be addressed. Treatment should include the following:

1. Healthy eating habits in order to reduce body fat, thereby decreasing weight to or near normal levels.

2. Addressing psychological issues which may have given rise to low self-esteem and depression. Meditation is effective in developing mental power and self confidence to combat obesity.

3. Exercise is useful in both a physical and a psychological context. It is helpful in weight loss and as the endorphin level elevates, depression disappears.

4. Acupuncture is an invaluable therapy in combating excess weight.

The Management of Obesity
It is virtually impossible for every individual compartmentalized into the varying categories of obesity, to attain his/her expected weight. However, we

can maintain reasonable health if we monitor our weight to some degree in order to avoid the hazards of an excess burden on our bodies.

In reality, to be uncomfortably overweight is tantamount to carrying a heavy weight. One is likely to collapse under the strain of managing too great a load. Constant over-eating causes the body to create excess fatty tissues; therefore we must take control of our eating habits.

If the eating disorder is psychological in origin, it is important for the contributory cause to be addressed before embarking on a weight loss regimen. For instance, people may find comfort in food as a substitute for an unfulfilled emotion such as love or the desire to become a parent. If the problem is not addressed, it may be difficult to lose the weight.

How many of us, after losing something, would compliantly give up what we have acquired as substitute for that loss? If the weight is lost and the emotional problem remains unattended, the individual might be left in a worse state of emotional deprivation as a result of giving up or losing his/her substituted comfort. This is why it is impractical for people to be bullied into losing weight by those who have no idea of the mental or emotional state of the individuals.

It is a well-observed fact that overweight people are often the happiest and nicest people to be around. This may be attributed to the fact that they are contented. On the other hand, they may be presenting an image of bravado and cheerfulness to be appreciated and liked by others, especially if they believe that they are resented. Yet, when they lose weight, some are often miserable and unhappy; they seem to behave as though something vital was missing from their lives.

Instructions. Eat according to the demands of the body. As we get older, we do not require the amount of food that we were accustomed to when we were younger. Our metabolic rate becomes slower, hence we burn up fewer calories and we are therefore likely to accumulate extra weight if we eat more than we should. That is why people tend to put on weight as they get older.

Diet. There are a number of diets, but it is important to eat a well balanced diet which can be tolerated for a long period. Establish a sensible manageable diet regimen by decreasing your energy intake. Additional energy needed by the body is then taken from the existing stores of body fat.

- Eat fewer fatty foods. Restrict intake of fat building foods such as potatoes, yams, bread, cakes, sweet biscuits, sweets, ice cream and coconut products.
- Drink lots of water.

- Avoid a 'crash diet' which is low in calories and which affords rapid weight loss. The weight lost with these diets is chiefly water, not fat. People on crash diets soon return to their former eating habit and gain back the lost weight because crash diets are not sustainable.

- Check your weight. Try to make the effort (if you can) to lose the excess weight. The main goal in your achievement to reduce weight should not be to satisfy others with your leaner physical appearance; it should be for the enhancement of your personal health.

- After a reasonable amount of weight loss, seek permission from your doctor to commence gradual exercise in order to maintain your new weight. There are several exercises such as brisk walking, stretching, swimming and skipping that are useful for weight control.

- Jogging is another popular exercise in controlling weight. However, for personal safety, women are advised not to jog alone.

I often jogged with my dog Yixi, though sometimes he would refuse to go if it was a cold or wet day. If I happened to meet a male in a secluded area in the park when jogging unaccompanied by my dog, I would pretend to be 'tough'. I would take a deep breath, then start to make loud consecutive exhaling noises through my mouth whilst I shadow boxed, punching the air as I jogged, thus giving the observer the belief that I was training for one helluva boxing match.

Early one morning whilst out jogging, I noticed a man approaching from the opposite direction. I immediately sprang into action by demonstrated my pretend 'training technique'. I punched the air so violently whilst I gyrated my neck like Mike Tyson, that the poor man might have felt somewhat terrified. He stepped out of my way and stood gazing at me alarmingly. I thought to myself, 'You may well be a decent bloke, but if you happen to harbour any unhealthy thoughts about defenceless women, this display should discourage you, mate.'

As I turned the corner, I looked back to make sure that the man could not see me. I then dashed behind the concealing trunk of the nearest large oak tree to rest and catch my breath. It is no fun for an unprofessional boxer to perform those antics whilst jogging. The heart and lungs are on overdrive as they try to cope with the sudden workload. The result is a feeling of exhaustion. Nonetheless, after composing myself and jogging home, I enjoyed a hearty giggle as I reminisced on my amusing escapade.

A crucial factor which should be taken into consideration when trying to lose weight is whether the weight is stable or rising. Some people find it difficult to get beyond a certain borderline on the scale despite determined efforts to lose more weight. This may be an indication that that is the appropriate weight for the individual.

It is in the interest of individuals to be sensible in determining whether they are comfortable with their size when carrying out regular routines. There are several telltale signs of weight-related problems such as lack of stamina in performing usual routine activities, breathlessness and tiredness.

When my dog Yixi increases the distance in beating me when I challenge him to a sprint, I become aware that I am gaining weight. However, being a bad loser, I promptly command my obedient competitor to stand still. As the pet complies with my command, I seize the opportunity to dash off ahead of him. Unfortunately, I generally fail abysmally to gain any advantage over him with that tactic, because he breezes past me like a greyhound in chase of the elusive hare on the racetrack.

It is not advisable to resort to extreme measures to lose weight; this can result in illness and even death. Although incidence of death from actual slimming is rare, there are reported casualties of slimming related diseases. Amongst such fatalities are two people who were very important to me, my mother and my best friend from the age of five. This chapter has therefore been understandably traumatic for me.

Reflection. It is evident that obesity is likely to predispose to health-related problems, therefore there is understandable concern regarding the welfare of individuals affected by it. However, it is not advisable that the 'sufferer' should be constantly pestered into losing weight. This tactic is counter-productive because in a desperate bid to appease depression incurred through nagging, it often leads to increase in comfort eating, especially in cases of psychological related obesity. Weight loss must be a subjective effort, not an objective exercise – it should be done for the health benefits of the individual, not for society's acceptance of him/her.

When anxious or depressed, some people find consolation in food. This is synonymous with a distressed infant trying to suck milk from its mother's breast. Although the child may not experience physical hunger, it may be trying to appease its emotional starvation. There are those who venture further than nagging by ridiculing overweight people. This insensitive attitude often drives the overweight victims to further depression and overeating.

Even if people have a weakness for food, what gives us the right to be unpleasant to them? Are we as sarcastic to people with other forms of disease and weaknesses, some of which stand the chance of endangering the health and welfare of others? Is it the fact that this condition, unlike others, cannot be physically concealed, which causes its sufferers to be victims of the onslaught of society?

'Heaviness in the heart of man maketh it stoop: but a good word maketh it glad.' (Proverbs 12:25).

Anyone experiencing a problem needs understanding, respect and compassion; not ridicule. Should a given number of people be selected at random for assessment on human weaknesses, it is likely that an astonishingly high percentage would have varying degrees of emotional discordance or abnormal traits of behaviour. This does not mean that those people are mad or bad; on the contrary, many are simply sad people.

A colleague once told me that her boyfriend had a habit of playing with her hair; then when he left her she began pulling out her hair from the roots (epilation) on occasions when she thought of him. Interestingly, at that period, she started to eat a considerable amount of chocolate and cakes. She later stated that she believed that whilst she was subconsciously removing the memory of her ex-boyfriend, she was replacing that vacuum with something she perceived to be a comforting substitute.

There may be other participants in the random testing who do not exhibit any peculiar traits of behaviour or they may have overcome them. Humans are a collection of differing personalities; some of us are impervious to emotional problems, whilst others are easily affected. This does not mean that those who show no signs of worrying are stronger or better that others. On the contrary, it is commonly assumed that people who are prone to emotional distress are often some of the most caring, loving and loyal people whose problems are often the result of their good-natured tendencies.

It is fitting that we should all show respect and fellow feeling towards those involved in the fight against obesity. We all have our individual demons to combat, but if we assist each other, collectively we stand a better chance of winning each battle. Let us imagine the torment of the afflicted, and then let us contemplate reaching out a compassionate hand to support them (if needed). By our deeds of kindness, we may emerge the catalysts in the obese person's victory, at the battle of the bulge.

Sickle Cell Disorder

What is Sickle Cell Disorder? Sickle cell disease, described as sickle cell disorder by some people, is the medical term for a chronic inherited genetic blood disorder affecting the haemoglobin which is situated within the red blood cells. This disease is the result of inheriting abnormal haemoglobin (Hb); this is the oxygen-carrying part of the red blood cell. A normal Hb is round like a doorknob and it is flexible, but under ce.... as sickle cell disorder, it becomes stiff and inflexible owing to dehydrati It resembles a farmer's sickle – hence the name 'Sickle Cell'.

People suffering from sickle cell inherit two faulty genes, one from each parent who is a carrier of the disorder. Likewise, the parents inherited the faulty genes from their parents. This cycle of inheritance is passed down the line for several generations (probably hundreds).

What are genes? Genes are minute particles inside the cells in our bodies; they pass on all the biological characteristics inherited from our parents and fore-parents. They are responsible for us inheriting traits of parental and ancestral looks, behaviour and susceptibility to certain diseases.

Genes are estimated to be between 50,000 and 100,000 in number. They double themselves to pass from one generation to another. They carry important information about us (how each of us is made and how we function) in long chemical strands that coil around each other, forming a double helix. This chemical strand is called Deoxyribonucleic Acid (DNA). DNA is often used nowadays to provide scientific evidence in determining proof in cases involving the paternity of children and criminology. It generally 'nails' the culprit.

If the chemicals become damaged, then the information is changed permanently. In sickle cell disorder, the gene responsible for the haemoglobin is damaged. That is why, despite the fact that there is now advancement in the management of this disorder leading to a decline in early death, there is no effective treatment (to date) in the eradication of this condition. Sickle cell disorder is a permanent biological abnormality.

It is important to note that sickle cell is not a contagious disease. One is born with it; it cannot be contracted as in the case of an infectious disease. This disorder is found in many parts of the world where malaria is endemic and the highest incidences of those affected are people of African descent. Others prone to be affected include Indians, Pakistanis and people of Middle Eastern countries. People of Eastern Mediterranean descent such as Italians and Greeks are also affected.

It is estimated that there are over 10,000 people with sickle cell disorder in Britain, and there are several thousands more with the trait: for example one in four West Africans, one in ten Caribbeans and one in a hundred Asians and Cypriots.

The History of Sickle Cell Disorder

Sickle cell disorder is believed to be an act of nature in providing protection from malaria. It has been discovered that blood from people with sickle cell trait who contracted malaria had fewer of the malarial parasites than those without the trait who had malaria. When the red blood cells containing sickle haemoglobin become infected by malarial parasite, sickling occurs. This process causes the parasite to be deprived of nourishment because parasites cannot survive unless they feed off living things.

Haemoglobin is made up of the iron-containing pigment haem and the protein called globin. The normal haemoglobin is identified as haemoglobin A (HbA). There are more than 800 variations of haemoglobin identified and the majority are conveniently labelled after their appearance or the area or towns in which they were discovered. Haemoglobin S is representative of people with the sickle cell.

Sickle cell disorder is somewhat lacking in sufficient mainstream medical dedication, therefore sickle cell organizations are actively educating professionals, sufferers, carers and the general public. It is not surprising to find that apart from some medical experts, some sickle cell sufferers here in Britain appear to be some of the most knowledgeable sources on this condition.

The inheritance of sickle cell disorder

At conception, half of the genes inherited by the foetus come from the mother and the other half come from the father.

- If one parent has sickle cell trait (AS), and the other is normal (AA), the children stand a 50% chance of being normal (AA) and a 50% chance of having sickle cell trait (AS).

- If both parents have sickle cell trait, the children have a 50% chance of having the trait (AS), 25% chance of having the disorder (SS) and 25% chance of normality (AA).

- If one parent has the disorder and the other is normal (AA), all the children of that couple will have the trait (AS).

- If one parent has the disorder and the other has the trait (Hb AS), the children born to that couple would have either the disorder, 50% (SS) or the trait, 50% (AS).

- If both parents have sickle cell disorder (Hb SS), all the children of that couple will have the disorder. This is by far the commonest and most serious form of the disorder.

NB: People with sickle cell trait are not normally affected with the disorder; therefore they are sometimes referred to as 'healthy carriers'. However, some may be predisposed to some minor symptoms of the disorder especially if they are deprived of oxygen. It is therefore important for people with sickle cell trait to inform doctors or dentists of their problem as they may require oxygen during anaesthetic.

Some symptoms of sickle cell disorder

There are several signs and symptoms associated with sickle cell disorder, and the most common ones are:

- Swelling of the hands and feet (dactylitis). This is often the first sign and this can appear from the age of six months.
- Chronic anaemia resulting from the shortened life of the red blood cells. This is due to the frequent destruction of the red blood cells. The average life span of a red blood cell is 120 days, but in sickle cell disorder it is an average of 8 to 30 days.
- Jaundice – a yellowish coloration of the skin and the white part of the eyes, resulting from the rapid destruction of red blood cells.
- 'Crisis Pain'. Blood is responsible for the transportation of oxygen and nutrients throughout the entire body. The transformation of the blood cells in a sickle cell crisis impedes the blood from passing freely through the smaller blood vessels. This causes clogging and back flow of blood, resulting in insufficient distribution of oxygen to the organs and other vital parts of the body. The lack of oxygen to the organs triggers the pain receptors, and they react by causing pain. Pain is a permanent feature of this disorder, but it may vary in severity.
- Enlarged spleen. The spleen is located behind the stomach, high up on the left side of the abdomen corresponding to the position of the 9th, 10th and 11th ribs. It is primarily associated with the function of the blood. It produces lymphocytes, one type of white blood cell, and it breaks down and removes worn out and damaged red and white blood cells and blood platelets (clotting agents). In sickle cell disorder, the spleen can be enlarged owing to the large volume of sickled red blood cells being destroyed. This leads to anaemia.

NB: It is common for the spleen to be enlarged during infancy, but it later shrinks, except in patients with certain conditions including sickle cell or sickle thalassaemia.

Other symptoms of sickle cell disorder

- Failure to thrive (stunted growth), pallor, weakness and delayed puberty.
- Owing to reduced immunity protection by the spleen and leucocytes, sickle cell sufferers are susceptible to bouts of infections, especially pneumococcal infections.
- Priapism: this is a condition in which there is a crisis in the penis, resulting in it being painfully erected for considerable periods. This situation is usually relieved by medical intervention.

- Organ damage: The kidneys are another contributing factor to anaemia. Damaged kidneys cannot concentrate urine in the normal way, therefore there is frequent urination and this is made worse by the fact that patients with sickle cell disorder must drink large amounts of fluids in order to decrease incidents of sickle crisis.

- Some sufferers may experience eye problems especially involving the retina, which is the membrane at the back of the eyes.

- Ulcers on the lower part of the legs, especially around the ankle. This is particularly common in Afro-Caribbeans.

- Red blood cells are responsible for taking oxygen around the body, therefore a decrease in the circulation of oxygen to the brain can result in headaches and occasionally, strokes. Incidents of strokes in children under the age of twelve years are a common feature of this disorder.

- Bones and joints are often areas for severe pain.

- Chest syndrome including discomfort in the chest and difficulty in breathing due to sickling in the lungs may occur.

Diagnosis: There are various ways of testing for the sickle cells, both before and after birth:

1. A routine request for this test can be made at the GP surgery.
2. Test is conducted before surgery.
3. Tests during pregnancy. Some hospitals routinely carry out blood tests for sickle cell disorder on all expectant mothers.

(a) *Chorionic Villus Sampling*: Testing a sample of the tissue around the foetus, which goes on to form the placenta or afterbirth. This tissue contains genetic material of the baby, and it may be obtained through the vagina and cervix, or by putting a needle through the abdominal wall. It is believed to be quite a painless procedure. Chorionic villus sampling is commonly performed before the 11th week of pregnancy. If performed later than the 11th week of pregnancy, testing is more difficult to perform and the baby could be exposed to the risk of miscarriage.

(b) *Amniocentesis*: This test is a simple procedure whereby amniotic fluid (the fluid surrounding the foetus in the womb to protect it from external pressure) is extracted. The test is performed between 14–20 weeks of pregnancy and it involves a sample of the amniotic fluid. This test carries a 1% risk of miscarriage.

(c) *Foetal Blood Sampling*: This procedure is conducted in a specialized centre. A sample of blood is withdrawn from the umbilical cord of the developing foetus. According to leaflet ref 7364 from the Brent Sickle &Thalassaemia Counselling Centre, 'Foetal Blood Sampling can be carried out at 16–24 weeks of pregnancy.' The leaflet also states: 'Foetal Blood Sampling carries a 2–5% risk of miscarriage.'

4. Tests after birth: In the United Kingdom, blood testing for sickle cell disorder is conducted in most hospitals. The dried blood spot test is routinely done on all babies on or after the fifth day after birth and the haemoglobin is tested for sickle cell and thalassaemia major. By the year 2006 there will be universal neonatal testing for sickle cell and thalassaemia throughout the United Kingdom.

NB: Apart from the medical tests mentioned above, in situations where infants have frequent abdominal pain, swelling of ankles and wrist, failure to thrive and are abnormally pale in complexion, sickle cell anaemia should be considered as a possible diagnosis.

Treatment and Management

Despite the severity of this disorder, the lives of those afflicted with it have greatly improved in recent years. Therefore there is much optimism that the quality of life for sufferers of sickle cell disorder can be reasonable, if the condition is carefully managed.

Care and advice

People with sickle cell disorder need plenty of rest. It is essential for them to be kept warm.

Some sufferers may need assistance and advice in order to cope with the disorder. Support group meetings are a good means whereby sufferers can meet together and communicate with others affected by the disorder. Contact with people affected by the same disorder, who are therefore likely to share similar anxieties and pass on relevant information, can be mentally stimulating and spiritually uplifting and therefore generally rewarding.

Fluids. Adequate fluid, particularly water, is of vital importance to the body, and whether we are healthy or sick, we need an average of 2 to 3 litres daily. People with sickle cell disorder require more than the average quantity of fluid daily.

Dehydration increases sickling within each cell. Blockage of blood vessels by the sickled cells causes severe pain. The kidneys can be quite susceptible to damage from sickling and could therefore be incompetent in their functions.

One manifestation of this is frequency in urination, as mentioned before. It is therefore important for patients to have regular intake of water to reintroduce fluids into the cells, thereby maintaining a reasonable balance of fluid in the body.

Diet. Due to the fact that patients with sickle cell disorder need to manufacture blood on a regular basis, they require a well balanced diet that is high in calories. This is of significant importance especially for children whose energy requirements are greater than adults. An adequate amount of protein is also of vital importance in helping to stimulate growth in children affected by sickle cell disorder.

Medication. Certain medications are essential to people with sickle cell disorder and some authorities on the disease advise that treatment should commence from three months old. Medication is often needed as prophylaxis (preventative) and also treatment against infection.

The commonly prescribed medications are:

- Antibiotics. The one frequently used in the treatment of sickle cell disorder is penicillin. It helps to provide protection from serious pneumococcal infection. It is not advisable to stop this treatment even if complementary medicines such as acupuncture or herbal remedies are also taken.

- Analgesics. Regular painkillers may be prescribed. If pain becomes severe, patients may require hospitalization where they would be prescribed stronger pain killers.

- Folic Acid. This is a vitamin sometimes given regularly to assist the bone marrow to make extra red blood cells. However, it is not a routine procedure in all treatment units.

- Immunization. Children should receive all the required immunizations. Additionally, they should be given Pneumovax, a vaccine providing extra protection against serious infections such as pneumocuccus. It is usually given for the first time around the age of two and repeated after five to ten years. Even if penicillin is taken, it is advisable for immunization to be also given. However, if the children are unwell, the parents/carer must inform the doctor before the children are immunized.

Blood transfusion. Taking into account that this is a serious form of anaemia, blood transfusion is necessary, when the Hb falls below a certain level that is normal for those individuals. However there are some people who, for religious or personal reasons, are opposed to blood transfusion. This does not mean that those people should be forced into complying with the treatment or ostracized for refusing.

Personal Comment. There is now a greater choice of medical alternatives, therefore it is time for substitutes that are compatible to health and people's moral and religious inclination to be made available. No matter how controversial it may seem to us, simply because we do not understand the reasoning of those patients concerned, we (especially those in the caring profession) must respect the wishes and beliefs of others in a world of diversity.

Exchange Transfusion. In some instances, children whose tests confirm that they have sickle cell disorder have some of their blood removed and replaced with transfused blood.

Other helpful suggestions. With the approval of the General Practitioner, the following choice of complementary therapies may be helpful in stabalising this condition.

- Aloe Vera or other herbal medicines prepared by a registered herbalist.
- Acupuncture.
- Meditation and visualization are also highly recommended.

One of the benefits of water. Water is beneficial for the proper function of the organs of the body. I must not omit its importance in assisting with brain concentration,

A few years ago I was deep in concentration on some written work in my local library, when suddenly I could not think clearly. That phenomenon is described as 'writer's block'. An eight year old friend happened to notice me closing my eyes in desperation to summon my mind into action. Tapping me gently on one shoulder, she asked whether I was 'trying to think what to write'. I replied in the affirmative.

She then told me that each time she found it difficult to concentrate, she drank water and it always worked for her. I was amazed by the advice of one so young.

I inquired the source of that valuable information. She told me that when she was younger, her grandmother who resides in Ireland always insisted on children drinking water instead of sweetened drinks, 'because water was good for the brain, it makes people clever,' she said.

I proceeded to ask her whether she shared that valuable information with her classmates. Staring at me with her eyes wide open, she said, 'Why should I tell them and let them be cleverer than me? I only told my friend and you; anyway my friend does not attend my school, so it does not bother me if she is clever; and you are old, so you have finished learning.' I smiled at that amusing answer from my clever little friend.

Lupus Disease (Systemic Lupus Erythematosus – SLE)

As in the case of Rheumatoid Arthritis, Lupus is an auto-immune or self-allergy disease. This means that the body reacts to an unknown stimulus and produces many antibodies, or proteins that attack the body's own tissues.

In normal circumstances, the body reacts against harmful invaders by creating antibodies (substances in the blood), which destroy or neutralize them.

In recent years, people are becoming more aware of conditions such as lupus and sickle cell diseases, however there are a vast number of people who are still ignorant of these conditions, especially lupus. Just as in the case of sickle cell disease, people affected by lupus seem to have a considerable knowledge of the condition.

Lupus is difficult to diagnose and it can be overlooked for a considerably long time, because some of those affected by it appear to look healthy. The majority of those affected by the disease are young women. It is estimated that about one in 800 women suffer from lupus in the United Kingdom, but men and young children also make up a small percentage. One of the classical symptoms of the disease is a healthy red rash on the cheeks. The name *lupus* is derived from the Latin word for 'wolf' because historically the pattern of the pinkish coloured facial rash was thought to resemble a wolf's mask or a wolf's bite.

Even as a qualified nurse during the late 70s, my knowledge of lupus disease was very limited. It was only after a nursing colleague of Asian origin was diagnosed with the disease that my eyes were opened to it.

There were times when my colleague would be her usual cheerful self, then she would suddenly become depressed and complain of every conceivable ache and pain. It was difficult not to believe that she was ill because she literally looked dreadful. She appeared to have bouts of attack during exams.

Although lupus is not popularly known like diseases such as multiple sclerosis and leukaemia, it is far more common. It is only after extensive publicity than several diseases are known to the public, which is why it is of crucial importance that lesser known diseases such as sickle cell and lupus are advertised so that they can be brought to public awareness.

Dr Daniel J Wallace, author of *The Lupus Book* (Oxford University Press 2000) wrote: 'In the United States, African Americans, Latinos, and Asians have a greater incidence of SLE than Caucasians. The prevalence among African

American woman was estimated by Kaiser-Permanente to be 286 per 100,000 in San Francisco. A Hawaiian study showed that Asian women have three times the prevalence of SLE compared with Caucasian women.'

Dr Wallace further stated: 'American Indians seem to have the highest prevalence of lupus ever reported, but the numbers surveyed were too small to confirm this trend.'

Lupus is neither infectious nor contagious. Someone can have the disease without showing any sign or experience any symptom of it until it is triggered by circumstances such as certain viral infections; exposure to strong sun; stress; after treatment with certain medication; hormonal changes occurring at puberty; after childbirth or during the menopause.

Signs and Symptoms of lupus

Lupus has the ability to mimic many other diseases. This trend can vary from person to person. Because lupus can cause problems in almost any part of the body, its symptoms can be numerous. The most common signs and symptoms are:

- Fatigue
- Arthritis
- Fever
- Anaemia
- Listlessness
- Chest pain
- Migraine & headaches
- Permanent rash over the cheeks
- Other skin problems
- Heart & lung problems
- Kidney problems
- Mouth ulcers
- General weakness
- Dry eyes
- Poor blood circulation, including Raynaud's Disease (obstruction of circulation in outlying parts of the body especially the fingers)
- Hair Loss
- Phlebitis

- Depression
- Psychiatric disorders
- Memory loss
- Flu-like symptoms
- Gastrointestinal problems

It is advisable for anyone experiencing some of the above-mentioned symptoms to request to be tested for lupus disease. Although doctors are generally good at diagnosing, it must not be readily assumed that they should recognize every disease as soon as they are consulted.

Treatment of Lupus

Although there is presently no cure for Lupus, the disease can be controlled thus affording sufferers a reasonable life. There are currently four main groups of drugs used in the treatment of lupus, depending on the severity of the disease. These are:

- Aspirin and Non-Steroidals – Anti-inflammatory drugs (NSAIDS). These are useful for patients who suffer mainly from joint and muscle pain. Aspirin in low dosage may also be prescribed to thin blood, thereby promoting circulation. The side effects of this group of drugs include gastro-intestinal irritation and bleeding. People suffering from lupus disease sometimes experience gastrointestinal problems, therefore NSAIDS should be given with caution and patients must be closely supervised.

- Steroids such as prednisolone have been vital in the management of lupus care and in some cases they are life saving. They have a profound effect on inflammation and they suppress active disease. The dosage depends on the severity of the disease. Once the disease is under control, under medical supervision, the patient can be weaned off steroids gradually.

- Anti-Malarials. These are helpful to patients with skin and joint involvement. These drugs may be sufficient for patients with moderately active lupus to use instead of steroids.

- Immunosuppressants. These drugs are necessary in curtailing the harmful immune reaction in the body. They are widely used to treat cases that are not responding satisfactorily to steroids and where patients have the severe form of the diseases, including kidney problems.

Other considerations for treatment:

- Meditation
- Acupuncture. Considering some of the effects of acupuncture, including immune enhancing, analgesia and sedation, it is beneficial in reducing some of the symptoms of lupus.
- Herbal remedies.

Advice For Patients

- Be informed as much as possible about lupus. Patients who are educated about their disease tend to do better than those who do not seem to know much. This is because they can recognize problematic symptoms early and seek medical assistance.
- Educate family and friends about the disease. Let them know of the signs and symptoms that you may experience. Signs are the manifestation of the disease that can be seen, such as skin rashes or mouth ulcers. Symptoms are indications of what patients may experience, such as feeling tired or depressed.

As I have mentioned in the section on diabetes, some people are inclined to conceal their illness. I cannot reiterate enough the need to be open about illness. Psychiatric disorder, depression and anxiety are high in young women with lupus. If those close to the patient, including family, friends and work colleagues, are unaware of the disease and its clinical manifestation, how can they be expected to be understanding and supportive?

Family and friends are therefore (at times) likely to distance themselves from the patient, because they may be fed up with the unexplained behaviour; colleagues may also complain about the person's irrational attitude. This can result in the sufferer being sacked from his or her job. These added psychological problems can lead to added stress, which is likely to worsen the condition.

- Join a support group. Being with people who understand the illness can be beneficial.
- Do not be afraid to discuss your fears or problems concerning the disease with your doctor, support group or close contacts.
- Rest is important for the body to cope with this disease. Do not try to make difficult tasks your priority. Learn to live at your own pace. However, as in most situations, exercise is important in maintaining

health, therefore people suffering with lupus must take regular, but non-aggressive, exercise.

- Eat a well balanced diet. Your body needs much nutrition to cope with the disease.

- Avoid direct and excessive exposure to the sun. People affected with lupus are usually sensitive to sunlight and also some artificial lights (such as fluorescent lights).

- Follow your doctor's advice. Take your medications as prescribed but always feel free to ask questions regarding your medical treatment.

NB: I would like to express my gratitude to Lupus UK for providing me with some information relating to this chapter.

PART 2

CHAPTER 3

The Causes of Disease continued

Traditional Chinese concept

The Bible informs us that God the omnipotent created man in his own image. If such an ingenious force constructed the human body, why then should we question its ability to function and maintain adequate health independent of chemical intervention?

It is quite obvious to the rational mind that, although God is intangible, He epitomizes health and strength. (He must be super fit to remain in charge of mankind this long. Many lesser forces would have resigned or been liable to suffer a most horrific irreversible emotional crisis commonly described as a nervous breakdown, incurred by the sheer stress of managing and caring for the human race today.)

Theorists of Traditional Chinese Medicine believe that if there is equilibrium or harmonious balance of the essential life forces within the body, we stand the chance of avoiding disease. This does not mean that we would all live happily forever, thus over-populating planet Earth.

If the prevailing vital forces within the body were balanced, then our health would be reasonably good. Even when we come into contact with some diseases, we would stand a chance of averting the symptoms or not being seriously affected by that disease. This is why some people are unaffected when there are outbreaks of cold, influenza and other contagious diseases. However if there is imbalance, there is a possibility of contracting diseases more easily.

In Traditional Chinese Medicine, promotion of the general health is of vital importance in the prevention of disease. Early detection and treatment of internal problems is also routinely undertaken, thereby preventing diseases.

According to the Traditional Chinese concept, there are four factors which are contributory causes to disease. These are:

(A) Environmental or External (those originating from outside the body)
(B) Emotional or Internal (those originating from inside the body)
(C) Miscellaneous (Causes which are neither outside nor inside)
(D) Phlegm

A. Environmental or External

There are six excesses responsible for the external cause of disease and these are directly connected with the environment.

They are wind, cold, heat, dampness, dryness and summer heat. They conform to the Five Elements. These excesses (apart from heat) are each related to a particular season. (Both heat and summer heat correspond to fire.)

The term excess as used in this sense can be interpreted as an abnormality, an evil or pernicious influence. When normal environmental forces become excessive such as a particularly cold spell in winter or an unseasonable occurrence such as a warm spell in the middle of winter (as experienced nowadays as a result of global warming), they contribute to disease.

Owing to individual physical make-up and an undetermined development period in some diseases, different people may suffer with different diseases at the same time or the same disease at different times. Clinical differentiation of the excesses is made on the basis of symptoms, not tests aimed at finding the causative agent of the disease as in Western diagnosis of disease. In other words the disease is described in terms as the body's response, rather than as a clinically identifiable disease entity.

(1) Wind Diseases (Spring Yang)

Diseases in this category arrive suddenly and change their symptoms quickly. They may be accompanied by symptoms of muscle spasm, dizziness as in vertigo (a feeling that one's surroundings are spinning), itching or a pain. The outstanding characteristic of a wind disease is that it often changes location. Wind is said to be the most harmful of the environmental diseases. It carries the other external excesses into the interior of the body. When the liver yang is excessively active, dizziness and convulsions occur; similar symptoms accompany high fevers. Both are caused by exterior wind travelling to the interior of the body.

(2) Cold Diseases (Winter Yin)

The main symptom of this excess is a feeling of coldness in the whole body or parts of it. Cold causes bodily fluids to solidify. An example to explain this scenario is when we make jelly: we place the liquid in a refrigerator and it later turns to jelly.

Solidified fluids in the body cause pain; this is due to obstruction in the flow of Qi (pronounced chee) and blood. Cold causes material substances to thicken in the channels; this results in cramps and spasms. When cold diseases are present, the body's excretions (mucus, tears, phlegm, urine and stools) become white, clear and watery. The tongue becomes pale in colour.

(3) Heat or Fire (Yang)

The principal characteristic of heat related excess is a feeling of hotness in the body or a part of it. Heat injures the body very easily and this causes the tongue and stools to become dry; there is also diminished urination and the patient becomes thirsty.

Heat may cause the blood to travel outside the channels; this can lead to haemorrhages or rashes. Some signs and symptoms of heat excess-related diseases are dark or yellow sticky and foul smelling body excretions. Sometimes the act of expulsion causes heat and discomfort in that area of the body. The tongue is abnormally bright red in colour. Diseases caused by one of the other excesses often transforms into heat or fire within the body.

(4) Dampness (Long Summer Yin)

This excess often appears during damp weather or when a person comes into contact with moisture for a prolonged period of time. Dampness is sluggish and stagnating. Disease caused by this excess takes a long time to be cured. When dampness is present on the external parts of the body the patient feels anxious, the limbs are heavy and the head feels swollen. When dampness invades the muscles and joints, all movements become painful and the affected parts become oedematous (water logged).

The spleen is the organ often affected by dampness. When the functions of the spleen are weak (especially the transforming and transportation of vital substances in the body), internal dampness may result.

(5) Dryness (Autumn Yang)

This excess attacks the fluids of the body and may result in dry skin, chapped lips, hacking cough and constipation. When the body's Yin substances are seriously depleted (as in the latter stages of the long fever-related illness) similar symptoms may appear. The tongue is deep red in colour.

(6) Summer Heat (Summer Yang)

The main clinical feature of this excess is fever with severe sweating. This is injurious to the energies. This excess is often accompanied by dampness.

B. Emotional or Internal

These are seven emotional states that are interconnected to our health; they are excessive happiness, anger, worry, pensiveness, sadness, fear and anxiety. They are linked with the Five Elements system of correspondences. These are all normal emotions, which can lead to illness if sustained for a long period of time.

These emotions can adversely affect those organs associated with the same element (e.g. the large intestines and the lungs in the case of metal, and the urinary bladder and the kidneys in the case of water). The Yin/ Yang balance in the body can also be affected by the emotions.

Worry and sadness correspond to metal, fear and anxiety correspond to water. Apart from the Seven Emotions, frustration upsets the free-flowing nature of the liver and not surprisingly, often leads to anger.

The Western labelled psychosomatic (mind and body) diseases are referred to as internal imbalance in ancient Chinese medicine.

NB: The Five Elements or phases comprise: Wood, associated with the liver and the gall bladder; Fire, associated with the small intestines and the heart; Earth, associated with the spleen and the stomach; Metal, associated with the lungs and the large intestines; and Water, associated with the kidneys and urinary bladder. This is a Traditional Chinese system of corresponding the twelve internal organs with the five mentioned elements of nature. The five elements were regarded as five properties inherent in all things.

C. Miscellaneous

These are syndromes due to causes that cannot be attributed to Internal or External causes of disease. Variation in the quantity, quality or time of eating causes indigestion and related diseases. Quality in this sense is representative of both the hygienic level of food and the traditional classification of food such as hot or cold, bitter or sweet. Each organ is associated with a corresponding taste according to the concept of the five elements: for example, the gall bladder and its corresponding organ the liver, associated with the element wood which corresponds to sour.

Way of Life

Ancient Chinese physicians emphasize the way people conduct their lives sexually and physically.

> (1) Sexual activity: Sexual intercourse and the reproductive function are linked to the kidneys in men, and the kidneys and liver in women. Excessive sexual activity can result in damage to the yin and yang (recessive and dominant energies) of organs associated with sex and

reproduction. Some associated symptoms are low back pain, dizziness and general reduction of sexual vitality. Women giving birth too many times can develop problems with menstruation and discharges.

(2) Physical Activity: The general activities of life are categorized under this section. The Chinese maintain that all of life's activities should be aimed or projected towards the goal of living in harmonious balance with the universe, the seasons, and one's own constitution and stage in life. Yang times – morning, spring, youth – should be active periods in a person life; Yin times – evening, winter, old age – should be resting periods.

However, although I agree with this philosophy to a certain extent, I would not encourage the seniors to over-indulge in rest. Inactivity heralds health-related problems especially in the case of seniors. We must maintain a balance, because when manual labour is performed in moderation, it benefits the body, while if labour is under or over performed, our health is liable to be affected.

Traditional Yin/Yang symbol

D. Phlegm

In traditional Chinese medicine the word *phlegm* does not refer to the secretion coughed up from the lungs, but to the stagnant fluids in the body. Traditionally its formation is due to dysfunction in the water metabolism especially in the transforming and transporting functions of the spleen.

The spleen is therefore the source of phlegm. When water in the body becomes stagnant, it is transformed into phlegm. There are many possible causes for this stagnation but the most common ones are Deficient Qi (energy) and Excess Heat.

Phlegm is both the result of dysfunction and the cause of further disease. When phlegm collects in the lungs there is coughing, wheezing and profuse expectoration. When it enters the stomach, there is nausea and vomiting; when it invades the channels swelling occurs locally; when it surrounds the heart delirium results.

NB: The concept of phlegm disorders includes what is described in modern scientific medicine as endocrine disorders e.g. problems associated with the thyroid glands; metabolic disorders such as diabetes and enzymatic and other biochemical disorders such as pancreatitis and thrombosis.

CHAPTER 4

Acupuncture

My first insight into the wonders of acupuncture was in the early 1980s, when I was nursing in Mount Vernon hospital. Located on the outskirts of London, this hospital is renowned for its pioneering treatment in cancer.

One of the patients on my ward was Mr G, an English gentleman in his mid-forties who was a consultant social worker. He had lived with his German born wife in China for a while and unfortunately on his return to England he became unwell and was later diagnosed with cancer.

Mr G refused to take diamorphine (pure heroin), which was prescribed for his pain. He, like a few patients I have nursed, refused to take strong painkillers prepared from opium. The reasons for refusal were sometimes ethical or because of the unpleasant side effects, such as drowsiness, respiratory depression and constipation associated with these drugs. There is also the likelihood of drug induced hallucination and although this may appear to be a better alternative to pain, there are some patients who prefer to remain lucid until the end. Nonetheless, it is a humane gesture to offer drugs to ease pain because pain is the most distressing symptom in the vicious sequence of disease.

It was customary for people to visit the patients on that particular unit at any time and ministers of various religions frequently visited hospitalized members of their congregation and other patients who were consenting to visits from them. One evening I overheard a clergyman telling one of his parishioners who had been prescribed large doses of opiate for her pain, that sickness, suffering and death were the consequence of man's sin in the Garden of Eden.

The following evening when I reported for duty on my ward, I was told that the patient had complained that the clergyman had told her that her cancer was the result of her sins. I am afraid to mention that some members of staff believed her story and were planning to have the minister banned from further visits to the ward, until I presented my version of the incident.

This was not a case of wilful lying. That dear lady was deeply involved in religion. She must have heard that very sermon preached umpteen times in her church by that particular minister and she probably agreed with his biblical interpretation of the consequence of mankind's sin in the Garden of Eden. However she was not lucid after continuously receiving diamorphine by pump to alleviate her pain, and so she misinterpreted the message on that occasion.

Mr G told me that he was aware that his cancer was too advanced to be cured, but he stated that he wanted to die with dignity. He told me that the only pain control he relished was acupuncture. He explained the benefits of that therapy and the varying conditions it was accredited to have successfully treated in China.

I approached one of the doctors on the unit on behalf of Mr G, requesting that consideration to be given for him to receive acupuncture in a London hospital where it was then available. The following day I was told that the medical team disapproved of the patient's request because they did not believe in the treatment.

Mr G and his wife were very disappointed after learning of the outcome of his request. Meanwhile he continued to refuse to take any pain-killing drug to ease his pain and discomfort.

Mr G's office of employment was based in the street where I lived; therefore we frequently conversed about the neighbourhood and other topics of interest. However he had a habit of diverting the topic of conversation to that of acupuncture.

To the surprise of everyone involved in his care, Mr G's condition rapidly deteriorated and he died within a short period after his request for acupuncture had been refused. Although his death was inevitable, none of us expected it to occur so rapidly.

My initial reaction was to speculate whether his death was a timely course of the disease; whether it was a result of his refusal to accept the medication that was vital in relieving his continuous pain; or whether he willed himself to die because his request for acupuncture had been denied. Each time I thought of that last possible reason for his death I felt a twinge of anger. No justifiable reason was given, apart from prejudice against a therapy that was not part of mainstream medicine. To me, not only was the refusal unjustifiable, it was also inhumane.

I felt that it was morally wrong to deny any terminally ill patient a last request; especially one which the patient believed would alleviate suffering. My anger was not levelled at the doctors who were responsible for the patient's medical care. It was directed at the general foundation of Western medicine, which perceived itself as the indisputable bastion of the medicinal territory.

The treatment would not have incurred any cost on the National Health Service because Mr G's wife had offered to pay for any expense. I felt that he should have been given the opportunity of trying out the treatment that he had so much faith in. I believed that if it was unsuccessful, he might have graciously acknowledged that acupuncture had been tried and he might have even accepted the opiate drug that he had originally refused.

After the birth of my last child I had a strong compulsion to pursue a different line of work in health. The primary reason for this change was to find a suitable working environment in which I could spend more time with my family.

I had worked on night shift for several years and I was becoming somewhat exhausted. I also felt the need to assert some form of autonomy in my career because I believed that I was capable of confidently working on my own outside the perimeter of the traditional caring establishment such as hospitals and medical centres. My husband and my children were also becoming unhappy with my absence from the family every night.

One evening as I was preparing to leave for nursing on the night shift at General Motors, my four-year-old held on to my uniform. With tears streaming down her little face she told me that the newscaster on the television warned people to stay away from General Motors, because there was a 'big fire there'.

I was astounded at the story my child had contrived to prevent me from going to work. She had never made up stories, nor lied to me before. I also felt saddened (not guilty, as proponents for mothers staying home would prefer me to state), that owing to her immaturity, the child could not fully comprehend the reason for my absence from home a few nights weekly.

It was quiet on that particular night, and when I visited Jack, the manager, shortly after my arrival and told him the story my daughter had concocted, Jack told me to close the surgery and then he instructed a foreman to take me home. I felt tremendously grateful for that display of human compassion from that kind gentleman and friend.

One day my husband showed me an advertisement in a popular magazine, inviting people with medical background to train as acupuncture practitioners. He told me that I had seemed somewhat fascinated with acupuncture since I nursed the gentleman who died. Then he said, 'Why don't you pursue a course in acupuncture?'

Suddenly I experienced an inward peace. I quickly glanced at the advertisement, then in a thrilled voice I shouted, 'Eureka!' I immediately contacted the Acupuncture College and they informed me that there were only two vacancies remaining. I immediately enlisted and commenced training a few weeks later.

I believe that I was divinely guided to practise acupuncture. It could have been the result of curiosity or a subconscious act of vengeance to work in the field of medicine that was denied to a dying person. Whatever the reason, I am extremely grateful to have been directed to this branch of natural medicine.

Since childhood, my only ambition was to become a nurse; I desperately wanted to be involved in caring for the sick. Today, acupuncture has become a gratifying bonus to my vocation. I feel that I have accomplished an added dimension that is fulfilling to my purpose in life.

The only sadness to this story is that I knew nothing of acupuncture before I met Mr G or I would have strenuously supported his dying wish. However, the fact that bureaucracy's refusal of that dying patient's wish may have contributed to my involvement with acupuncture has given me added incentive and determination in my commitment to this branch of medicine.

What is acupuncture?

Acupuncture is the ancient Chinese art of curing disease by inserting very fine needles into selected areas of the body to restore health. It is estimated to be about four and a half to five thousand years old.

Other traditional Chinese therapies include: Herbal medicine; Acupressure, which is basically using the fingers to do what needles do in Acupuncture; Diet; Moxibustion, which is the application of heated powdered leaf of the moxa plant (*Artemesia vulgaris*) on selected sections of the body.

It is said that experimentation into acupuncture began after Chinese warriors wounded by arrows were miraculously cured of diseases affecting parts of the body unrelated to the actual wound.

Needles made of stone were initially used. These were followed by needles carved out of bones and bamboo. Nowadays the needles chiefly used are made of stainless steel and some are as thin as a hair.

Theory behind acupuncture

Although it is somewhat difficult to translate the meaning of Qi in the English language, it is an integral medical composite within the basis of Traditional Chinese Medicine. Qi can be defined as a matter on the brink of becoming energy, or energy on the verge of materializing. According to the ancient Chinese, Qi, life force, or vital energy of life, is responsible for the maintenance of life. It is an invisible force, which gives life to all living matter; this is why it is frequently described as 'the vital energy of life'. Qi can be found in everything in the universe, whether organic or inorganic.

Qi is made up of two opposite but equally important components: Yin the recessive and Yang the dominant.

Some examples of yin and yang are as follows:

Yin	Yang
winter	summer
cold	hot
night	day
woman	man
black	white

The theory behind acupuncture is that if there is imbalance of Yin and Yang, there will be disharmony and subsequent disease.

Similarly, if there is disunity between a couple, the situation can cause a strain on the partnership. This may escalate and result in the breakdown in that relationship. In order to restore the union, the couple must settle their differences in a neutral manner.

How acupuncture works

Qi or vital energy of life flows along invisible pathways in the body known as meridians. There are hundreds of acupuncture points located along these pathways.

Traditional Chinese understanding in the treatment of disease is in direct contrast to that of Western trained doctors, whose primary aim is dealing with the symptoms and causes of disease. The traditional Chinese practitioner does not treat symptoms. Diagnosis and treatment is focused towards the whole individual.

In Western medicine pulse examination plays a role in diagnosis and in some instances prognosticating or forecasting the course of disease. But more importantly in traditional Chinese Medicine, examination of the pulse is the keystone in establishing a diagnosis. However, pulse diagnosis is an art, which can only be perfected after years of training with traditional acupuncturists who are familiar with its practice. Six main pulses are checked on the radial side of each wrist (below the base of the thumb). Three of these pulses are superficial and three are deep. Each pulse corresponds with the position of a specific organ of the body.

In Traditional Chinese Medicine, the tongue also plays an important role in establishing a diagnosis. A normal tongue is light red in colour and it is of the proper size. This enables it to move freely. It also has thin layers of whitish coating, which is neither too dry nor too moist.

The following are a few examples of abnormal tongues:
- **Pale tongue.** This is an indication of low energy, circulatory problems associated with low haemoglobin or anaemia.

- **Red tongue.** This indicates internal heat caused by over-consumption of alcohol, inflammatory related conditions, stress, and tiredness due to heavy workload.

- **Cracked tongue.** This is an indication of dehydration as seen in severe lack of fluid, high fevers and shortage of water-soluble vitamins (vitamins B and C).

- **White-coated tongue.** This can be an indication of sluggish digestion whereby there is retention of food and problems associated with excess weight.

- **Thick yellow-coated tongue.** This is an indication of persistent accumulation of food in the stomach and intestines leading to constipation.

Apart from pulse and tongue examination, other information, including the history and life style of the patient and the presenting symptoms, is pieced together like a jigsaw to form a picture of the individual's problem.

After gathering the relevant information, the practitioner is then in an informed position to establish a diagnosis and proceed with treatment.

Acupuncture therapy is amazingly successful especially when given for the duration specified by the practitioner. Despite approval by some, there still remain a body of hardened sceptics who unrelentingly demand a scientific explanation regarding the validity of this ancient art of treating disease.

The principal objective effects on the body following acupuncture are:

1. **Pain relief or analgesia** – This is the best known effect and one of the primary reasons why Western doctors are of the opinion that acupuncture is only effective as a pain control regimen.

2. **Sedation** – Acupuncture is useful in the treatment of mental and behavioural problems, insomnia, addictions and anxiety states.

3. **Regulatory** – This means creating a state of balance within the internal body. Mechanisms responsible for some of the essential bodily functions such as heart rate, breathing, the body's temperature, sweating and urination are sometimes damaged in the process of disease. Acupuncture is beneficial in restoring balance to these functions.

4. **Immune enhancing** – This simply means that the body is strengthened to resist or fight off disease. It has been proven that antibodies (substances formed in the body to kill or neutralize invaders such as bacteria), white blood cells and other agents in the fight against disease are increased after acupuncture. Therefore, acupuncture is beneficial in the treatment of infections.

5. **Psychological** – There is a calming and tranquillizing reaction on the body.

   NB: On each occasion that I needle a certain point on a young man who practises martial arts, he drifts into a meditative state. Despite the reason for treatment, he would insist that I include that particular point in his treatment regimen.

6. **Motor Recovery** – Acupuncture has been proven to speed up recovery in some paralyzed patients.

The argument in favour of acupuncture

Acupuncture has been practised for thousands of years in China – the world's largest population (home to a quarter of the human race). Evidence of its effectiveness has astounded Western practitioners visiting China. The World Health Organization has been so impressed with the Chinese system of health care that it has endorsed the use of traditional medicine in many countries, including the developing nations. Acupuncture is safe and it is economical.

Modern conventional medicine is easily accessible and affordable to people living in the West, where traditional medicine is an alternative treatment. However, to the poor underprivileged developing nations, traditional medicine is the principal armament in the battle against disease. To those nations, this branch of medicine is of vital importance in the maintenance of health and the treatment of disease. It is therefore unfair that some choose to ridicule and challenge the use of every branch of traditional medicine.

'Scepticism is the chastity of the intellect.' (Santayana).

Owing to convincing evidence that acupuncture releases endorphins and other chemicals from the brain, some Western scientists are now convinced of its importance. Nonetheless, there still remains a degree of scepticism and resentment by others of this age-old therapy.

One of the reasons for Western cynicism towards acupuncture is the absence of scientific evidence as proof of its effectiveness.

'Part of the problem is that Western trained physicians demand the validation of any therapy by comparison with an ineffective placebo in a manner in which neither the therapist nor the patient knows which treatment the patient is receiving at the time it is being administered (double-blind controlled trials). Assessment of a new drug or medication is possible by such comparison, but the assessment of a physical therapy such as acupuncture is clearly not feasible in this manner. Since the demand of proof by such clinical trials of a specific action of acupuncture is unreasonable, scientific credibility has to be achieved by exploring the mechanisms of its action.' (*The Scientific Basis of Acupuncture* by Anton Jayasuriya).

In a paragraph titled 'Drug treatment And The Rise Of Pharmacology', Professor Roy Porter writes: 'It has always been much easier to believe optimistically in a remedy than to prove its worth in even a faintly scientific way.' (The *Cambridge Illustrated History of Medicine*).

Professor Anton Jayasuriya also states in his book *Clinical Acupuncture*:
'It is against the backdrop of such present day practices and the spiralling incidence of iatrogenic diseases, that the safety and efficacy of acupuncture should be judged.'

Jayasuriya continues:
'Theories, hypotheses, conjectures and speculations are interesting, and essential for scientific research to proceed, but they should not be regarded as immutable. Theories in medicine change from decade to decade. Books on Western pharmacology and therapeutics have changed face almost completely with each decade over the past century. In no other system, as in Western medical science, has one decade rejected so decisively the therapy of a previous decade, not only as useless, but as being harmful.'

'Man is a political animal.' (Aristotle).

It is evident that the scepticism levelled at acupuncture is dominated by political (nationalistic) arrogance and not wholly based on scientific evaluation, as they would have us believe. One wonders if its credibility would have provoked such prolonged antagonistic cynicism, had acupuncture originated in the West.

There are several Western trained doctors who are now fully pledged complementary practitioners, or who practise complementary medicine (especially acupuncture) in conjunction with their main profession. Doctors within the NHS are referring some patients requesting acupuncture to colleagues. These are some of the very doctors who complain of being overworked within the NHS. Therefore, in the light of this revelation, acupuncture must be a credible therapeutic asset.

It appears that the use of complementary medicine is dictated thus: 'Some branches of complementary medicine can only be recognized if administered by Western trained physicians.' This way of reasoning reminds me of the following personal experience.

Several years ago when I was a young fresh-faced student nurse, I associated with two other female nurses and Jock, a Scottish male nurse. We were all single people and we had a lot in common. We were therefore supportive of each other.

One day a male nurse from another hospital asked our friend Jock to be introduced to me, 'the new kid on the block'. He had already met the two other female nurses. No sooner were we introduced than he started ridiculing Jock to me. I immediately felt a twinge of resentment towards that male nurse.

Jock was a decent young man with a strict religious background. His only vice was his sports car. If necessary, he would go without food in order to maintain the upkeep of his precious car. He took us driving on several occasions.

I was surprised one day when the male nurse visited me. He told me that he called to warn me about driving around with Jock because the car was dangerous. He went on to say that Jock was once involved in a terrible accident and his female companion almost lost her left leg.

I was so psychologically dazed on hearing that awful 'story', that before I realized what I was doing, I found myself automatically clutching my left leg and lifting it up to make sure that it was still intact. Although I was rather stunned at hearing that news, I was somewhat unconvinced. I also wondered why he had decided to reveal that incident just as Jock had left for his holidays.

A few days later, the male nurse telephoned to ask whether he could take me out some time in the future. To my surprise, he told me that on Jock's return, he was going to borrow his car to take me out driving if I agreed. *That was the very unsafe car that he had warned me about just days previously.*

I was momentarily speechless with anger. I declined his offer and further asked him never to contact me again. Not surprisingly, I later found out that the story about the accident was untrue.

The fact that a Western trained doctor practises acupuncture, or that people are taught acupuncture at a Western college, will not necessarily ensure greater success in treatment. Acupuncture is a different medical model to Western medicine. The ordinary people in China originally practised it and today some of the most successful acupuncturists are undoubtedly the 'barefoot doctors' in China; these are villagers with little or no Western medical background.

It is important to note that just as the children of farmers or bakers become expert in those occupations because it is ingrained in their culture, the Chinese also have an authoritative command in mastering the art of their ancient medicine. However, it is essential for people in the West with no medical background, who wish to pursue a career in acupuncture, to have an understanding of the structure and function of the human body, because unlike the Chinese, they are treading on unfamiliar territory. Therefore, traditional Chinese medicine must be taken seriously in order to preserve its credibility, not simply as a pastime activity or a fascination which anyone can meddle with.

'Politics is not an exact science.' (Otto Von Bismarck).

Nationalism attracts admiration when demonstrated in a positive and sensible context, but, to the rational mind it is perceived as an unpleasant obstacle when brandished in a manner intent on depriving the human race of adequate health care. By disregarding politics in medicine, we would be more inclined to an unbiased recognition of the truth. Politics has no positive contribution in the health of humanity; on the contrary, in several instances it has proven to be the ultimate ammunition for catastrophes.

'... doctors' increasing preoccupation with the technology of their trade, have driven many patients in rich countries to search for methods of healing that they regard as more 'natural'. Doctors, proud of their high-tech gadgetry and their scientific interventions, are now reluctant to see themselves as healers. Yet healers – individuals who offer more than technical solutions to biological problems – are what many people obviously want.' (*The Cambridge Illustrated History of Medicine* by Roy Porter).

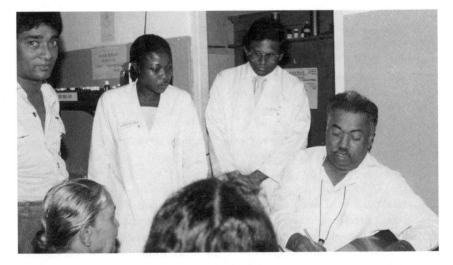

The author (centre back) at university with Professor Anton Jayasuriya (front right).

If we are to be successful in our continuous struggle to manage health costs and at the same time promote health by eradicating disease, we must be prepared to offer unbiased accreditation to traditional and complementary medicine. We need to focus on universal solidarity in order to expedite improvement in health. If we do not work collectively as 'the family of man' in our battle against disease, then consequently, we are likely to be constant casualties in pandemic proportions to the onslaught of disease.

In the concluding chapter of his foreward to the first edition of *Clinical Acupuncture* by Anton Jayasuriya, Professor Bruce Pomeranz, one of the pioneering scientific workers on the endorphin mechanism of acupuncture analgesia states: 'It does not worry me much, if acupuncture yet defies scientific explanation; after all Einstein's discoveries were made by studying the exceptions to *Maxwell's equations. If acupuncture is an exception to the Western medical model, all the better; perhaps this will be the chance for a major breakthrough in the future understanding of the human body complex.'

Maxwell's equations. These are four equations, which together form a complete description of the production and interrelation of electric and magnetic fields. During the nineteenth century, the physicist James Clerk Maxwell based his description of electromagnetic fields on these four equations, which express experimental laws.

CHAPTER 5

Acupuncture Case Histories

Case History No. 1.

Where better to start than with my own?

Our eldest daughter suddenly developed eczema-like symptoms (an inflammatory condition of the skin) on her face at the age of one year. The child was so uncomfortable with the condition that she often cried and scratched her face so severely that it bled. Her condition improved for a few years and then at the age of five it returned severely.

Our doctor prescribed a medication to control the itching along with a mild painkiller, but neither seemed to have much effect on her condition. A few months later, she was prescribed a steroid-based cream to be used in conjunction with the two previously mentioned medications.

One of the foremost actions of steroids is to suppress the symptoms of disease. Therefore the steroid had been prescribed to reduce the itching, puffiness and redness of my daughter's face.

Although a nurse for several years I have always had reservations regarding the use of some prescribed medication. Part of my aversion to this is a direct result of awareness of the side effects, although these are minimal in some cases. Although the benefits of some medication are often greater than the side effects, I am nonetheless often concerned about possible adverse reactions; however, concerned about the child's discomfort, I apprehensively applied the cream prescribed hoping that it would improve her condition.

After using the medication for a few days, I observed that although she was not in as much discomfort as she had been previously, there was not much improvement in her condition, so I gradually decreased the medication, and then stopped it completely.

A health visitor suggested that I apply oilatum emollient in the child's bath. This liquid preparation, containing light paraffin, softens, relaxes and smoothes the skin. It is also a skin cleanser therefore there is no need to use soap. This seemed to ease the itching and discomfort to some degree, but unfortunately periods of remission (temporary disappearance of symptoms) of the disease were often followed by bouts of relapse (recurrence of symptoms).

I clearly remember the day I when I took my daughter to visit the dermatologist (skin specialist) at our local hospital, on my doctor's suggestion. Her little face was swollen and terribly marked as a result of her constantly scratching it.

As we awaited her appointment in the reception area with other children and their parents, my daughter noticed a little girl playing with some toys. As she approached the little girl to play with her, the child's mother dashed forward quickly and lifted her away from my daughter.

My daughter ran over to me then burst into tears. The other adults seemed astonished at the action of the mother in question and one lady in particular turned to the others and said, 'Isn't that awful?' I lifted my daughter, gave her a reassuring kiss, and then I took her outside.

My daughter sucked the index and middle fingers of her left hand from the age of three months, but she had stopped just after her first birthday. To my astonishment on that day (just over four years later) as I held her in my arms, she held me tightly around my neck with her right arm, then she placed the very two fingers she had originally sucked into her mouth and started sucking them again. I did not discourage her because I felt that she had her fair share of psychological barriers to contend with at that particular period in her young life.

As I returned with my daughter to the clinic, the mother in question approached me and apologized. As soon as my daughter saw the woman, she cowered and held on tightly to my skirt, and then she literally hid her face under it.

Although my daughter was a mere child, in her young mind she seemed to have assumed that the woman resented her because of her facial appearance. That experience was a typical example of the way in which a complex can be developed from a young age; however I was not prepared to encourage it. I gently removed my daughter from under my skirt, then I publicly told her not to be embarrassed to face the lady in question or any other individual.

The child instantly removed her fingers out of her mouth, then boldly thrusting herself forward, she replied, 'Yes, Mummy, I shan't hide no more.' Her reply was spontaneous, but so amusing that some of the parents laughed and even the mother in question seemed amused.

The dermatologist told me that there was nothing further that could be prescribed for my daughter, but she advised me to resume giving her the original medications.

That night my daughter was in severe discomfort; she cried for hours as she scratched her face in agony. As the noise from her crying resonated in my head, I told my husband that she must be experiencing extreme agony. It was then that he suggested that I should try treating her with acupuncture.

I was somewhat astonished at my husband's suggestion, but it was a compassionate cry for help for his child and one of desperation for himself. He was greatly affected by her condition because her constant crying prevented him from having adequate sleep. He told me that on a few occasions he was so tired whilst driving to and from work on the busy motorway that he had to try desperately to stay awake.

At that period I had just completed my first year of training for my diploma in acupuncture. I had no practical experience in needling skills, though I regularly practised needling myself in preparation for the ensuing practical part of my training.

I therefore decided to have a go on my daughter in the hope of reducing her discomfort. I had no indication whether or not she was destined to become one of the statistical 80–90% of acupuncture successes; nonetheless I was determined to try.

I was somewhat apprehensive of her reaction to treatment involving needles. It generally took two adults to restrain her whilst a nurse administered her immunization injections and the screams from her must have caused those present to have tinnitus (ringing in the ears) for days. Nevertheless, I was determined to try.

The more I contemplated the prospect of treating the child, the more determined I became. The following day, after my son had arrived from school and my husband from work, knowing that I had the necessary back-up team to restrain the child, I decided to launch into action.

Operation Mater

(Mater in French is slang for mother and when translated, it means to subdue or tame).

I told the child that I was going to try to assist her body to rid itself of the awful stinging sensations. I also asked her to sit very still or I might be forced to ask her father and her brother to hold her down, because it was important for the needles to find the correct tiny acupuncture points. Had I dared mention that if she did not sit still needling would be painful, she would not have complied with the treatment.

As I prepared for the procedure, she became weepy when she saw the needles. I needled myself to show her that it did... then as I quickly proceeded to insert the first needle into her arm, the child sat motionless, gazing in amazement at what must have appeared to her as a fascinating tiny little object stuck on her arm. I quickly seized the chance to add another four needles into selected parts of her body whilst the situation was favourable, then after a few minutes, I gradually removed them.

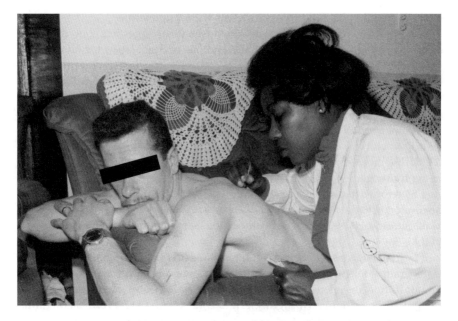

A client receiving acupuncture treatment from the author.

At the end of her first acupuncture treatment, my brave daughter gleefully said, 'Oh Mummy, the needles did not hurt me like those horrible injections did.'

I explained that needles used for injection are much thicker than those used in acupuncture; however it is the fluid used in injections that causes pain as it is pushed into the tissues. I also told her that acupuncture needles are solid therefore they do not contain any liquid. Furthermore the needles are very fine; some are as fine as a human hair. That is why there is little or no pain. I informed the child that I would give her a few more treatments.

The following evening my daughter prepared herself for her treatment by lying on her bed, then she promptly called out to me to treat her immediately. Deserting my chore, I immediately proceeded to execute what to me was one of the greatest tasks I was destined to undertake.

On the second session, I started treatment by needling a point called Hegu (large intestine four), which is located at the back of the hand, between the thumb and the index finger. This is one of the most painful acupuncture points for most people and yet, to my amazement, the child did not move an inch as I manipulated the needle to stimulate the point.

I gave my daughter five treatments within nine days and even to this day, as a teenager, she has never had a recurrence of her original skin condition. We are all astounded by the result. She seemed to enjoy the treatment and she complied better than was expected and within days her condition gradually improved. Then within a few weeks, there was no visible indication of the condition. Her recovery was so remarkable that she was the subject of an article on acupuncture in a local magazine a few years later.

Even to this present day, she has had no problem with teenage-related skin conditions such as acne. She probably had acupuncture as a booster about four times per year, for two years following her initial treatment.

Having treated numerous patients since my daughter, it is reasonable for me to state that her recovery was one of the most rewarding cases for me. This is due to the fact that she was my first case and my first successful result in this ancient Chinese art of treating disease. She is also my daughter and ironically, I was in the early stages of my pregnancy with her when I met Mr G, the gentleman who enlightened me about the benefits of acupuncture.

Naturally, I experience a sea of emotions when I recall this particular case. For a mother, the birth of a child brings insurmountable joy. Every aspect of that child's development is scrutinized with curiosity and maternal protection.

Therefore seeing a child suffer physical discomfort and self-mutilating injuries on its tender little body causes parents to be consumed with sadness, despair and in some instances guilt. These emotions are compounded by the psychological injury that is sometimes incurred to the child by the insensitivity of some elements of society.

Parental obligation and my professional skill were instrumental in the improvement of my daughter's condition. Equally, her cooperation was also an important contributory factor in the healing process. She did not ask to be born, we chose to have her, therefore it was our parental obligation to explore appropriate avenues to improve her quality of health.

Parental responsibility should be an instinctive immeasurable act of love. This can be expressed in different ways in order to enhance and maintain the holistic healthy development of children. Oftentimes parents are faced with the dilemma of making the right decision regarding the welfare of their children and many opt for a course of action that they hope would prove to be the right one.

Case History No. 2

In May 1992, Loryn (a fictitious name), a 19-year-old police cadet, contacted me for acupuncture treatment after reading my daughter's story in a local magazine. This beautiful young woman had suffered with psoriasis, a chronic inflammatory skin condition, since the age of seven.

Diagnosis

On examination of her pulses and her tongue, there was indication of what is described as 'solid blood' in Traditional Chinese Medicine. This situation can lead to irregular, or absence of, menstruation.

When I asked Loryn how long it was since her periods became irregular or absent, she appeared to be alarmed at that line of questioning. She told me that she had had a stressful childhood and adolescent life and that she had never had a normal period; they were irregular, then they stopped completely. Many people are aware that stress is one of the dominant factors for a vast number of health related problems.

Loryn informed me that she was treated with hormone treatment to correct her menstrual problem for a considerable amount of time, but the problem did not respond to the treatment. Her doctor even told her that she might not be able to conceive children naturally; therefore in due course if she would like to have children, she would have to consider receiving fertility treatment.

Loryn also stated that she had received acupuncture for her menstrual condition two years prior to her consulting me, but her acupuncture practitioner, with whom I was fairly well acquainted, died suddenly, therefore since his death she did not have any further treatment.

On Loryn's first visit to my clinic, there were patches of psoriasis on her head, back and parts of her legs. These are raised rough reddened areas on the skin. She was accompanied by her mother and during the course of our conversation, it became clear to me that there was an extremely close bond between mother and daughter. But even more noticeable was the fact that there seemed to be a reversal of roles particularly on the part of the daughter. Quite unaware of her actions, Loryn behaved as if she was the carer or protector of her mother.

When I offered Loryn a seat, she gave it up to her mother before I had a chance of seating the mother. Then when she was receiving acupuncture treatment, she glanced across at her mother several times asking her, 'Are you all right, Mom?' At one point I interjected by saying, 'But it is you who are having needles stuck into your body, not your Mom, so why are you asking if she is all right?' They both seemed amused at my observation and they started to giggle.

Later the mother revealed that she had experienced a period of psychological and psychiatric turmoil several years earlier and Loryn, who was then a very young child and also a good little companion, assisted in nursing her back to health. She continued, 'I don't know how I would have coped without her, she was my rock.'

Treatment

After taking Loryn's history I was of the opinion that her condition relapsed whenever she was anxious or worried about specific situations, although she stated that she was not consciously aware of worrying. I also felt that her anxiety had induced a considerably amount of stress on her system. The vicious cycle of anxiety and stress was liable to induce an added health hazard – nutritional imbalance.

I therefore decided to apply acupuncture to some vital points to cope with her anxiety. I also used a few selected health points to regulate her energy and her blood.

As the sessions of treatment progressed, I combined acupuncture with moxibustion, a traditional Chinese method of treating disease and maintaining health by burning moxa punks at specific acupuncture points. I advised her to take evening primrose capsules, which I felt would be beneficial for both her gynaecological and her skin problems. I also recommended oilatum and emulsifying ointment to be used for baths and for washing her hair.

By the seventh session, there was a marked improvement in Loryn's condition. She phoned to inform me of her progress, whilst giggling for most of our conversation. Loryn has an infectious giggle and despite her disorder, she smiled and giggled a lot. That was one of her many pleasant attributes which I found captivating.

Her progress continued and within ten sessions of weekly treatment, there was scarcely any visible sign of psoriasis. She had a few more sessions, and then I gradually decreased her treatment.

Within six months of treatment Loryn gradually started having periods, although irregular at times. To this date, Loryn's condition remains controlled and she only consults me when she feels the need for the occasional treatment.

She was married a few years after she first consulted me and I am happy to report that today she is the proud mother of two of the most adorable boys. She did not have any need to receive fertility treatment. Actually, her first pregnancy was a pleasant surprise because it was unplanned. She told me that she went to the doctor fearing that she was suffering with appendicitis; instead, after she was examined she was told that she was pregnant.

Since treating Loryn, I have also treated her husband and every member of her immediate family, except her children, who I am happy to state are very fit and healthy. Loryn constantly tells me that as soon as anyone mentions an illness, she immediately blurts out, 'You ought to make an appointment to see my acupuncturist.'

Her mother has described me as the angel who healed her daughter. However, as I have often explained to people, I cannot accept the claim that I have cured or healed anyone. I am only one unit in the chain linking people to a healthy or manageable life. I am of the opinion that my involvement in the healing process is to work with people to assist them in overcoming or coping with illness.

If therapists are prepared to take full credit for successful cases, then I feel they must also be accountable for the unsuccessful ones. I believe that each patient is contributory to his/her own recovery by cooperating with the treatment and complying with the instructions or advice from therapists.

CHAPTER 6

Herbal Medicine

'And God said, I have given you every herb bearing seed, which is upon the face of earth, and every tree which is the fruit of the tree yielding seed; to you it shall be meat.' (Genesis 1:29).

What is a herb? A herb is part of a plant used for food, flavouring or medicine.

"For the turning away of the simple shall slay them and the prosperity of fools shall destroy them.' (Prov 1: 32).

Man's dependency on vegetation dates back to creation. It is worth mentioning that apart from medicinal and culinary uses, vegetation provides homes for an inestimable number of people. It is nature's way of providing us with oxygen and protecting us from the ravages of disasters such as torrential rain and floods. Vegetation also provides shelter for animals and birds in the wild.

This is a poignant reminder to the 'I am all right' wealthy multi-nationals who it seems are oblivious to the consequence of deforestation. Moreover, even if they were aware of the effect of their folly, it is doubtful whether some of them are capable of showing compassion to the underprivileged inhabitants of the rain forests. This may be due to the fact that the reasoning of some wealthy people is often synonymous with monetary profit and loss scenario; therefore demonstration of human compassion would be tantamount to loss in revenue in the eyes of a materialistic culture.

There are people who are gravely distressed by this apparent raping of the rain forests. To those with moral conviction, this action is perceived as sacrilegious and contemptuous and it has resulted in the formation of an army of anti-deforestation protesters.

To its people, the rain forest is synonymous with blood running through the blood vessels of any life force. It is the natural habitat of some of the richest and finest herbs; therefore destruction heralds starvation, disease and death in some cases. This may subsequently lead to the annihilation of the inhabitants.

It is an irrefutable and consequential danger for humanity to exist outside the boundary of a natural world. We must realize that we are a part of nature;

by destroying it, we are also unwittingly ruining the very existence of the human race.

'And the fruit therefore shall be meat, and the leaf therefore medicine.' (Ezekiel 47:12).

The nations actively engaged in using herbs have an older civilization than the West. Those people have survived on herbs for thousands of years and it is the principal source of affordable medicine for many in the developing countries.

Similarly animals and birds out in the wilds have no access to veterinary medicine and yet they seem to fare well (apart from the unfortunate occasions when as a result of man's indiscretion to nature and the environment, these species become affected by pollutants).

Modern medicine is accredited for improvement in our health, but it is obvious that improvement in health is primarily due to better health education (including healthier diet), wider use of complementary medicine and better living conditions.

Prior to the advent of Western medicine man satisfactorily maintained health and was also cured of disease by using herbs. The numerous centenarians in the Caribbean, especially Barbados, can substantiate this claim. Many of the senior citizens have never used or rarely use Western medicine. However in recent years, the number of people living longer has fallen. This is because the younger generation seem to have ignored the natural and have developed a fetish for seemingly more exotic medications including antibiotics. This is a dangerous practice, which could progress to drug resistance.

Herbal medicine is predominantly used in China, with the world's largest population. It is also widely used in other Asian countries, in Africa and South America. It is not unusual to find that some of the inhabitants of those countries have no formal teaching regarding the precise pharmaceutical action of herbs on the body; however they are knowledgeable about herbal treatment for specific conditions.

People are generally contented to be relieved of some of the symptoms of their illness or they are happy to be cured (when it appears that the symptoms have disappeared and a better quality of life is experienced). Sufferers of disease are not interested in the mechanism of the healing process. They simply want to get better by any reasonable method. This irrelevant questioning of how, why and when does it work, is a never-ending bone of contention within the Western scientific fraternity. Nonetheless, there are a growing number of people in the West who are converts to traditional medicine.

Like acupuncture, herbal medicine, when used traditionally, addresses the root cause of disease. Similar to the actions of other branches of traditional medicine, herbs have a holistic effect on the body. They tackle the general health of people. Many of those who have used this branch of medicine can substantiate this claim.

Hostile Reaction

When science competes with nature, it sometimes propagates derogatory evidence in support of its case. For hundreds of years the West has been intolerant of herbal medicine. As a matter of fact, any remedial treatment not invented in the West is liable to be ridiculed or dismissed as nonsense or evil. As late as the eighteenth century Europeans caught using herbs were burnt to death, simply because they were believed to be witches.

Ted Kaptchuk, a renowned American practitioner of Chinese medicine, stated in pages 1–2 of his book, *Chinese Medicine -The Web that has no Weaver*':

'... many Westerners have strange notions about Chinese medicine. Some of them see it as hocus pocus – the product of primitive or magical thinking ... They assume that current Western science and medicine have a unique handle on Truth all else is superstition.'

The reason for this negative reaction to natural medicine may well be an expression of power by those involved in modern medicine. Wealthy pharmaceuticals are not prepared to be on a parallel foothold with herbal or any other complementary medicine, therefore they are understandably dismissive of the health promoting potentials of these remedies. Yet it is estimated that a vast majority of Western medicine consists of herbs.

'Although we should not discard the notion that science is a quest for truth about the world, we should take heed about the psychological and social factors which oppose this quest.' So wrote Tony Morton in an article called 'Schools in Conflict: The Motives and Methods of Scientists'. 'Yes, it seems that fame, financial gain or even political gratification has sometimes influenced scientists' findings.'

As far back as 1873, Lord Jessel expressed concern about such influences in court cases when he said: 'Expert evidence ... Now it is natural that his mind, however honest he may be, should be biased in favour of the person employing him, and accordingly we do find such biases.' (*Awake* 8 March 1998).

The need for discipline throughout the whole spectrum of the medical profession

A report by The House of Lords Select Committee on Science and Technology Sixth Report which was released in January 2001, stated: 'In 1999 the Department of Health commissioned ... the University of Exeter to produce an information pack on the regulatory prospects of complementary and alternative medicine [34].' This pack states that the purpose of regulation in healthcare is:

'To establish a nationwide, professionally determined and independent standard of training, conduct and competence for each profession for the protection of the public and the guidance of employers. To underpin the personal accountability of practitioners for maintaining safe and effective measures to deal with individuals whose continuing practice presents an unacceptable risk to the public or otherwise renders them unfit to be a registered member of the profession [35].'

It is of crucial importance that every healthcare procedure is safely carried out by competent practitioners. However, before implementing the proposed regulatory laws on complementary and alternative medicine, it would be in the interests of all concerned, for the medical profession and the pharmaceuticals to lead the way by meticulously regulating themselves.

The apostle Luke, who incidentally was also a physician, stated in his Gospel: '*Either how canst thou say to thy brother, Brother, let me pull out the mote that is in thine eye, when thou thyself beholdest not the beam that is thine own eye? Thou hypocrite, cast out first the beam out of thine own eye, and then shalt thou see clearly to pull out the mote that is in thy brother's eye.*' (Luke 6:42).

Orthodox medicine is responsible for some outstanding achievements in several areas. However, although this is obviously not a wilful act of extermination of the overpopulated human species, it is a generally well known fact that it is also responsible for a staggering number of unnecessary fatalities, some of which appear to be unnoticed, or in some cases unchallenged.

Campaign for Truth in Medicine, based in Kent, UK, stated that 'The Journal of American Medical Association (Vol 284, 26 July 2000) reports statistics that show Western healthcare is now the third leading cause of death in the US, inflicting some 225,000 unnecessary deaths annually. These fatalities are categorized into the following headings':

Unnecessary surgery	12,000
Medical errors	7,000
Correct drug prescribing	106,000
Infections in hospitals	80,000
Miscellaneous	20,000

Herbal contribution to Western medicine

Some well known herbal extracts in Western medicine are:

Digoxin – an extract from the foxglove, which is one of the commonly used drugs in the treatment of heart failure.

Steroids – an extract from the wild yam, which reduces symptoms of disease by suppressing them.

Aspirin – an extract from the white willow tree, frequently used as a painkiller and an anti-pyretic (reduces fever).

Antibiotics. These are a group of drugs including penicillin, ampicillin and streptomycin (to name a few), used to treat bacterial infections.

In 1929 when Sir Alexander Fleming discovered penicillin it was hailed the ultimate ammunition in the war against bacteria (commonly known as micro-organisms, microbes or germs). Since the introduction of penicillin in 1940, several other antibiotics have been produced. It appears that as fast as these drugs are being produced to tackle a specific type of bacterium, other more difficult strains of bacteria are forming and creating a growing problem of drug resistance, which means that in some cases, antibiotics have little or no effect on these so called 'supergerms'.

There is no doubt that antibiotics are useful in the treatment of some infections, including those that can proceed to become serious and life threatening; however there is concern regarding the frequent and inappropriate use in some minor conditions. Overuse or incorrect use (when the drug is not taken as prescribed) causes the responsible micro-organism to become resistant to the drug. The body's natural defence against infections is also suppressed if antibiotics are taken too often and this can cause repeated bouts of infections.

If a country were under the threat of invasion, it would not be tactical to deploy troops only in the most vulnerable area, whilst leaving other parts of that country unguarded. If that were the strategy, the invaders would overrun the unmanned areas thereby gaining a reasonable foothold in the country. Later the dominance of the invading force is likely to be increased and the country may well be taken.

Similarly, it is reasonable to assume that a general approach to health seems the most logical course of action in aiding the body's defence against disease instead of sporadic intake of antibiotics at the first sign of feeling unwell. It is the whole body that needs to be fortified in order to protect or defend it against disease. Therefore, herbal medicine and other credible forms of traditional medicine can be enhancing to the whole system.

The acceptance of traditional medicine would not herald the end of modern medicine. Western medicine is undoubtedly an important aid in the battle against disease. There would always be a place for it within the realm of experimentation and treatment of disease, therefore it is doubtful whether anyone can substantiate a justifiable argument against its continuity. However, it is not the panacea that it is made out to be in the fight against disease, therefore some branches of alternative and complementary treatments should be equally accessible to the public as mainstream medicine.

Some frequently used medicinal herbs:

Garlic: Garlic is one of the most useful universally used herbs. Clinical trials conducted by several hospitals have proven its therapeutic value in the treatment of certain disorders. It can be taken cooked in food, in capsule form or eaten raw. People are often discouraged from taking garlic because of its pungent smell; this is due to allicin, the substance responsible for its protective properties.

Actions of garlic. Anti coagulation – thins the blood; anti-hypertension – reduces blood cholesterol and lowers high blood pressure, therefore it is useful in the prevention of heart problems; microbial – kills bacteria (germs); antibiotic – kills, treats and prevents bacterial infections; anti parasitic – destroys parasites; anti fungal – kills fungi; immune enhancing – increases the body's resistance to disease, fights infection and repairs damaged white blood cells; **anti ageing** – delays the ageing process; and anti oxidant – gives some protection against cancer.

'The smell of garlic may keep others away, but, according to a report in the spring, 1993 edition of Optimum Nutrition, it may also keep cancer away! According to a 1998 study conducted by the National Cancer Institute in China, people who lived in provinces which used garlic liberally in their cooking had the lowest rate of stomach cancer.' (*Hot News* (Vol. 1 Issue 2) England, May 1997).

Other uses of garlic. Garlic can be taken as a tonic in the prevention and the treatment of digestive and respiratory diseases. It can be taken as treatment for flu, whooping cough and colds. It can also be applied to the skin for the treatment of insect bites and parasitic infestation such as ringworm.

Caution! Some people may be allergic to garlic, therefore if there is gastric upset such as heartburn, burping, vomiting or diarrhoea, discontinue its use until you have consulted your doctor.

Recommended daily intake: Three to five cloves daily according to the size of the bulb. If taken in capsule or powered tablet form, follow the instructions. *Crushing and overcooking will destroy allicin, the principle ingredient of garlic.

Cinnamon. This is a warming remedy which benefits the digestive system and assists in stimulating the circulatory system. It has a tonic effect on the kidneys and it is also an antiseptic. Other uses of cinnamon: treatment of the common cold, exhaustion after flu, cold limbs and promotion of urination.

Eucalyptus oil. This is an antibacterial, therefore it is useful when inhaled or applied directly on the skin, for the treatment of infections and chest problems. Australian Aborigines once used eucalyptus as a general treatment.

Peppermint. An excellent herb for respiratory problems. Due to its menthol constituent, it is one of the most frequently used herbs for the reduction of mucus. It is also good for the relief of wind, which also leads to the relief of colic (spasmodic abdominal pain).

Other uses of peppermint: It is also one of the most effective herbs in the treatment of problems such as indigestion, ulcerative colitis, Crohn's disease and irritable bowel syndrome. It is also good for colds, aches and pains such as headaches and certain types of migraine, nasal catarrh, colds, influenza and painful periods.

Thyme (leaves and flowers). A warming agent, therefore it is good for respiratory problems including laryngitis, tonsillitis, whooping cough, asthma and bronchitis.

Ginger (root). A warming herb. It is very good for coughs, colds, chills, fever, sore throat, wind, menstrual pain, cramps and reduced circulation in the outer parts of the body. It is also good for stomach chills and diarrhoea. It can be used as a mild antiseptic to cleanse the skin in cases of cuts and infections.

Ginseng. This is said to be one of the oldest herbs in history. It is mostly cultivated in China, Korea, Siberia and north-east America. The root of the plant is the part used medicinally.

General uses of ginseng: It stimulates the circulation, alleviates stress and fatigue, regulates blood pressure, improves vitality and boosts physical performance.

Other uses: It is helpful in cases of exhaustion and anaemia. As a result of some of its pharmacological potential including stimulating circulation, it is a natural Viagra (sexual enhancing drug).

Onion. One of nature's best mucus cleansing agents, it is therefore effective for colds, catarrh, abdominal pain, headache due to nasal congestion and diarrhoea (because of its warming effects). Just as in the case of garlic, it is also a natural antibiotic.

Some Popular Natural Remedies.

Honey. Effective in arthritis, anaemia, dry cough, hoarseness, cramps, fatigue, sinus problems, potassium deficiency, stomach and intestinal ulcers and high blood pressure. It is also a mild sedative, therefore it can be helpful in inducing sleep. Two teaspoonfuls of honey in a teacup of hot water, taken in the morning on an empty stomach, is very effective for constipation. Honey is quickly absorbed into the body; therefore it is an effective treatment for hypoglycaemic attacks in diabetes.

Guava. Boiled guava fruit or leaves are effective in treating diarrhoea.
N.B Caution. Eating too many guavas at a time can result in distressing acute constipation.

Lemon: This is a rich source of vitamin C and is therefore useful in the treatment of colds, cough, sore throat, allergies, infections and arthritis. It is useful in the prevention of scurvy – a condition where there is deficiency of vitamin C (ascorbic acid) due to lack of fresh fruits and green vegetables. This disease was common amongst early explorers who spent lengthy periods on the high seas. In a bid to avert it, British sailors consumed substantial numbers of limes. That is why they were referred to as 'Limeys'.

Vinegar. This is another good source of potassium. Gargle with two teaspoons of vinegar in a glass of warm water to ease sore throat. For treatment of hiccups, slowly sip one teaspoon of cider vinegar in a glass of warm water.

Other indications for vinegar. For arthritis and overweight – drink one teaspoonful in water before or after meals. Consult your doctor for advice before resorting to this method to lose weight; even with permission, do not use vinegar as a weight control regimen for long periods.

One to two spoonfuls of apple cider vinegar taken in a glass of water before a meal, is said to be a good remedy for the prevention of food poisoning.

Caution! Avoid vinegar if you have a tendency to acidity or digestive problems.

Acknowledgement. I am immensely grateful to the late Professor Mark Yu, Dean of the Academy of Chinese Acupuncture in London, for incorporating several tradition Chinese therapies including herbal medicine into the curriculum, thus giving his students basic knowledge of other holistic therapies.

CHAPTER 7

Aloe Vera (Liliaceae)

Alleluia!
Long leafy distinguishable plant
Origin of the lily family
Exceedingly acrid in taste
Variety of interesting species
Enriched with nutrition
Renowned for its historic past
Ameliorates various afflictions.

My Personal Experience of Aloe Vera

As a child growing up in Guyana, the unusual beauty of this seemingly plain plant always fascinated me. Although I had never noticed flowers or fruits on our aloe plant (as was customary with the majority of plants) I was attracted to the appeal of its plainness.

During the latter part of 1995, I twisted my right hand and chipped a bone in the middle finger, as I landed heavily on that hand, to break the impact of a heavy fall in the ice.

A few days later, with my right hand still swollen and the injured finger enlarged to twice its normal size, I set off for a scheduled holiday in Guyana. My right hand was in such a bad shape that I had to use my left hand to complete the routine travel documents.

Aloe Vera plant

118

Two days into my holidays, my hand had swollen to such enormous proportions that I could not make a fist. My finger was throbbing so much that I had to resort to taking painkillers, a remedy I had not used for several years, but as it was difficult to administer acupuncture with my left hand, I had to improvise a quick workable pain control regimen. The painkillers merely lessened the intensity of the pain, but I was still aware of great discomfort in my hand.

My nephew Lenny advised me to apply a leaf from a herbal plant known locally as Noni. Lenny's diet was richly supplemented with various herbs and he seemed knowledgeable about the medicinal properties of various herbaceous plants.

That night I applied the Noni leaf to my hand. I used a rubber glove to keep it in place. The following morning the swelling had subsided remarkably, but although the pain was controlled to some degree, it was still causing me some discomfort. Later that morning as I sat on our stairs my eyes became hypnotically transfixed on the large bitter aloes plant that was approximately 20 years old according to my family's estimation.

I tried to recall whether Aloe Vera was ever served medicinally to my siblings and me when we were children. I recalled that on occasions nursing mothers applied it onto their nipples to deter toddlers (who were past it) from sucking breast milk.

Another recollection of the use of Aloe Vera was on the occasion when my mother applied a small piece of its thick glue-like gel onto my youngest brother's finger to deter him from sucking a finger which appeared withered and cracked as a result of him sucking it habitually.

After application of the aloe sap to his finger, each time the toddler stuck his finger into his mouth, he quickly pulled it out again and cried in desperation. I felt so sorry for the unhappy child that when my mother was not looking, I took the corresponding finger of his opposite hand and quickly placed it in his mouth to appease his frustration. The child sucked the finger ravenously for a few seconds, and then he lashed out at me as if to suggest that I had given him a tasteless substitute. The following day my brother ceased sucking his finger after my mother reapplied the aloe sap to it.

As I continued to stare curiously at the seemingly large Aloe Vera plant, I wondered whether the plant standing so majestically before me possessed healing qualities. After gazing at it for what appeared to be ages, I approached the plant and broke off a piece of one of its largest leaves to examine it closely. Inside that particular leaf was a thick jelly-like substance, which was slightly yellowish in colour. This coloration was an indication that the plant was old.

I was becoming very concerned about my health. I thought that if I had been healthy, my finger would have improved. I truly believed that there was a marked slowing down in my body's natural healing mechanism.

I allowed fear to overlook fact. The lengthy course of my injured finger was dictated by the situation that it was presented with. The right hand should have been bandaged and rested from the time of injury. Not only had I not applied a bandage, I even placed the injury under more punishment by lifting and carrying heavy luggage during my journey. The change of temperature from cold to intense heat was also a barrier to healing, and swelling was likely to be intensified.

As John Billings observed: 'It is better to know nothing than to know what ain't so.' Self-diagnosis by people with a medical background is a dangerous predisposition; the worst scenario creeps into the imagination.

That day after thinking deeply about the Aloe Vera plant I decide to apply a poultice made from it on my affected hand. During the night, I renewed the poultice and surprisingly, for the first time since my injury, the pain was amazingly minimized the following day and the swelling was reduced by 60 per cent.

I continued using the poultice every night and within one week from commencing the treatment I was completely pain free and the only evidence of injury was a slightly swollen middle finger.

Ironically, upon my return from holidays, a company in England selling Aloe Vera products approached me to become an agent for them. I became involved with the company for several years.

What is Aloe Vera?

The Aloe plant is popularly known as bitter aloes in many countries where it is commonly grown. This is simply because of its bitter taste.

This cactus looking plant is really a member of the lily family. It is believed that there are over 200 species of aloes and most are non-toxic, but there is a small percentage that are poisonous. Credible researches have found that *Aloe barbadensis* Miller, a species from Africa which was taken to Barbados in 1650, is the best and most commercially used variety in the Caribbean, North America and South America.

The leaves of the aloe plant, which contain a thick fleshy gel, are triangular and they grow in a spiral shape resembling a rosette. When broken, the leaves immediately drain out the sap (or plant fluid). Just as blood is enriched with essential properties vital to the function of the body, the sap of the Aloe Vera is said to contain compounds of laxative, painkilling, antibacterial and anti-fungal properties, all of which are important in maintaining healthy bodily functions. Other important ingredients of the Aloe leaf are discussed later.

The History of Aloe Vera

Aloe Vera is believed to be one of the oldest plants recorded in history. It was noted in carvings on Egyptian temple walls as early as the 11th millennium BC, where it was known as the 'plant of immortality'.

It is believed to have been used by the ancient Egyptians in the preparation of their dead. The Roman naturalist Pliny was one of many who recorded its use in embalming the Pharaohs and nobility. He stated in his *Natural History* that Aloe Vera was also good for headaches, bleeding mouths and gums, restoring hair loss, removing piles and as an enema.

Aloe has been mentioned on a few instances in the Bible; examples are: Numbers 24:6, Psalms 45:8, Song of Solomon 4.14. Also in John 19:39–40 it is written: *'And there came also Nicodemus, which at the first came to Jesus by night, and brought a mixture of myrrh and aloes, about a hundred pounds weight. Then they took the body of Jesus, and wound it in linen clothes with the spices, as the manner of the Jews is to bury.'*

Cleopatra, reputed for her natural beauty, is said to have used Aloe Vera as her secret beauty ingredient. Nowadays Aloe Vera is one of the most popularly used hair and beauty products.

It is recorded in history that on the advice of Aristotle, Alexander the Great captured the island of Socotra in the Indian Ocean. However it is assumed that this particular island was not captured to add to the collection of Grecian conquests as was traditional during the period 333 BC, when Persia and Egypt were taken by Alexander. It is believed that Socotra was taken because of its vast aloe crops, which were needed to treat Alexander's wounded soldiers.

It has also been reported that when the soldiers left after capturing Socotra, they took a quantity of aloe, which they grew in their wagons. This was to provide them with fresh supplies of this valuable herb to treat the wounded soldiers.

Likewise, nowadays Aloe Vera has also attracted the attention of many governments because of its therapeutic ability, especially in healing burns. Because of its nutritional qualities, Aloe Vera is an excellent general tonic and it is widely sold by distributing agents and chemists. Hair products, body conditioners, skin creams for several conditions, toothpaste and lip balm, are among some of the many other Aloe Vera supplements on sale.

Mahatma Gandhi was reputed for his frequent drinking of the aloe juice. In a letter to his biographer Romain Rolland, Gandhi said: 'You ask me what were the secret forces that sustained me during my long fast. Well, it was my unshakable faith in God, my simple and frugal lifestyle, and the Aloe whose benefits I discovered upon my arrival in South Africa at the end of the 19th century.'

Some properties of Aloe Vera

To date Aloe Vera is the only plant known to man to be enriched with such a large variety of nutritional properties. Its chemical composition is of numerous varieties. I would only mention some of its basic properties:

Vitamins: A, B1, B2, B6, B12, C, E and Folic Acid. Vitamins are a group of complex organic substances that are necessary in small quantities for the normal function of the body. They are therefore essential in the maintenance of life. The word vitamin when translated means 'agent of life'. (See chapter on vitamins.)

Minerals: These are chemical elements that are essential in the diet. Amongst these are calcium, sodium and potassium, zinc, manganese, magnesium, copper and chromium. (See chapter on nutrients.)

Sugars: glucose, fructose, cellulose and aldonentose. Some sources of these compounds are said to have lowered cholesterol and improved blood pressure, arthritis and liver function.

Enzymes: Enzymes are important agents in the breaking down of food, thereby aiding digestion. When food is broken down, nutrients are absorbed in the body. There are numerous enzymes in Aloe Vera; some of the important ones are amylase, lipase and catalase.

Amino Acids: There are roughly eighteen to twenty of these required substances in Aloe Vera. These are products required in the body for the formation of proteins, which are necessary for the development and repair of muscles.

Saponins: These have a natural cleansing and antiseptic ability. They also foam in water solution and are therefore useful as detergents, shampoos and cosmetics. Nowadays, shampoos containing aloe are a popular commodity.

Lignin: This is a pulplike substance that can penetrate the skin; hence it is beneficial for skin problems. Skin problems are the main conditions treated with Aloe Vera.

The Anthraquinones: These are about one dozen. These compounds are found in the sap of the aloe leaves and are believe to be antibacterial, antifungal and antiviral. They are also excellent painkillers and laxatives. There have been several anecdotal reports of Aloe Vera induced lowering of blood sugar levels in diabetic patients and two of my patients have also had this experience.

Some conditions that may be relieved by Aloe Vera

- Allergy, arthritis, acidity, acne, some asthmatic conditions and anxiety.
- Bad breath (halitosis), high blood pressure, bowel problems, burns, bleeding conditions, bruising, blisters and some blood diseases.
- Constipation, cradle cap, chigger (trombicular autumnalis or harvest mite), cramps, conjunctivitis, colic, and cancer – by assisting to combat unpleasant side effects of treatment and providing the nutritional requirements of the body.
- Diabetes, digestive problems, diarrhoea, duodenal ulcers and depression.
- Eczema, eye and ear problems.
- Fevers and fungal infections such as ringworm.
- Gynaecological conditions such as problematic menstruation due to hormonal imbalance.
- Headaches, hair and scalp problems, heat rash and head lice.
- Influenza, indigestion, insect bites and stings and impotence.
- Jaundice, joint diseases.
- Kwashiorkor, kidney infection, knee-joint.
- Lumps and liver problems, low libido (low sex-drive).
- Mouth ulcers, menstrual problems and marasmus
- Nipples (sore or chapped), nausea, nose problems including sinusitis and rhinitis.
- Operations – both before and after care management.
- Piles, palpitations, pain, palliative tonic for the terminally sick.
- Rashes, to combat unpleasant side-effects of radiotherapy.
- Sprains, strains, stretch marks, sickle cell anaemia, sunburn, stomach problems including ulcers, skin problems.
- Thrush, toothache, tendon problems. Aloe is also a good tonic.
- Ulcers and urinary problems
- Veterinary medicine and problems with varicose veins.
- Warts, whooping cough, wounds.

Kwashiorkor

The name of this disease is believed to have been given by the Ga tribe living in and around the Ghanaian capital Accra.

'It is a form of malnutrition due to a diet deficient in protein and energy-producing foods, common among certain African tribes. Kwashiorkor develops when, after prolonged breast feeding, the child is weaned onto an inadequate traditional family diet. The diet is so inadequate that it is physically impossible for the child to consume the required quantity in order to obtain sufficient protein and energy. Kwashiorkor is most common in children between the ages of one and three years.

The symptoms are oedema (excessive accumulation of fluid in the body tissues), loss of appetite, diarrhoea, general discomfort, and apathy; the child fails to thrive and there is usually associated gastrointestinal infection.' *Concise Medical Dictionary*, (Oxford Reference, 3rd edition).

The traditional diet eaten by people whose children develop kwashiorkor, includes plantain, yam, cassava, potatoes and rice. This diet is deficient of first class protein, which is needed for the healthy development of children.

Other notable symptoms of kwashiorkor are: Loss of weight. The child becomes miserable and cries a lot, there is muscle wasting especially in the chest and upper arms, the child has a flabby appearance, the skin is dry and the hair becomes brown, reddish grey or white. The hair may also become brittle and sparse. In severe cases the skin may change colour and may appear as if it is burnt. Later oedema is more prominent and the liver becomes enlarged.

Some of the hundreds of thousands of infants in Darfur, Sudan, who are facing starvation, disease and death after being driven out of their homes by Arab militia in 2004 are presenting similar symptomology. Unfortunately, soon after they are displayed on TV for the world to observe their devastating tribulation, they die.

Treatment: A diet rich in first class proteins is usually satisfactory in treating the disease during the early stages; however during the late stages, the child must be carefully observed as there is a possibility of developing infection.

Marasmus

This is another nutritional disease in which there is progressive wasting in infants under the age of one year. It is due to inappropriate feeding.

Marasmus has been described as

'Severe wasting in infants when body weight is below 75% of that expected for age. The infant looks 'old', pallid, listless, lacks skin fat and has a subnormal temperature. The condition may be due to malabsorption, wrong feeding, metabolic disorders, repeated vomiting, diarrhoea, severe disease of the heart, lungs, kidneys and urinary tract, or chronic bacterial or parasitic disease (especially in tropical climates). Maternal rejection of an infant may cause marasmus through under eating. Acute infection may precipitate death.' (Oxford Reference *Concise Medical Dictionary*).

Other symptoms of marasmus are: Frequent watery diarrhoea or partially formed stools. The stools may also be bulky. There is stunted growth. The abdomen may be noticeably enlarged due to the presence of gas.

Treatment: This depends on the underlying cause. Initially very gentle nursing and the provision of nourishment and fluids by gradual steps is important. In some instances, babies are weaned from breast milk too early and probably due to poverty they are given substitute diets that are low in calories and protein.

Frequent pregnancies are another contributory factor to marasmus. If a woman becomes pregnant too soon after giving birth, she can no longer nourish her young existing infant by breast-feeding. She is also likely to feel tired; therefore there is a probability that she will be less inclined to focus on the general care and welfare of her children.

Noni

Similar to Aloe Vera, this plant is believed to be useful in treating a wide range of conditions. It has always been accredited for its analgesic and anti-swelling effect on the body.

In recent years, the juice of its fruit has been hailed as a 'miracle' treatment for various illnesses. Although claims to the success of this herb are anecdotal, recently several people in North America and the Caribbean (especially Guyana) have claimed to be greatly relieved of their symptoms. Even some cancer sufferers are believed to have maintained a lengthy remission by taking regular prescribed doses.

Nonetheless, although I would not doubt the claims of this herb, it is always advisable for people to consult a qualified herbalist before taking this or any herbal preparation. Also, those receiving prescribed medication for serious illness must not discard it in order to commence noni. Always consult your doctor before embarking on a different treatment regimen.

Aloe Vera Case History

Case one

During a routine eye examination, Mr R, a middle-aged diabetic, was told that he had diabetic retinopathy, a serious diabetic eye condition involving the retina.

There are two types of diabetic retinopathy. In a leaflet produced in London by the Royal College of Ophthalmologists and the Royal National Institute for the Blind, with sponsorship from Alcon Laboratories UK Ltd in Hertfordshire, the two types of diabetic retinopathy are described as follows:

'(a) **Maculopathy** – a condition in which the blood vessels in the retina start to leak, sometimes causing impairment of central vision (the vision responsible for recognizing people's faces or reading small print). The amount of vision lost varies from person to person. However navigation vision (the part of the vision responsible for getting around) remains unaffected.

(b) **Prolific diabetic retinopathy** – a condition in which the blood vessels in the retina become blocked. When this occurs, new blood vessels form to replace the blocked ones.'

This is a clever act of nature in repairing the damage, thereby providing the retina with an alternative method of receiving blood. Providing conditions are favorable this act of natural reconstruction is common in almost every aspect of life.

Fortunately, with early detection, both of these conditions can be treated satisfactorily as in the case of Mr R, who was referred to the eye clinic at his local hospital to be treated with laser, a beam of high intensity light that is focused on the retina. Laser cannot rectify the problem, however; it merely prevents it from worsening.

After the first treatment, Mr R was given an appointment for a following appointment six months later. Meanwhile he commenced taking Aloe Vera gel on a regular basis to boost his general health. Then on the second appointment, a doctor examined his eyes. It is routine practice for patients to be examined before receiving further laser treatment.

Mr R told me that after the doctor's initial examination of his eyes, he proceeded to re-examine them a few more times. The doctor then requested the consultant eye specialist to examine the patient's eyes. The consultant did this for a lengthy period.

Concerned about the attention his eyes were attracting, Mr R inquired the reason for the continuous examination. He said that the consultant told him that there was no sign of the problem that he presented with on his initial visit. The consultant further told Mr R that according to the severity of the problem when he was seen for the first time, it was impossible that one treatment of laser could have corrected it.

At the same time Mr R's blood sugar which had risen on several occasions, became reasonable stable and tests indicated a considerable drop to near normal reading.

There is a strong possibility that Aloe Vera had improved this gentleman's condition. There have been several reported cases of people, including diabetics, who benefited from taking Aloe Vera. However, I would like to stress that it is imperative that diabetic patients taking Aloe Vera should be under the supervision of a GP, a nurse or a qualified herbalist, because as the level of the blood sugar decreases, the dosage of anti-diabetic medication taken should be reduced. Diabetics must be well supervised.

Case two

After periods of hospitalization and tests dating back to 1970, Mrs C was diagnosed in the early 1980s with multiple sclerosis, a degenerating disease of the brain and spinal cord. She was treated by her General Practitioner for symptomatic relief of the disease. Unfortunately there is no known cure at present for this medical illness, though a lot can be done to delay deterioration, thereby enabling sufferers to maintain a reasonable quality of life.

On the advice of her doctor whom she described as 'caring and understanding', she commenced acupuncture treatment soon after diagnosis was established. This was mainly to delay deterioration of her condition and to ease the symptoms associated with MS.

She commenced acupuncture treatment with me five years later after her acupuncture practitioner emigrated to the Far East. She has a few sessions of treatment annually and considering that she has had symptoms of her illness for nearly three decades, her general condition and ability to cope remain reasonably satisfactory.

Although it is not always possible to predict the course of disease (prognosis) in individual cases, I believe Mrs C's success in maintaining reasonable control of her illness must be attributed to her admirable determination and sensible management of her health. This lady loves life and despite her debilitating condition she continually makes the best of life by socializing and having recreation whenever necessary. She is not predisposed to feeling sorry for herself. On the contrary, she often seems to think of other people's predicaments, which are sometimes minimal when compared to hers.

She is also actively involved in her church and it appears that her spirituality and her friends have cushioned her with insurmountable courage and strength, which seems to take precedence over her ill health.

In 1997, I showed Mrs C a leaflet on the many benefits of Aloe Vera and she immediately decided to try the product. Within days of commencing Aloe Vera she reported that she was having normal bowel movements on a daily basis.

Prior to taking aloe, despite taking prescribed medication to evacuate her bowels, she was constantly constipated for as long as seven to ten days. She also reported that her legs were often swollen and the bottoms of her feet were scaly and broken. Since commencing Aloe Vera, however, those problems, which are symptomatic of her condition, are greatly minimized and some have disappeared.

Further reading on Aloe Vera: *The Essential Aloe Vera* by Dr Peter Atherton; *Aloe Vera the Natural Healer* by Paul Horsey-Pennell.

CHAPTER 8

Meditation

'If you stand very still in the heart of a wood – you will hear many wonderful things – the snap of a twig and the wind in the trees and the whirr of invisible wings ... If you stand very still in the turmoil of life – and you wait for the voice from within – you'll be led down the quiet ways of wisdom and peace – in a mad world of chaos and din ... If you stand very still and you hold to your faith – you will get all the help that you ask – You will draw from the silence the things that you need – hope and courage, and strength for your task.' (Patience Strong).

I strongly believe that meditation purifies the mind, thereby incurring a renewed activation of the spirit, thus resulting in a fortified bodily structure. A cleansed mind and an active spirit are contributory to the perfection of people's thoughts and actions. If we strive to change our contaminated mode of thinking and behaviour today, we can influence and sustain positive transformation destined to benefit the world tomorrow.

Since the early 1980s there has been a noticeable increase in the number of people of varying lifestyles who have become actively involved in meditation and other positive mind-enhancing disciplines. Amongst those trying to redirect the course of their lives by seeking spiritual enlightenment through meditation are a noticeable number of academics, wealthy individuals and celebrities. This highlights the fact that academia, money, power and popularity do not necessarily bring fulfilment in life; on the contrary, they can sometimes herald a tormented and insatiable life if the spirit is stagnated.

In his book *The Conscious I*, Andy James states: 'Our environment is changing rapidly. Runaway science and technology has given us enormous power, but as Einstein observed, there has been no corresponding increase in our wisdom to use that power. In other words, our intellectual development is out of balance with our stunted emotional and spiritual growth.'

If we were spiritually fortified, we would be mentally prepared to address affluence with some degree of modesty. Some of us have met wealthy people who are the epitome of humility and decency. These are people who are aware of who they are; they are not reliant on wealth or celebrity status to forge an illusive identity tag of self-importance for themselves. If we operate without spirituality, we will be caught up in a climate of seemingly endless problems so commonly experienced by many today.

Signs of hazardous times

We are now living in 'perilous times' as foretold in Timothy 3:1. Owing to insurmountable pressures the by-products of a modern, selfish and materialist world, people are unable to control themselves. This fact is revealed in trends of increased selfish behaviour, brazen attitudes and heightened patterns of insensitivity toward others.

Some of us may appear to enjoy an admirable lifestyle and yet we may not necessarily be happy. Despite the fact that we are advanced technologically and intellectually, we are yet unable to interact rationally with each other. In spite of advanced wisdom today, world leaders are impotent in conceiving amicable solutions to problems and even as we enter a new millennium, instead of resorting to rational discourse and resolutions, they continually resort to hostile formulae as a means of solving disputes. But, as we observe, war is a futile and insensitive exploit. Its main objective is to exacerbate situations, not ameliorate them as the warmongers would have us believe.

If world leaders are prepared to verge upon belligerent methods in order to solve their differences, then what hope is there for our stressed up young people with personal problems of varying descriptions?

Speaking on non-violence, Martin Luther King stated, 'Christ gave me the message; Gandhi gave me the method.' Why can't our leaders (some of whom profess to be religious) adopt that formula when they are confronted with disagreements, instead of deliberately promoting the iniquitous 'fashion' of sacrificing innocent lives?

Yet, as we observe, those very leaders, who charismatically influence others into senseless combat, seem to lack Samson-like qualities themselves. Neither they nor their family members and colleagues are ever physically involved in battle. Whilst leaders callously devise war, it is often ordinary folks (some of whom are parents of young children) who are intimidated into trading their lives for the honour of leader and country.

How can an unconditioned young mind be expected to function rationally in this tirade of pandemic commotion, reeking an utter stench of despair?

Some of the problems associated with the younger generation are understandably self-inflicted, but others are the results of living in this stressful modern world.

Recent Dilemmas

Some young people wrongly emulate unsavoury patterns of behaviour, which to their confused minds seem justifiable in order to cope with life. It is therefore not surprising that so many try to find solace by being literally doped up to the eyeballs with drugs.

Murder is now so commonplace amongst some factions of young people that they make it look like a trivial game of cowboys and Indians.

These problems are the manifestation of a generation caught up in a perilous age and being devoid of spiritual guidance, they do not know who they are, or what to do. They are understandably bewildered, therefore some cannot rationalize that their behaviour is illogical and self-destructive.

Some of these young people are resentful of family and factions of society. Therefore, it is an arduous task to assist with the restoration of rationality and normality to the lives of these 'victims of perplexity'. They are often deluded and would often argue that others in society have problems whilst they do not.

If people are in denial, how can they be assisted?

The need for self-evaluation through mental and spiritual contemplation

In recent years, the suicide rate in young men in Britain has spiralled. In the late 1990s, it was estimated that 1500 young men commit suicide annually in Britain; this is four times more than young women. It has been observed that young black men are included amongst this unnatural mortality.

Those who are aware of the history of the early Afro- Caribbean immigrants to Britain can verify that suicide was never a part of that culture. Those pioneers, who bravely ventured to an unfamiliar country with the minimum of financial aid for their upkeep, found themselves employment and made the best of life.

They struggled on despite hardship and several were successful in achieving their goal, which was to obtain employment, purchase their own homes and raise a family. Suicide was never part of their agenda; they were too busy carving out a respectable future for their children, who are now today's generation.

Like a relay race for the survival of their offspring those pioneers ran an arduous yet tactical race, lunging forward to hand over the batons – symbolic of hope and prosperity – into the hands of their descendants. Regretfully, some of those pioneers observe in bewilderment the young members of their team deliberately drop their batons. This catastrophe heralds a difficult life for the irresponsible progeny.

In order for the younger generations to enjoy a satisfactory life, they should emulate the positive attitude and example of their forebears. However for those at the brink of despair, with the appropriate meditation techniques, many would find spirituality the only true link to God and the discovery of 'self'. By establishing a link with God, they can find the answer to their specific purpose in life and they will find atonement for their troubled life. This discovery would act as a buffer in fortifying them from the impact of any further problems encountered throughout life.

What is meditation?

According to the Oxford dictionary, meditation is 'serious and sustained reflection and mental contemplation'. A vast number of practices are included under the banner of meditation. However from a 'Christian' prospective, I choose to focus on God for direction in my life. He is the only guide whom I can truly rely on to illumine my path in life. He created me; He alone knows my innermost needs and therefore the course that my life must take in order to fulfil the specific goal or goals which He has in store for me.

I believe that meditation is an important requisite in coping with life in the world today. It is to a certain degree contributory to my mental conditioning. Through mental clarity comes spiritual awareness, therefore meditation is contributory (to a degree) in assisting me to discover who I am.

Meditation has also been instrumental in the elimination of distractions in my life. I can now identify the things I need, as opposed to those which I was conditioned by society to think that I wanted and therefore **must have** in order to have a successful life.

Finding the true me (the spiritual embodiment) with the help of meditation is tantamount to liberation. Not only do I feel freer, I am also carefree of negative issues that once tormented my mind and stagnated my spirit. I am not perfect, but who except Christ would dare proclaim to be flawless?

Although I am not a staunch devotee of meditation, I often practise it whenever I feel the need and the outcome is always satisfactory.

My transformation

I have always been a worrier and my husband often hinted that if I had nothing to worry about, I would deliberately conjure up something to set me off on the worrying pathway of all races. Well, that was not difficult, because I would easily resurrect painful events in my past to set me off on that worrying trail.

I doubt very much that I was mad, or that I was seeking sympathy. In my quest to obtain wholeness, I simply needed pacification for my emotional problems. I could not operate satisfactorily as a person with unresolved problems. I wanted to know what or who was responsible for them.

I would sometimes ask myself: 'Was it my fault and if so, how did I contribute? The most worrying aspect was if I could not find out why a problem had occurred, how then could I prevent its recurrance?

Several years ago, a senior nursing colleague who was experiencing problems of a personal nature told me that she was reluctant to discuss her problems with people, for the simple reason that they were likely to misunderstand, misjudge and therefore misdirect her. She was not entirely against the idea of sharing her dilemmas with others; however, she was a very philosophical individual and she indicated that even with the best of intentions it was not realistic for people to understand and empathize with others satisfactorily.

That day after completing my shift I pondered deeply on the nurse's narration on human reaction to dilemmas of others, then suddenly it began to make sense to me. I thought of popular reactions, including mine to other people's problems. Comments are often as follows: 'If it had been me, I would not worry about it, don't let it bother you'; or 'It was all your fault'; or 'You should be more confrontational, don't let them get away with it.'

We simply expect others to react or address their problems the way we know best – our way. People are individuals; therefore they should not be expected to attend to their problems in the same manner as 'advisers'.

I wanted to be involved in a self-help regimen that would assist me in coping with my problems. I did not contemplate a means of completely ridding myself of my problems because I am of the opinion that we are allocated our individual quota of problems (although some of us are endowed with an over-abundance). Nonetheless, through self-discipline, we can each learn to cope or coexist with problems.

I do not advocate that we should all try to manage our problems even if assistance from well-meaning and trustworthy people is offered. There is no reason why we should not consider and explore the possibility of assistance, if offered.

My moment of enlightenment

Shortly after that discussion with my nursing colleague, the professor at my acupuncture college in London invited his students to freely participate in his meditation classes. I must admit that owing to adverse revelations concerning some forms of meditation practice by members of certain cults, I was somewhat apprehensive to participate. I was of the opinion that meditation was not a 'Christianly' thing to do.

There is an element of extremist speculation of some philosophies, including meditation and acupuncture. Those who are unfamiliar with the true facts sometimes find fault with every aspect of those disciplines. (Even the concept of religion has experienced a thorough bashing by sceptics whose primary purpose is to denounce the very idea of a God.) This form of prejudice can be interpreted as truth by the unsuspecting mind, therefore although I felt a strong compulsion to pursue this branch of self-discipline, I did not know what to expect of meditation. Professor Yu was a trustworthy and highly respectable individual, so I felt safe in that sense but I still had a bit of reservation. However, I decided that I needed some form of self-discipline to condition my hyperactive mind, therefore following the decision of a few other students, I decided to join the class.

Day dreaming

Day dreaming, an elementary form of meditation which we all unwittingly occasionally indulge in, is the closest I had ever reached in the act of reflection and mental contemplation on a situation.

In the past I have often gazed captivatedly at birds as they soar majestically in the sky and wished that I too could emulate that freedom of escalating myself from the stresses of earthly life. I changed my mind about being a liberated feathered friend after I caught sight of a large tomcat as he galloped down the street strangling a poor defenceless little bird in his mouth. He then dashed into his back yard.

The following evening the owner of the cat, whom I was well acquainted with, invited me to her home for tea and a chat. I was so upset by the incident involving her cat and that poor bird, that during the course of our conversation, I made it my business to relate the natural yet disturbing behaviour of her beloved pussy.

I told her that I was aware that cats were hunters, but judging from the amount of expensive cat food he consumed at home, he should not have had the need to kill in order to survive. She sadly confessed that he frequently attacked birds, even after he had eaten, then piled them up in her back yard, whilst she was left to revive or dispose of the unfortunate creatures.

Perhaps poor pussy would have been a more contented domesticated animal if he were not pampered. On the other hand he was probably languishing for his natural source of food instead of human manufactured sophisticated meat.

As I complained, the cat was perched in a chair. He seemed a bit fidgety and he purred occasionally. He then glanced at me with half closed eyes as if he understood what I was saying about him and was none too pleased about my presence on 'his patch'.

Becoming somewhat uncomfortable and wary of his intention, I inquired the reason for his uneasiness. His owner explained that owing to an unforeseen lengthy working schedule, she returned home late, therefore he was hungry because he should have had his meal one hour ago.

She then picked him up and stroked him. Then as she attempted to kiss him (which she often did), he lashed out with one of his front paws across her face. This made me jump backwards rather nervously. To my astonishment, as he boxed her in the face, he looked at me intimidatingly as if to say, 'You watch it, mate, you are next to receive a swing of my paw!'

I clutched my handbag tightly just in case the need arose for me to go on the defensive. I thought to myself, 'You spoilt brat! If you are fed on time and yet have an appetite to seek out innocent birds for dessert, only God knows what you are likely to do whilst hungry, to someone protesting about your baneful deed.' I soon made a hasty retreat.

As I pondered the awful fate of those carefree innocent birds, I certainly did not relish such an awful fate by a cat. I promptly decided to remain as God created me – human. At least I stand the chance of defending myself against predators, and I am somewhat optimistic that should a member of the feline posse plan a dastardly attack on me, I am more likely to scare it off than to succumb a helpless victim of its assault.

My first meditation lesson went well and at the end, the professor spoke to us about our individual performances. When it was my turn, he told me that he was surprised that it was my first lesson but as he had observed, I had a natural knack for that art.

I felt delighted that I had impressed my tutor. However he was not aware that although I appeared to have participated well, I was a bit frightened initially. Therefore when no one was looking I dashed into a vacant room, and quickly but quietly recited Psalm 23.

When I reached the part that says: *'Yea though I walk through the valley of the shadow of death, I will fear no evil, for thou art with me; thy rod and thy staff they comfort me,'* I repeated it very slowly and deliberately as I looked up in the direction of heaven (hoping that God would see and shield me from any imminent danger). I was not prepared to take any chances without God's presence. Afterwards, I could not help giggling at my pre-meditation appeal for divine protection from above.

I felt that my initial meditation performance was fairly encouraging, but I was not totally satisfied with the technique used. We were instructed in a particular form of meditation whereby we focused on our respiration, internal organs and a few of the main acupuncture points on the body.

As soon as I arrived home, I went into a quiet room, closed my eyes, then I started to practise the technique again. I felt that I was achieving success because I felt very relaxed and tranquil. Then I literally felt the energy in my body swirling around gently as I concentrated and mentally directed it.

Then there was a feeling of weightlessness and to my astonishment, I suddenly felt as if I was levitating. As I gently opened my eyes, I expected to find myself floating a few metres towards the roof, but to my relief I was still on the floor. It was a pleasant experience, but I felt that I needed a different technique.

That night before retiring to bed, I noticed that I had retained some tranquil feelings. I thought deeply about my meditation experience; however, although meditation shuts off the mind in order to gain insight, I felt that God should be the focal point in my technique. I sensed that as my creator, He was responsible for my very existence including the air I breathe and all the things we were supposed to concentrate on during the brief meditation session at my college. I therefore decided to focus on God instead of the basic format taught to me. This does not mean that I am critical of the original method; it means that I simply cannot operate satisfactorily unless God is involved to some degree, in every aspect of my life. As my creator, He is able to foresee my needs much more than I can, therefore by abiding in His grace during meditation, I believe that I stood a better chance of fulfilling my personal spiritual needs through meditation.

Let us suppose we are given a gift which was specially designed for us, which later became faulty. Do we in ignorance of the construction of that gift simply set about repairing it ourselves or do we return it to the maker to rectify the problem for us? The sensible thing to do is to ask the makers to locate and rectify the problem. Likewise, in the case of meditation, I believe we are obligated to God to direct and influence our path.

Another reason for my reliance on God during meditation may well be attributed to my 'clingy persona'. I like to stick to my beliefs. I will not easily adapt to changes, especially if I am not familiar or comfortable with the conditions stipulated in the process of those changes.

That night I seriously thought about the subject of meditation, then I decided to practise once more, but instead of following the instructions of my tutor, I focused on my imagery of God. To my surprise I was totally immersed in a state of profound peace and tranquillity, the likes of which I had never experienced before. That was my moment of conversion to meditation and it is truly another amazing transformation in my life.

Pre Meditation Consideration

In order to get the best use of a piece of equipment, we renew or recharge it. That principle is also applicable to the body. Even minute cell in the body is believed to be revitalized during appropriate meditation techniques. This is why we need to integrate meditation as a vital link in our quest for a holistic and healthy existence.

Consider some of the basic facts about life as stated by the late Brother Mandus of the World Healing Crusade, in his book *Relaxit and Get Fit*, pages 14 and 15:

'You are a spirit, a life force functioning through the mind; through your conscious thoughts and sub conscious patterns and influences. This is the real and subconscious you – never forget this!

Your body is like a precision instrument or delicate machine in which you are temporarily dwelling. You are in spiritual and mental charge of this 'machinery' through your brain and nervous system.

On a subconscious level, the mind automatically controls many physical functions, such as the formation of new cells, digestion of food, breathing and sleeping, to name a few.

Being so interlocked, mind and body, there is a constant communication between the two. The mind is constantly motivating the physical system. The body is continually flashing messages back to the mind about the environment, people and, of course also any physical danger, pain or discomfort.

When any part of the mind or body is subject to sustained tension, discord, distress or disease, the whole spiritual – mental – emotional and physical system goes out of balance and we suffer from lack of health, peace, happiness, energy and well-being.'

Meditation for beginners

Choose a time when you are less likely to be disturbed.

Prepare yourself by dismissing any negative thoughts from your mind. Unless our minds are representative of a sacred temple, we cannot achieve the benefit of meditation.

'*How can a mind that is fearful, envious, acquisitive, discover that which is beyond itself? It will find only its own projections – the images, beliefs and conclusions in which it is caught.*' (J. D. Krishnamurti. Adapted from *The Conscious I* by Andy James).

Some religious devotees take off their shoes before entering their place of worship. To me that act is symbolic of discarding impure or contaminating particles before entering the sacred place to communicate with an unblemished God. Likewise, it is difficult to receive the benefits of holism through meditation if we cling on to impure thoughts such as anger, hate, spite, malice and greed (amongst others).

Meditation Technique

'You cannot teach a man anything; you can only help him to find it within himself.' (Galileo Gallilei).

Sit upright in a comfortable chair or lie on your back. Breathe out slowly, and then fill your lungs with air. Breathe out again. Now start breathing naturally. Smile throughout the entire session.

Think of the following words or quietly utter them: 'I am a spirit, an eternal being. I was created by God, therefore I will abide in His infinite love.'

Let your mind be filled with that thought for a few seconds. Now repeat: 'My life is in your hands, Father. Impart in me your vision and give me an insight of the works you desire of me. I surrender myself to you.' Now imagine God responding to you in these words – *'BE STILL AND KNOW THAT I AM GOD, YOUR CREATOR ... MY GRACE IS SUFFICIENT TO GUIDE AND SUPPORT YOU TOWARDS YOUR GOAL IN LIFE.'*

Let those words of assurance echo in your mind for a few minutes as you remain quietly in your assumed position. Do not think of anything; simply enjoy the beautiful tranquillity and profound love that you feel within. Abide in that love, totally accepting that it comes from God, because He is the embodiment Love.

Next, briefly visualize each of your organs for a few minutes; imagine that they are healthy. When you have finished this mental imagination of as many organs as you can locate, you may pray if you feel the desire to do so, or you may utter an affirmation, such as: 'Today I am going to eat less, because I am filled with something much more enriching to my mind, spirit and body than food, or, today I am going to succeed in whatever I do, because I am guided by my own revitalized spirit.' Then gently and quietly arise from your assumed position and commence your usual task.

There is no specific time limit for this form of meditation; however 20–30 minutes is the average time limit for most people.

Post-Meditation

After visiting the hair stylist, we try our utmost best to keep our hair intact for as long as we can (that is if we are satisfied with the hair style). The feeling and benefits from meditation cannot be bought, it is a self-acquired accessory to health, therefore we must try to maintain that feeling of elation for as long as possible.

Some benefits of meditation

During meditation, the level of endorphin (the morphine within the body) is raised, therefore this would account for the feelings of tranquillity we experience. It would also have a positive affect on our general performance and our physical appearance.

The following are manifestations of some of the benefits of meditation:

1. Tranquillity. A feeling of calmness, contentment and happiness.

2. Spiritual regeneration and better understanding of one's self and others.

3. An alert mind, leading to greater mental clarity.

4. A younger physical appearance.

In the 1999 issue of *Pink Ribbon*, the breast cancer awareness magazine, Lulu, the bubbly British singer, was amongst several celebrities interviewed on staying positive. Lulu's response was as follows: 'Through meditation, I have discovered equipoise – an equal and balanced state. This is such a gift. How can I feel anything other than optimistic?'

Several years ago after commencing meditation, I contacted members of the World Healing Crusade in Blackpool, England to ask their opinion regarding this discipline. The minister who responded to my enquiry stated that meditation was unquestionably helpful in man's search for holism. He also sent me the following short story written by a member of the Crusade.

As I opened the door

As the students streamed out of the college, John could see Mary heading towards the tree-lined avenue beyond the campus. He had always wanted to make friends with her but she appeared to prefer her own company. He had heard that she was a young widow but she seemed contented as if she had a rare secret.

Hurriedly he caught up with her and plucked up courage to say, 'Hello Mary, going my way?' 'Which way is that?' she asked. 'I'm just looking for a quiet spot to meditate,' she replied. 'Oh, that sounds interesting,' said John

'Hasn't that to do with those Eastern cults, Gurus and things like that?'

'Oh no,' answered Mary, 'It's just another name for prayer. I think you'll find it says in the scriptures: May the words of my mouth and the meditations of my heart find favour in thy sight. The one big difference I see between Western nations and those of the East is that when Westerners speak about prayer they are always asking God for something or telling Him something. The people from the East spend more time listening to what God has to tell them.'

'Oh, I can't get with that stuff at all,' said John.

'Well,' said Mary, 'take last week for instance. I hadn't been feeling my usual happy self and I began to suspect I was becoming depressed. I decided to sit down and meditate. The last thing I remember thinking about was that if my body is truly a temple of the Holy Spirit as Jesus says (He even said he would destroy the temple and build it up in three days), I would like to see into the part that was my mind. I drifted off and found myself looking into a dark room. In one corner was seated a miserable creature resting his head in his hands. He was rocking back and forth, moaning and groaning and repeating to himself: If only. If only.

'I must have conveyed my thoughts to him for he looked up and said: My name is Grief. I got in when your husband died and I've been so well nurtured and cared for since that I've stayed on. Every time you looked like cheering up and getting rid of me someone would say how sorry they were about Jim and you would go over the whole story again. You never got the chance to forget and this kept me warm and comfortable.

'I realized how true this was, I had wallowed in my grief and actually began to feel cheated if people didn't say how sorry they were about Jim.

'My attention was drawn to another corner of the room. Here was another miserable creature, worse than the first. It also began wringing its hands, muttering: What can I do? How can I manage? Tomorrow, next week, next year. Maybe I'll die, there is no hope.

'I was aware that Grief was speaking again: This is my wife, Anxiety, and those are my two children, Fear and Gloom.

'Poor Fear cowered in the corner, a veritable bundle of bones, his knees rattling together, saying: I'm so scared. I'm scared of the dark because I don't know what's there and I'm scared of the light because everyone can see me. I don't know what to do because I'm afraid of life and terrified of death. There's nowhere to turn.

'From the other corner came a muffled voice: I'm his little sister, Gloom, I hate it in here, there's nothing to do and no hope.

'As I surveyed the melancholy quartet I thought: So that's what I've been harbouring in my mind. I must put them out, but how? It was then the voice of

God said within me: They are too weak to do anything, you must make the first move. Let in a little light.

'I murmured a little prayer: Please send the Light. The door opened, there was a blinding flash and a gust of fresh air. I suddenly knew what people meant when they said they have seen the light, they mean enlightenment.

'Something rushed past me and the whole room illumined. I saw the previous tenants rushing out into the darkness where they were obviously more at home. I was struck dumb and gazed at the empty corners. With a voice like a tinkling bell he answered my unspoken question: My name is Faith. You know they can never live in the same abode as me. Grief cannot live by himself – he has to have company.

'I knew I should have been able to get rid of him long ago, but when I looked sad and got all the sympathy I think I really came to enjoy it. I became too apathetic to bother to read my Bible, or to meditate, or I would have remembered the words: 'consider the lilies of the field how they grow – they toil not neither do they spin, yet Solomon in all his glory was not arrayed like one of these. How easy it is to fall into the slough of despondence.' Kitty Brisbane, Caloundra, Australia.

Reflection. It is not easy to cope with living in this modern age. We are constantly bombarded with insurmountable burden, stress and, consequential afflictions; therefore we cannot be totally reliant on an over-active mind. We need to condition the mind (the centre of all bodily activities), so that our spirit, the true self, the guard, the guide and the pacifist, can be activated.

During the latter part of April 1999, a woman in the United Kingdom made medical history by undergoing major surgery on her foot without the aid of anaesthesia. She simply used mind control. We must never underestimate the power of the mind. With the appropriate motivation, we are capable of controlling our minds, and subsequently our lives.

When we operate in our true form, we are less likely to be stressed because we would know who we are and what we need, as opposed to what we want. Apart from other roles, our spirit acts as our link with God, our guiding force and a pacifist in troubled times.

Although the mind is a dynamic part of our being, we must not be wholly reliant on its impulses and actions, but through meditation, the mind nourishes and activates the spirit, which in turn feeds back positive ideas to the mind. It is only when the spirit is under God's control that the mind can operate satisfactorily.

Selwyn Hughes, the renowned Christian counsellor, stated, 'We cannot reach God by mental action. The mind is an area of conflict in many Christian lives.

When we bring our spirits into subjection to God, our minds are filled with the word of God, then our thoughts which are harnessed to God, can become positive and powerful' ...

Spirituality

In the same way that the hunter traditionally searches for food to feed his family and they in return attend to his needs, I have based my mind/spirit relationship on that scenario.

Taking into account the marvellous dynamics of the spirit, it is incomprehensible why some people ritualistically visit 'specialists' in the supernatural for guidance and assistance. It is no secret that for various reasons some people seem to be addicted to this practice. This is a sensitive issue and I am of the opinion that the majority of clientele of the supernatural are troubled people who are desperately seeking help and guidance, therefore one can only be sympathetic. However, I would like to state that in seeking such help, one is empowering another human to control one's life, whilst forfeiting one's God-given right to enhance one's own spirit, the most fundamental part of one's very existence.

It is well known that constant dabbling with some aspects of the supernatural may seem to reveal encouraging signs on the periphery, but there may follow deepseated repercussion in the form of apathetic spirituality (unresponsive attitude by one's own spirit). The consequence is a never-ending spiral of dependency, similar to the unfortunate drug addict who cannot function without the next 'fix'.

Suppose we constantly leave our vehicles parked outside our homes whilst we travel by other forms of transportation. When we do decide to use our own vehicle it may not start or if it starts, the engine may develop problems that would cause the vehicle to stall. This scenario is representative of the consequence of an inactive or abandoned spirit. We must activate our spirits through self-discipline.

CHAPTER 9

Counselling
Evaluation of popular model:
Recommendations for changes

Counselling is undoubtedly an invaluably contribution to modern therapies. It is a new therapy, which has become increasingly popular in recent years.

What is Counselling?

Counselling is working with people and providing psychological support in order to assist them in either solving their problems, or learning to live with irresolvable problems. A therapeutic result is not dependent on professionalism; it is the result of good counselling skills, demonstrated by the approach and attitude of the counsellor.

Counselling is a much sought after therapy. It is big business today, therefore an increasing number of people are attracted to it. Moreover, like any new money-making idea, there are likely to be some practitioners whose interests in pursuit of this therapy are solely financial fulfilment.

There are a wide variety of issues that are addressed through counselling. Some are as follows:

- Eating disorders (too little or too much)
- Relationship problems
- Teenage problems including coping with bullying
- Employment issues
- Coping with childlessness
- Support for the lonely or bereaved
- Family issues
- Drugs and alcohol dependency
- Coming to terms with incurable diseases such as Aids
- Issues relating to sexuality or gender

Interpretations of behaviour

Counselling is a valuable therapy if conducted in a manner which is supportive of the individual's innermost needs; it can be a gateway to the solution or management of diverse problems. However, in order for it to be beneficial to those who are in need, it is necessary for counsellors to be familiar with the racial characteristics and cultural customs of the clientele.

Conditions affecting the mind and the emotions often affect the way we behave, but it is erroneous and somewhat dangerous to stick a universally recognizable identity label on every dysfunctional condition. This is simply because contributing factors vary in individuals and people of different race or cultures.

As a practitioner of complementary medicine, I am rigid in my belief that because the causes of disease vary in individuals, people should therefore be treated as individuals. For instance, one person's headache may be due to an eye problem, another person's may be caused by a blow to the head, which may have been sustained in the past, whilst a third person's headache may be due to anxiety.

If each of the above was diagnosed as suffering from headaches and given the same prescribed painkiller for the relief of the discomfort in the head there might be some relief of pain. However there might be episodes of increased headaches and additional symptoms if the real cause of the headache was not investigated and adequately treated.

Criticism of mainstream counselling model

'Let no man presume to give advice to others that has not first given good counsel to himself.' (Seneca).

During my research for this book in the mid 90s, a senior white counsellor, with over twenty-five years of experience, told me that although counsellors may empathize (understand and share the feelings of others), they do not fully understand the cultures of ethnic minorities.

I am therefore of the opinion that despite all good intentions, mainstream counselling can hardly be perceived as the appropriate approach in helping members of the minority ethnic community with their problems.

How can anyone with no insight into my background and therefore uninformed of my basic needs in order to function according to my biological and cultural dictates, profess to have the ability to assist me in resolving my problems?

If I am not understood by professionals (including psychologists and psychiatrists) trying to assist me to alleviate my problems, there is a possibility that my behaviour may be misinterpreted. Through ignorance in perceiving the genuine cause for my behaviour, they may be inclined to diagnose my relatively innocent problem as a serious case as indicated or dictated by a general textbook. This may necessitate the prescription of unnecessary medication, which may prove to be potentially harmful to me. Although it is primarily the role of doctors who are involved in the process of diagnosing disease and prescribing medication, nonetheless, everyone (including counsellors) involved with patients/clients with psychological problems needs to be perceptive in diagnosis.

Reaction of some black children to institutional prejudice

An article under the caption 'Racism Drives Black Children To Drugs', was featured in *The Voice* newspaper 1/5/2000. The article stated that according to a report released during the end of April 2000, black children aged 11 to 16 exposed to racism are turning to drink, drugs and cigarettes. The problem is believed to be worst in instances where children had experienced racism from their teachers.

It was stated that one in five black children has been excluded from school because of disruptive behaviour or violence towards fellow pupils. The report stated: 'Clearly these are all very worrying, negative experiences. It appears that the pressure, stress and inner conflict experienced by the victims of racism creates in black children, a higher propensity for negative behavior.'

However the survey revealed that the majority of black children were happy with school and home life. The report was conducted by the Peoplescience Intelligence Unit, which is designated to be a source of information for those seeking an understanding of life for blacks and Asians in Britain today.

Compelling argument for Ethnic counsellors

Those children mentioned in the above report who are now psychologically 'messed up' supposedly by racism, are now a potential clientele for counselling and they are likely to be sent to white mainstream counsellors. It is in the welfare of the children that the primary choice of counsellors should be black or alternatively anyone having a fair knowledge and perception of black people. If counsellors who can realistically empathize with ethnical issues are put in a position of helping to heal, there is every likelihood of successful therapeutic results.

Another factor for concern is that the children counselled may be likely to identify a similarity between teachers and counsellors in the role of helpers.

Good teachers are expected to assist students educationally, not hamper them. Therefore, if those children featured in the Peoplescience report were to be sent to white counsellors, some are likely to prejudge the counsellors by remembering their experiences in school. The very experience that consequentially landed them in the therapeutic couch to be faced by white counsellors. Some might even verbalize thus to the counsellor: 'Hold on, mate! It was your kind who is responsible for my present predicament in the first place, so why should I believe that you can assist me in overcoming my problem?'

Personal Comment: I am somewhat reluctant to accept racism as the single cause for the plight of the children mentioned in the Peoplescience survey. I believe that another contributing factor to this problem is ignorance of understanding black children by white teachers. Anyway, whatever the reason or reasons, what were the parents' reactions when those children were getting into trouble in school or coming home smelling of drugs, cigarettes or alcohol, or even drunk in some instances?

Did they not have any indication of the children's behaviour in class from the teachers during parents' evenings at school (an occasion when teachers discuss the progress of each child with his/her parent(s)?

Parents should be actively involved in their children's academic progress by communicating with teachers as often as possible. This would be an indication that they are concerned for the children's welfare. This action is likely to be a psychological boost for the children, because they would have the impression that parents are accompanying them on their education journey, therefore they need not be fearful. With this assurance in mind, incidents of education phobia whereby children are so frightened of school that they abscond, misbehave and later drop out, would be minimized.

Parents' evening is in some ways synonymous with counselling. After consultation with the family (or individual in some instances), the counsellor has a clearer insight into the family and the issue(s) in question. They then have an indication of how to assist or guide those needing help.

Likewise, when parents are actively involved in their children's welfare (which includes supporting teachers), teachers must grasp the opportunity of gleaning information regarding the family by careful and discreet observations. This would place them in a more informed position of knowing and understanding the child and its situation at home.

Success is the best form of revenge

Young people need to realize that education (not only at school, but that which incorporates the wider spectrum of knowledge) is a vital necessity for the progression of mankind. Not only does it play an important part in our economical improvement, it also contributes to improving the power of the mind. An inactive mind is likely to under-function owing to lack of mental stimulation. This is why some young people who are not actively engaged in studying or working become depressed. Then because depression gets them down, they turn to drugs or alcohol to pick themselves up. Thus commences a far greater problem than putting up with education.

Although I greatly sympathize with those children who have experienced racism from teachers, I have difficulty in understanding their self-destructive reaction. Why seek revenge by incurring injury to themselves and also to parents/carers and other family members, who in some instances have endured great hardship in trying to secure a meaningful life for them?

Why subject others to the hurt incurred by authority, instead of seeking positive solutions whereby problems can be overcome? The best solution would be the determination to achieve academically, and then if the children were truly the victims of racist teachers, their accomplishment would be a psychological defeat for those who set out to impede their progress. This courageous defiance of perseverance and achievement on the part of children would also be compensatory for parents and carers, for nurturing and guiding them towards a satisfactory life.

We have all encountered problems of one nature or another at some stage of our lives (including childhood), but most of us seek ways of addressing those problems in a responsible and positive manner.

Often, when I encountered problems during my youth, my mother would solemnly utter the following citation: 'Must Jesus bear the cross alone and all the world go free?' This particular quotation has had such an indelible effect on me that it often springs to mind, particularly when I listen to those who seem to think that they have a God-given right to sail through life unscathed.

Although my mother often got on my nerves for over-using that quotation, I sensed that she was insinuating: 'Why should you flow through life unaffected by problems when others, especially Christ, have endured much more that you have?'

The following inspirational song by Cecil Frances Alexander was often sung at morning devotions during my school days. As it was a Church of Scotland School, religious devotion was an integral part of our education. I believe that it was intentionally selected by the teachers to instil courage and determination into the minds of pupils:

We are but little children weak,
Nor born in any high estate,
What can we do for Jesus' sake?
Who is so high and good and great?

When deep within our swelling hearts
The thoughts of pride and anger rise,
When bitter words are on our tongue
And tears of passion in our eyes.

Then we may stay the angry blow,
Then we may check the hasty word,
Give gentle actions back again,
And fight the battle for our Lord.

There's not a child so small and weak
But has his little cross to take,
His little work of love and praise
That he may do for Jesus' sake.

If young people are prepared to destroy themselves by smoking, drinking and taking drugs, then if their problems are the result of racist teachers, the perpetrators would have succeeded with their evil ploy. As people can observe, life in Europe today is not a bed of roses for some black people. Racism in Europe has soared proportionally within recent years, so is it not time that young black Europeans assert themselves realistically? Why not try to instigate positive changes in order to curb the stench of racial intolerance, instead of continuously acting out the role of the victim?

It is estimated that the majority of black children experiencing problems in schools are boys. I personally have a problem with the fact that some young black men are being perceived as 'weak'. From a young age I saw the role of men as protectors; therefore I have been psychologically conditioned to look up to men as guardians, because of several experiences.

During the senseless politically motivated racial tension in Guyana during the 60s, when several innocent people lost their lives, my father armed himself with a stick and patrolled our property, whilst we attempted to sleep. One night one of my younger brothers who was twelve years old decided to join our father in keeping vigil. The child armed himself with a brick. My father promptly sent him back indoors, and although we admired his bravery, we could not help laughing at his daring tactic in defending the family.

Racism is as old as the hills and just as children can easily clamber up steep hills, so too must they be encouraged to rise above prejudice. However, although I am not dismissive of the findings of the Peoplescience report, we must not easily accept every child's claim of racism as the contributory cause for his/her problems in school. If children were wise to the idea that they can get away with that sensitive topic as an excuse, they would constantly trump up the race card to justify their unacceptable behaviour. If parents readily believe all stories concocted by children (without investigating), then they would unwittingly assist in the promotion of children power, which for those children involved would later lead to adult sorrow.

There is at present a rising climate in multiculturalism in Britain and some other European countries. It is therefore imperative for those countries to realistically acquaint themselves with the racial culture and patterns of behaviour of minorities, before using terms such as 'unacceptable behaviour', 'mad' or 'mentally disturbed' in describing traits of behaviour that are unfamiliar to them.

Innate curiosity and the craving for excessive power predisposes man to spasms of exploration, discovery and conquest at a cost of billions of dollars. Would it not be more beneficial for us to educate ourselves (to a greater degree) with the family of man and assist in the improvement of the lives of those in need, wherever necessary?

'Since education is fundamental to the progress of the individual, nation and the world, we should all embrace the vision of ever multiplying its effectiveness as quickly as possible.' (Brother Mandus of the World Healing Crusade).

As we enter the second millennium, there is a need for education, greater understanding and acceptance of the diverse peoples of the world, especially those of the disadvantaged nations. This would hasten the unification of humanity, because it would inevitably break down stereotypical barriers, often the result of prejudice induced by ignorance and fear, which invariably lead to racial intolerance, injustices and tension.

Conclusion

Counselling is undeniably a useful therapy, but there are instances when its use is questionable. Recently there is an increasing tendency to misuse it. Instances of this can be observed when specially trained bereavement counsellors are rushed off to assist people in dealing with grief in emergency cases involving stress and trauma. Several people have questioned the validity of this strategy.

Why are people in the West psychologically coaxed into believing that the only emotions they are meant to experience in life are the happy ones such as joy and jubilation? People should be encouraged to cope as best they can with sadness and suffering, because like happiness it is also part of the package that comes with human existence. However, if it is obvious that an individual is still unable to cope with grief after a reasonable period, then intervention in the form of counselling may be accessed. But it is preposterous for anyone to readily assume that counselling will automatically dispense with grief.

In countries where people openly show their emotions, grief counselling or problems associated with repressed emotions are unheard of. There is nothing more therapeutic than a good hearty cry or even contained volumes of the occasional holler. It is no wonder weeping has been described as 'the anti-freeze to the soul'.

How can a total stranger (who incidentally is usually a paid professional), descending on a mother who has just lost a child in horrific circumstances ever understand that woman's pain? It is not unusual for the counsellor who is assisting the bereaved mother to come to terms with the loss of her child to be a young childless woman. And as the grieving mother clutches her lower abdomen (as if psychologically compelled to reach out to her womb – the garden in which that child was cultivated), the young conditioned counsellor sympathetically looks her straight in the face and tells her, 'Yes, I know how you feel.' What an act!

Is that not a preposterous statement considering that the only discomforting experience of the womb for the counsellor is the odd spasm of menstrual discomfort, which can never parallel the pain of giving birth or the emotional trauma of losing a child?

Is it not reasonable to assume that at that particular devastating period, the only people most of us would care to be around us are a few close relations, genuine friends and the minister of religion (in the case of those of us who are religious)?

Not many people would relish the thought of professionals invading their personal space at times of profound sadness and grief saying to us, 'Tell me, how do you feel?'

There is a Red Indian cliché which invites others to 'walk in moccasins to know what it feels like to walk in the snow'. It is no good cruising up to the reservation in an expensive jeep and a good pair of warm boots to monitor the conditions of the impoverished Red Indians limping in the snow because of their painful frostbitten feet.

How can one truthfully and honestly profess to understand the plight of those people unless one has had personal experience of wearing moccasins in the given conditions, or having knowledge and understanding of their situation? Familiarization with the way of life of the Red Indians and the nature of the work on the reservation is pertinent information in understanding their situation.

Mental Illness

Today it is a dangerous predisposition for psychological and psychiatric diagnoses to be decided purely on the theoretical analysis of the original founders of psychoanalysis. Those theorists were white Europeans; therefore the basis for their findings was the result of studying, observing and treating white people, whose pattern of behaviour especially in those days bore little similarity to that of black people.

Questioning the period of psychoanalytical discovery, let us ascertain how many of those learned men came into contact with an African, an Indian or a Chinese, let alone observed the cultural characteristics and patterns of behaviour of these individuals.

An example of misunderstanding black people

Several years ago when I was actively involved in nursing, a middle-aged Caribbean gentleman was admitted as a patient on my ward. He was a hardworking gentleman, who suddenly suffered a stroke, which resulted in difficulty in speaking and paralysis of his right limbs. He found communication very difficult and often when he struggled to converse, he would kiss his teeth or cry in total frustration.

One day, after one of my white colleague observed him kissing his teeth, she turned to me and whispered 'Isn't he rude!'

I told my colleague that the gentleman was behaving in a manner that was typical of some black people when frustrated and that his expression had nothing to do with bad manners. I further explained that although there are times when kissing of teeth can be construed as blatant rudeness, the gentleman's behaviour was easily distinguishable as mere frustration. I have also had justifiable reasons for expressing myself in that manner on some occasions.

There are occasions when people's innocent natural reactions and patterns of behaviour are wrongly interpreted by individuals. Therefore, although psychiatry and psychology are invaluable strides in the history of man's understanding of mental and emotional complexities including behaviour, it is unreasonable to accept them as a panacea for the whole of the human race.

'One of the most vociferous critics of the medical model of psychiatric disorder was Thomas Szasz (1961). Szasz asserted that the whole concept of mental illness was a myth, which could not stand up to close examination.

Although people use medical terms to describe mental illness, Szasz argued, they use social criteria to define it, not medical ones like how well the person was coping with family and friends, or keeping up with their social responsibilities. Psychiatric diagnosis, unlike physical diagnosis, was all about social judgments.' (*Foundations of Psychology* by Nicky Hayes 1994).

Behaviour can be an individual attribute; it is also biologically and culturally linked. It can also be due to diseases affecting the brain and central nervous system (neurological disorders). Some of us may intentionally choose to adopt a trait of behaviour that is foreign to our background. There is nothing wrong with people pleasing themselves or trying to please others, but this does not mean that we must all adopt mannerisms and patterns of behaviour perceived as correct in the eyes of mainstream society.

Why must it be assumed that someone who happens to be an introvert or another who is an extrovert are both outside the perimeter of normality? That is an absurd conjecture.

In 1997, the well-published case of a British nanny accused of the murder of a baby in the USA captured the attention of the world. When the nanny was found guilty, her parents remained dignified in a manner that was typical of traditional Britain. Those who were ignorant of the disposition of the British seized the opportunity to debate the relaxed demeanour of those two people by stating that they were aware of their daughter's guilt and therefore they had expected the verdict.

The question of the young woman's innocence or guilt is irrelevant to the point I am making. However, the reaction of her parents was not surprising to me, because it was a reaction that is common in white Britain.

'*It is harder to hide feelings we have, than to feign those we lack.*' (La Rochefoucauld).

There are not many people from ethnic minorities, including myself, who could have displayed or maintained such a calm composure as that nanny's parents. As for me, I would have had to be very heavily sedated or in a deep meditative trance with endorphins dripping out of my ears in order to cope so calmly.

And yet, had I managed to display such passive deportment, it would not have been an accurate exposé of my true persona. Later that sham would have greatly affected me because I would have felt that in my child's hour of need, the real me was absent. Nonetheless, that does not make me a better parent than the nanny's parents; neither does it make them better parents than me. People are individuals, not automatons, therefore we must not be expected to think and act alike.

People with psychological problems are sometimes encouraged to behave in a pretentious manner by being coaxed into addressing their problems in a manner that is quite contrary to the dictates of their genuine needs. That is a formula for the escalation of emotional and mental problems.

If people's behaviour does not contravene the safety of society, then they should be encouraged to get on with their lives as best as they possibly can, not coaxed into changing their personality.

Are drugs the main solution to mental illness?

Like any disease, the treatment of mental dysfunction should be addressed holistically. The mind does not function as a single unit; it is part of a cohesive team, which also incorporates the spirit and the body. What then is the logic of prescribing a drug to work on the mind whilst the spiritual and bodily needs are ignored?

It is now assumed that second and third generation young Afro-Caribbeans in Britain are six times more likely to be detained in psychiatric hospitals as victims of mental illness, especially schizophrenia. Comparative research conducted in Barbados and Trinidad by King's College Hospital in London in 2002 revealed that the percentage of mental illness in young black people in those islands was much lower than in Britain.

This revelation substantiates the claim by many that the generic labelling of the term 'mental illness' is a misnomer attached to some conditions which are socially induced. These young people, unlike their forebears, were born in Britain, therefore they rightly perceive it as their country. However, unlike their white compatriots, they are often treated differently. They experience inequality in the education system and in employment; therefore they perceive the system as grossly disparaging and biased against their welfare. This scenario is synonymous to a mother favouring one child whilst rejecting the other.

It is reasonable to believe that many of those affected by the 'mental health bug' are also victims of changes of lifestyle (including social and religious deprivation). It is a well-observed fact that in their countries of origin, Afro-Caribbean people socialize a lot and many tend to be religiously inclined. They often appear happy despite financial restraints. It is not unusual to find that for every twenty people (including the old and the young) passing on the streets, ten would be singing or whistling a tune, only pausing to greet each other. Despite financial stagnation and materialistic idolization, those people have an inherently cheerful disposition. They are unrestrained in behaviour; they are not afraid to sing out loud for fear of offending others and probably being deemed as 'mad', therefore they freely express a natural state of joyfulness.

Some Afro-Caribbean people in Britain find themselves relinquishing their natural happy trait, either voluntarily or through unavoidable circumstances. The family is an integral part of their social life, but the limited family connection in Britain, modern tendencies including separation of parents, voluntary or involuntary isolation of families and selfish tendencies, there is an evident evaporation of traditional family bonding. This is destined to induce mental-emotional apathy in young black people needing to connect with their own, in order to experience cultural awareness.

Those diagnosed with supposed mental illnesses might simply need to develop a greater level of cultural awareness, thereby reconnecting with their traditional way of life. This process includes socialization that would enlighten the process of self-identification, uninhibited self-expression and spiritual and religious fortification. These factors may be influential in the prevention and amelioration of some forms of so-called mental illnesses.

Addressing the question of education in *Questions & Answers* Book 2, Brother Mandus of the World Healing Crusade states,'Its central defect is that we have not yet fully conceived or recognized that the teaching of spiritual principles should be the foundation upon which personality, character and intellectual growth must be created.

'A person functions best when centred on an awareness of God as the source of light, and the spiritual laws which keep the whole being in peace, balance and receptivity to inspiration.'

PART 3

CHAPTER 10

Some Hindrances to a Healthy Existence

Loneliness

'No man is an Island entire of itself; every man is a piece of the Continent, a part of the main.' (John Donne).

The above is one of my favourite quotations. To me, it summarizes the interdependent and interconnected existence of humanity in order to live satisfactorily.

Loneliness is a melancholic feeling that can affect and transform the most fortified mind into a state of total despair.

One middle-aged widower told me that I would never imagine what it is like to be lonely, neither would I like to experience it. He stated that after completing his part-time job, he would deliberately linger and search for other chores to do, so that he could be around people for as long as possible.

Another divorced gentleman in his 60s told me that he couldn't understand why people make such a fuss about dying, because he believed that death is a relief for lonely people. That particular gentleman was one of my most frequent acupuncture clients. He often had treatment for genuine ailments and then after his condition had improved, he would request more treatment to prevent recurrence of the initial problems.

Sometimes I was under the impression that the gentleman requested treatment for the sake of being with other people at the acupuncture clinic. I did not believe that he was seeking longevity by having frequent treatments, nor was he a hypochondriac. He simply was a shy and lonely man who took the chance of frequenting a place where he could freely mix with a limited number of people.

A few months into treating the gentleman in question, I became concerned at the frequency of his visits, simply because I felt that he was paying too much financially to address his loneliness. I decided to speak to a senior colleague about the situation. She stated that it was obvious that the therapy was psychologically beneficial to him; therefore it might be a bad decision to discharge him. She therefore suggested that I charge him less.

I felt that if he was charged less, he might be encouraged to increase the frequency of his visits; therefore I decided to discuss the situation honestly with him. I advised him to have less treatment and I encouraged him to join a bachelors' club. To my relief, he agreed to my suggestion.

On a purely ethical basis, I am against the notion of people attending private clinics for lengthy periods, unless in situations of severe chronic medical conditions. I have heard of patients attending private clinics for years. One female patient, who was referred to me with chronic backache, told me that she had received fortnightly manipulative therapy privately for twenty-seven months, but her condition remained unchanged. When I inquired of the private practitioner's reaction to her situation, she told me that she was advised to persevere with the manipulation, but she should also continue taking the painkillers recommended by her general practitioner. I was astounded at that information.

What is the point in taking prescribed medicine on a regular basis whilst receiving private treatment? How is one likely to determine which treatment was effective? What is the point in paying for private medicine, when one is also dependent on National Health Service medicine (the less costly of the two)?

I personally find it both morally and professionally unacceptable when private practitioners seem to adopt an insensitive disposition towards patients/clients. I strongly believe that it would be advantageous if those contemplating a profession in private medicine were placed in an environment whereby they could actually witness the varying affects of illness on people.

If there is conscious awareness of the physical and psychological effects of disease, then it becomes much easier to have empathy and consideration for the sick. One is less inclined to focus on extracting money, instead of genuinely assisting people to overcome affliction.

Loneliness is one aspect of life that people in countries such as Europe experience and it is so traditionally entrenched in some of the population that it has become an acceptable way of life to them. This is understandable and in some ways admirable. If one is born into a particular traditional way of life, then one accepts and adapts to the prevailing condition (such as keeping oneself away from others). One's outlook on life should be respected, even if it is difficult for others to understand. However during the early days of migration to Britain, immigrants, especially the isolated ones, felt the full brunt of loneliness because they were faced with a new experience in life.

I smiled when the gentleman indicated that I did not know what it is like to be lonely. I am a jovial person by nature, but my happy persona does not afford me immunity to every prevailing adverse situation, including mental and emotional problems. I have been down 'lonely valley' and like others, I perceived it to be an absolutely distressing abyss, but like so many others, I dealt with it in the manner I believed to be suitable for me.

My husband told me that when he first arrived in England from his native country of Barbados, he was so desperately lonely that he would venture out in the cold to get to places where he could meet and associate with people. Sometimes he would even sit in the park during the winter just to have a glimpse of people as they passed by. Owing to frequent exposure to the cold whilst inadequately dressed, he soon contracted repeated bouts of acute bronchitis.

Coping with loneliness

During my early years in nursing I knew of some foreign nurses (particular Afro-Caribbean, Asians and Africans) who sometimes took turns sleeping in each other's rooms. Then unkind tales incriminating some with lesbianism began to circulate. Nothing could have been further from the truth than those rumours. Most of those nurses were from large extended families and separation was a traumatic experience, so they simply created a surrogate family by bonding with others who were in a similar situation.

It is customary in Britain for young infants to be separated at nights from their parents at a very early age. Also some children leave home during teenage years, hence those children develop independence quite early in life. British children are therefore mentally and emotionally conditioned to deal with changes in living situations and some can bravely and confidently take on the world for all that it is worth.

This early independence is not commonly experienced in the developing countries. It is not unusual for infants to sleep with parents even at the age of four years or later, and adults often live in the parental home until marriage, some remaining even after marriage. This lengthy bonding results in closer familial ties, but unfortunately it results in a lack of independence. Therefore people from the developing world who experience separation for the first time are understandably unprepared to cope with it and are therefore in need of support.

Another way in which foreign nurses were relieved of loneliness and boredom, was through the benevolence of other foreigners and relations. In addition, on several occasions we were invited by our British nursing colleagues and patients to spend a day or a weekend at their homes. This act of kindness was a frequent occurrence by some British people who were in direct contact with foreigners and it was an admirable and greatly appreciated gesture of generosity. I am greatly indebted to those people for their charitable act at a time of need.

The positive side to loneliness

It is not possible for me to empathize with people who have experienced extreme or continuous periods of loneliness, as in the case of some seniors, because I have not been subjected to that experience (as yet). Nevertheless, I believe that loneliness should not always be perceived as a negative experience. It can be used as an opportunity for self-exploration in order to determine who we really are (self-identification). Loneliness can strengthen and harness us for adverse situations in life.

It can also be used as a time of penitence, whereby one can reflect on one's life, then strive to implement changes necessary to achieve personal and spiritual accomplishment.

The lonely seniors

We must not leave seniors to get on with loneliness. These are vulnerable individuals whom we should be concerned about. We should not be hesitant in offering genuine unconditional friendship and help if necessary to the lonely, but we should not be too forceful in our offer.

I use the term 'if necessary' because some seniors are natural or conditioned loners, therefore they do not relish what they sometimes perceive as intrusion from others. However, I am of the opinion that some seniors are not necessarily bothered about being lonely, they are simply fearful of the dangers of being alone. This is understandable.

Nowadays heartless human predators habitually target defenceless seniors. Those who believe that they are entitled to molest, hurt and steal from others set upon these defenceless people. In some cases the reason for this seeming inhuman behaviour is downright evil or greediness, and the perpetrators are often remorseless.

In recent years these dastardly attacks on seniors have reached disproportionate levels and the impact of the offence seems worse for the victims and society when the offenders cannot be identified and brought to justice.

The fact that criminals appear to escape with offences against seniors probably gives them a feeling of triumph, which in turn spurs them on to pursue a tirade of contemptible acts against other vulnerable people.

My experience

I am the second child of a large family, but being the oldest daughter, my role was that of a deputy mother.

I was a manageable individual, nonetheless; I functioned in an automaton-like manner. I simply acted in accordance with the way I was expected to. I carried out tasks given to me by my parents and elders without consciously thinking of the reasons for doing them, though at times when my given chores seemed obscure or senseless, I managed to summon up the courage to question the relevance.

Spiritual Workout

When I arrived in the United Kingdom, I became abruptly weaned from my conditioning and home environment. My transition was not easy, but I was determined to improvise a formula to cope with the situation that I was faced with. It was during that period that I started to think deeply about slavery.

I tried to equate my loneliness in a foreign land to that of the slaves, but I soon came to the realization that there were no comparisons between the two cases. The slaves were forcibly taken to distant foreign countries into a hostile and inhuman situation of servitude, whilst I had made a conscious decision to leave my home, relations and friends to pursue a caring career in Britain, which at that time was 'the mother country'. I was also fortunate to be accepted and befriended by my white colleagues, a situation which the slaves were not likely to have experienced.

That was one of the most important periods in my life; it was then that I started to discover who I truly was and I began to realize my mission in life. By spending ample time on my own, I found myself developing my spiritual awareness and I also started to frequent the church.

I truly believe that I was spiritually and psychologically conditioned during that period to cope with loneliness and I now view isolation in a different light. It appears that I was purposefully subjected to loneliness in order to find Self.

Those who are familiar with me can affirm that I truly enjoy my own company. There are times when I have an overwhelming compulsion to be alone. Sometimes when I am alone, it appears as if I am transferred back to my penitence-like experience during my early days in nursing. I often experience a transient feeling of inner peace and tranquillity during that period. But in a strange and inexplicable way, during that period, I consciously believe that I am never alone.

Conclusion

Life throws several challenges at us and because some are unexpected, we are therefore unprepared. Loneliness is one of those challenges and if we do not confront the situation in a positive and constructive manner, we may find ourselves dismally entrapped in a gloomy and meaningless existence.

In order to inject some form of vigour in our lives, we may easily seek comfort in negative and destructive patterns of behaviour. We need to be positive in addressing loneliness. Loneliness is often a period of testing our mental, emotional and spiritual endurance, therefore the outcome of that test can be educational in the sense that we can evaluate ourselves by strengthening our weakness.

Advice for students

Each year, large numbers of young people leave home to commence university education. Some are away from their families for the first time, therefore initially they can experience varying degrees of loneliness.

Some students are tempted to visit clubs in an attempt to relieve loneliness and the pressures of coping with studying. There is nothing wrong with having recreation in the form of reasonable socialization, but it is not sensible to combine regular clubbing with studying. A reasonable amount of recreation is of vital importance, but a low energy level is a disadvantage to concentration.

The alarming rate of stress-related illness in students is indicative that those affected are not having enough rest (although other factors such as studying and working to pay for their education are also contributory causes).

Living away from home does not mean that students should automatically be transformed into different people. There is going to be some degree of change in character; this is a preparatory stage for adulthood and independence. However, if students incorporate (instead of dismantle) the years of parental grooming and nurturing into their moral curriculum, they may find coping with loneliness more manageable.

Above all, always remember the comforting assurance of the Lord, in which he promised 'never to leave us alone', as demonstrated in the following story that I have included for students and others experiencing loneliness:

FOOTPRINTS

'One night a man had a dream: he dreamt that he was walking along the beach with the LORD. Across the sky flashed scenes from his life. For each scene, he noticed two sets of footprints in the sand; one belonged to him, the other to the LORD.

When the last scene of his life flashed before him, he looked back at the footprints in the sand. He noticed that many times along the path of his life, there was only one set of footprints. He also noticed that it happened at the very lowest and saddest times in his life.

This really bothered him and he questioned the LORD about it. 'LORD, you said that once I decide to follow you, you'd walk with me all the way, but I've noticed that during the most troublesome times in my life there is only one set of footprints. I don't understand why when I needed you most you would leave me.'

The LORD replied, 'My precious child, I love you and I would never leave you. During your times of trial and suffering when you see only one set of footprints, it was then that I carried you.' (Anon).

Envious Rivalry or Insensitive Competition

'A sound heart is the life of the flesh: but envy the rottenness of the bones.' (Proverbs 14:30).

This biblical quotation is applicable to all negative emotions, including malice and greed. These emotions are not only destructive to the soul; when sustained for long periods, they can lead to psychological, emotional and physical illnesses. They also hinder our peace and prosperity in life. A wise man once said, 'If you think and act with a pure thought, happiness follows you like a shadow.'

Although the notion of disease induced by negative emotions is part of the philosophy of Traditional Chinese medicine, even some people with no formal knowledge of this branch of medicine are aware of the fact that people of a jealous and spiteful disposition (often labelled 'badminded' individuals) are prone to self-imposed health problems.

I often wonder whether man's predisposition to compete with others results from a pattern of acquired behaviour originating from creation. From a relatively young age, children find themselves in a ridiculous situation whereby they are being led to believe that the only way to be acknowledged by teachers, parents and society is by achieving a top of the class performance. This form of brain-conditioning can consequently give way to baseless competitive tendencies throughout life. It is also a formula for mental, emotional, spiritual and physical illness and unhappiness.

Those who have the capability to learn faster than others are conditioned by the attitude of some teachers to feel superior and they often become teachers' pets. I presume those teachers interpret the so-called clever children's achievement as a reflection of their (the teachers') personal success. This may bear some semblance of truth, but I feel that some teachers are equally accredited for the failure of children. This is due to the fact that whilst the fast learners are given too much attention, the slower students are neglected. Nonetheless, there are teachers who pay special attention to children in need of assistance.

My experience: During my childhood, I was moderately academically gifted, but as I emerged into my early teenage years, I became less focused on my education. My academic performance was so abysmal in one examination, that although I managed to score enough for a pass, my headmaster summoned me to his office.

That headmaster was Benjamin Augustus Hope, a maternal relation and one of the most brilliant and respected headteachers in the history of our school, during my school days.

After stating his dissatisfaction at my performance in the examination, he added that drastic measures would have to be taken, because I was wasting my natural talents by 'playing the fool'.

To my utter dismay, that afternoon after school, my headmaster mounted his bicycle and rode to my home to discuss my performance with my parents. One week later that caring teacher offered free extra tuition after school to a few students including me. That experience has greatly enriched my life in many positive ways and I am deeply grateful to that gentleman, who was not only my headmaster, but also one of the most influential mentors in my life.

The other contributory factor to the problem of the slow learning was corporal punishment and humiliation implemented by teachers. During my schooldays in Guyana, some teachers exerted insurmountable pressure on children who underachieved. This ridiculous form of Gestapo-like discipline was a common feature throughout the former British colonies in the Caribbean.

Once I sat in awe as I watched a teacher place a cap with the word 'dunce' on an embarrassed slow learner, whilst some of the children in the class erupted in laughter. Is this extreme form of punishment not likely to sink a child's confidence much deeper into a state of worthlessness and despair? The embarrassed child left school shortly after that incident.

As the curriculum and code of practice for schools in the British colonies was dictated by Britain, I often wondered whether children in Britain were subjected to such indignity during those days. I am of the opinion that each child is born with his/her individual inbuilt potential, which should be identified by discerning teachers, who should then encourage the child to develop his/her ability.

It is questionable whether the current multidiscipline education curriculum for children is workable. I am in favour of a system whereby the child is encouraged to pursue its favourite subject; this is likely to increase its confidence with a positive psychological attitude. This approach is likely to instil confidence in him/her to pursue and probably excel in other subjects in due course.

It is good practice for everyone to have an understanding (not necessarily thorough), of varied topics that are of relevance in life.

Parental influence

Parents are sometimes responsible for influencing their children with envious tendencies. This may be due to several factors, but some of the foremost ones are:

- Direct influence. Innocent supposedly loving gestures such as purchasing a child an expensive pair of trainers to match or upstage those worn by other children. This can foster envious tendencies in later life.

- Indirect influence. Children often observe and cultivate patterns of behaviour from parents; therefore parents who compete with other people are likely to pass on this negative trait of behaviour to the observing children.

Envy is described as discontent or resentment because of another person's success, advantage or superiority. Why should someone harbour envious feelings towards another when we are all individually talented? Envy is the gateway to stronger negative emotions, which are destructive to the mind, body and soul of the discontented person. Likewise, it can affect innocent victims of its intent in similar manner. It is an injurious 'dis-ease'.

Some other causes of enviousness

(1) **Lack of identity and direction in life.** There are many of us who operate in an automaton-like existence. We have no idea who we really are, therefore we do not know what we are supposed to do. To establish some form of meaningfulness in our lives we set out to mimic others.

This tendency to imitate others is an interesting observation concerning the popular assumption that humans are pack animals and that their behaviour is interconnected and interdependent with each another. This pack animal instinct is probably the reason why we notice cases in which people senselessly compete against others.

During the quest (or conquest) to find purpose in life some people are impervious to the feelings of others. Like a battle for survival, some humans are prepared to knock others down mercilessly.

This problem of enviousness has been endemic in man since creation;

nonetheless we must adopt a more contented attitude and we must not crave for what belongs to others. These may be possessions acquired through sheer hard labour and downright determination. It is only in identifying ourselves and our true purpose in life that we are in the position of determining our individual vocation in life.

(2) Lack of self-discipline. As I have stated before we were all born with individual talents. God does not discriminate. However, through lack of self-discipline or idleness, some people concede their chances to capitalize on their natural God-given talents. It is however fair to assume that there are others who, for various justifiable reasons, are incapable of utilizing their abilities in an effective manner.

The increased numbers of chat shows on television have exposed many alarmingly sad features of present day life. I am amazed to see how many young people have let themselves be catapulted into a life of punishment.

These unfortunate children have become mothers, some as young as 12 years old. It is customary to listen to some telling the chat show hosts, 'Ama going back to school to get me an egucation.'. In as much as I admire their courage in trying to complete their education, one cannot help imagining the difficulties these children may encounter in coping with studying and raising a family.

Children must realize that having babies is not likely to be viewed as a complimentary attribute on their part. Education and commonsense is foremost in the quest for accomplishment and fulfilment in life. I cannot generalize, but it seems that those who fail to prepare themselves by pursuing their talents are the most resentful of the success of others. How many times have we not heard, 'I wish I had a nice home or a nice car like that individual.'

Why don't we applaud those who apply themselves sensibly in the pursuit of their vocation instead of imitating a crab-like mentality in trying to haul them down to the bottom, thus impeding their ambition of reaching the top? I believe that if we were supportive of the success of others, then we would be likewise compensated for our good gesture by being successful ourselves.

Sibling Rivalry

'A friend loveth at all times, but a brother is born for adversity.' (Proverbs 17:17).

Rivalry is common amongst siblings. It sometimes starts early in life as innocent competition in gaining parental approval. This can result in serious consequences if allowed to escalate. Some popular examples regarding this nature of rivalry can be seen in the Bible.

Cain slew his brother Abel, because Abel's offering to the Lord was more appreciated than his. Jacob deceived his father Isaac by pretending to be his older brother Esau (although he was influenced by their mother Rebecca). He offered his father a meal which the father requested of Esau, the hunter, thereby receiving the blessing meant for his brother.

Again we read of the jealously of the sons of Jacob towards their younger brother Joseph because he was his father's favorite. His resentful brothers sold him to the Ishmaelites.

'Jealousy is the most radical, primeval and naked form of admiration – admiration in the form of war, so to speak.' (Robert Louis Stevenson).

The accounts of the above-mentioned cases of rivalry or jealousy amongst siblings were all recorded in Genesis, the very first book of the Bible. Therefore, it is evident that some of the earliest people to inhabit earth were grudgeful of others. Cain and Abel were the very first humans to be born of a woman (Eve) and one killed the other because of jealousy. Nonetheless, today we are aware of the adverse consequences of negative emotions, because we have more evidence of its disastrous consequences than those early biblical characters, therefore we should not subject ourselves to its continuity.

Distraction

If we focus on our own potential, we can accomplish our goal. It is when we become embroiled in the struggle for power within the family enclave or organization that our specific mission becomes blurred to us. We are then entangled within a system whereby we constantly strive for supremacy by competing against others.

The snobbery of society is somewhat responsible for this system of occupational politics. People in certain so-called respectable professions are perceived as more intelligent and important and therefore superior to others. They are therefore more appreciated and respected than others. This can result in a feeling of worthlessness and low self esteem by those who feel they are less acknowledged. It can then progress to a feeling of resentment in the form of enviousness.

How often have we not witnessed or heard of people desperately trying to destroy those who strive to be a success in life? In a devilish tendency to bring the aspiring victim down to their level, those beset with jealousy sometimes concoct false accusation against the innocent.

This action is a replica of childhood misdeeds. Some children are often grudgeful of others who seem to be doing better than they are. The resentful children sometimes even go to the length of concocting stories about the successful ones, although in a less cruel manner than adults do.

Life would be more successfully managed if we operated as a team. We are dependent on the contribution of a varied selection of people in society.

An architect may design a laboratory which would be constructed by builders. Cleanliness including good hygiene is of vital importance in laboratories therefore specialized cleaners would be employed. The valuable work of refuse collectors must not be excluded from the team because if they did not remove the garbage from laboratories, hospitals, industry and homes, we would be besieged by an army of germs, insects and vermin, and this would contribute to the outbreak of various diseases. How do we know that it is not God who imparted a special DNA to the refuse collector so that he can cope with his specialized task? Despite desperation for employment, try as some will, many people cannot cope with that occupation.

It is not practical to expect scientists and doctors to readily adapt to other occupations such as cleaning and refuse disposal, because they are accustomed to dealing with man microbes and medicine. Likewise, others should not be expected to carry out the work of scientists and doctors.

We must be contented in our area of employment, although if we are working in an environment in which we are uncomfortable, we are perfectly entitled to change it for another form of employment that is more fulfilling to us.

Conclusion

Enviousness is a 'cancerous' entity which eats away the conscience and soul of its victims. It depletes the body of positive creative energy as it charges along its trail of destruction. When positive energy is injured, one is restricted in making rational choices and decisions. One is therefore entrapped within a spiral of worthlessness and destructive behaviour.

What is the point in inflicting injury on oneself by an envious disposition? We need to be less hasty with our analysis of situations. We often equate monetary riches with happiness and contentment. If we listen to some wealthy people and observe their behaviour, we would ascertain that money is not the key to happiness and fulfilment in life.

Do we ever consider how some of those people who are envied because of their wealthy financial assets acquire their status? Some have done so legitimately, but others have reportedly resorted to methods that would seem unbecoming to many.

No one should be resentful of another simply because of his/her achievement. This is a symptom of internal turmoil. What is needed is spiritual fulfilment, which would alleviate resentment by channelling peace and contentment into that vacuum.

We must bear in mind that we are the authors of our own fate. It is therefore up to us to model our lives in a pattern that can yield fulfilment. It is unreasonable for us to compare ourselves to others who have prepared or sacrificed for a situation, whilst others remain nonchalant about the prospect of using our talents sensibly.

Example: I bravely entered the annual local 10-kilometre road race in Dunstable (a section of my community) at the youthful age of 40 plus. Although I am a regular jogger, I had never competed in a road race before that event. Racing my children and my dog in the grass-cushioned park was the closest I had got to any competition in my adult life.

There were 51 competitors and the majority were members of athletic clubs. As the race progressed, I targeted one particular woman who appeared younger than me, but she ran somewhat uncharacteristically for an athlete, so I felt that I stood a chance of beating her.

About 2 kilometres from the finishing line, I decided to seize the opportunity to pass the lady simply because she annoyed me by running in front of me throughout the race. I therefore proceeded to fill my lungs with extra air, then unwisely sprinted past her. Within 100 yards of completion, I felt as if my distressed lungs were about to explode under the stress of the athletic battle, so spotting the winning line ahead of me, I relaxed a little. To my astonishment as I glanced over my left shoulder, the woman whom I had targeted was advancing to overtake me.

I thought to myself, 'After all the effort I have invested in beating you, don't tell me you are going to get the upper hand over me!' I was so charged up with adrenalin that I momentarily lost reality. In a desperate bid to impede my rival, I felt a strong impulse to thrust my arm out or to grab hold of her T-shirt in order to prevent her from passing me. That unsportsmanlike impulse soon left me. However, even if I had managed to slow her down, I doubt whether I could have mustered up enough energy to outsprint her, as my poor legs were on the verge of collapsing.

I finished thirteenth in the race, which was not a bad achievement. My 7-year-old daughter was so excited that to the amusement of spectators, she danced with joy on the track as I stumbled in. My older daughter, who entered at the last minute for the fun of it, finished sixteenth.

Aged 11 years, my daughter was the youngest competitor in the field and her performance was so impressive that she was invited to join one of the clubs, but she declined. She later told me that running was boring. That remark was a proverbial slap in my face for me, because my husband and I are such ardent athletic enthusiasts that we named the child after a reputable British ex-100 metres sprinter.

Although everyone seemed happy with my performance, I felt a sense of failure. I was not bothered by the fact that I had been beaten by the first twelve people, neither was I concerned if those who came in after me had managed to pass me during the race. My frustration was purely down to the fact that that particular lady had beaten me. As she stepped forward to receive her medal, I thought, 'It should have been me receiving my medal in that position.' I felt gutted. I looked around in childish anticipation, hoping that one of the stewards would announce that she was disqualified for cheating. I had hoped that they would perceive the manner in which she clumsily overtook me to be a violation of the rules. My hopes were dashed because no one disputed her success. Later, after meeting the lady in question, as we drank beverages on the racecourse, she revealed that she had been running for some years for an athletic club based in a bordering county. She then asked me the name of the club that I represented. I told her that I was not a member of any club; I simply took part in the race for the fun of it. She remarked that for an amateur, I ran exceedingly well.

At that point I suddenly felt an immense sense of guilt for my reaction towards that competitor who ran me into the ground. It was only then that I mentally, graciously conceded defeat. I also admired my rival, because I acknowledged that she was a dedicated and experienced athlete, therefore she was a worthy winner. I consoled myself by thinking, 'Finishing behind this lady should be a commendation, not a condemnation for me.'

Give credit when it is due

Just by looking at the athlete in question, I 'picked' on her believing that she was someone whom I could easily beat. As it turned out she was the competent athlete, whilst I was inexperienced in tactical distance running. In all sincerity, I was not prepared for that event. If I was not prepared, then why should I expect to win?

This should be a learning experience for all. We must never underestimate people simply because they may exhibit a peculiar feature. As someone aptly stated, 'Do not judge a book by its cover.' Neither should we begrudge others because of their achievements, especially when they have prepared themselves for it by working hard. Jealousy must not be easily overlooked. King Solomon stated, 'Jealousy is as cruel as the grave,' therefore we must try to avoid letting ourselves be consumed by this devious emotion. Similarly as we sensibly avoid the life-threatening under-currents of an unpredictable ocean, victims of jealousy must seek protection in the form of alertness and evasive action. If not, they may suffer emotionally and psychologically and in some cases, even physically, as a result of the grudgeful actions of others.

CHAPTER 11

Damaged emotions

Part 1

Some emotional issues in life are the most difficult health related problems to cope with. This is even worse if the problem stems from early childhood experiences. No matter how physically well victims of emotional problems may look, at times they experience more psychological suffering and pain that we can possibly imagine.

One of the saddest cases of emotional turmoil that I have encountered is that of a young man whom I will refer to as Sam.

Several years ago I was consulted by a young man who requested acupuncture treatment for a badly injured shoulder. I immediately assessed him in order to determine whether his complaint was treatable by acupuncture.

Sam's problem resulted from an injury to the left trapezius muscle (the flat triangular muscle extending over the back of the neck and upper half of the trunk). This injury was sustained during one of his rigorous training sessions. Sam was a keen fitness enthusiast and by looking at him, one would be inclined to believe that he was a professional bodybuilder or a weightlifter.

My initial impressions of the 19-year-old blond Englishman, whom I nicknamed Schwarzenegger (after Arnold Schwarzenegger, the well known bodybuilder), was that he was a courteous and disciplined individual. However, he possessed another characteristic – shyness, which to me was as noticeable as the others. Although he dwarfed me in height, he would constantly avoid eye contact by staring towards the roof, bending his head downwards to look at the floor or even glancing from side to side to avoid looking at me.

I treated Sam and to my delight, his response to acupuncture was amazingly satisfactory. Although he had experienced severe pain and discomfort on effort when using the affected shoulder, he had an 80% recovery after the third treatment.

Three years later Sam phoned me requesting acupuncture treatment for a problematic gastrocnemius or calf muscle (the thick muscle at the back of the leg), which he had injured during gruelling training. He was running for several miles a day, with fifty pounds of weight strapped to his back.

During his treatment I inquired about his academic progress and I was very pleased when he informed me that he had been successful in obtaining his degree. He further stated that it was difficult to get meaningful employment in England at that period so he had applied to join the French Foreign Legion. That was the reason why he was engaged in a painstaking training schedule, to improve his fitness and promote his chances of acceptance in the FFL.

I was astounded that that 'gentle giant', who obviously was an academically gifted young man, would opt for a career in the French Foreign Legion.

The French Foreign Legion

The French Foreign Legion was founded in 1831 by King Louis Philippe, for services outside France. It was established as an aid in controlling French colonies in Africa, and its headquarters was at Sidi bel Abbes in Algeria.

The army is believed to comprise foreigners who were primarily from several European countries, and it has been reported that Frenchmen were forbidden to join. However in his book, *The French Foreign Legion*, Nigel Thomas states: 'Many Frenchmen were admitted illegally. Some of them were criminals whom the French authorities wanted to get rid of. Others were simply escaping from lives of drudgery and hardship. They, and many Frenchmen after them, pretended to be French speaking Swiss, or Belgians, and enlisted in the legion under a false name.'

Hugh McLeave, author of *The Damned Die Hard*, wrote: 'Men joined for their soupé and the chance to grab some of the fabled treasures of Africa. Behind them pressed the hungry and jobless, the vagrant and felon.'

Even if the information regarding the FFL is sensationalized, one cannot help but wonder why a genteel and academic young man like Sam would be inclined to join any army, far less one of such notoriety.

Incidentally, at the same period I was treating Sam, I was also treating an ex-British soldier who told me that he had had first hand information about the FFL during his army days. I asked Sam if he would like to meet the gentleman so that he could get an insight into the FFL. He smiled at me and with his usual poise of head bent downwards, he said, 'Jac, I know what yo   'e up to, but no one is going to persuade me to change my   e to enlist with the FFL, but if I fail I would try to enlist with another foreign army.' However Sam decided to meet the gentleman and I arranged the meeting soon afterwards.

After introducing Sam to the gentleman, I made myself scarce by becoming involved with clinical duties, whilst they became engaged in light conversation.

They eventually got around to the main agenda of discussing the FFL.

After Sam told the gentleman that he was hoping to be enlisted with the FFL, the statement from that gentleman sent a chill up my spine.

He quietly stared at Sam for a while, then he said, 'Son, you may think that you are tough, but I knew strong ruthless men who cried like babies when they were in the FFL, because they found the discipline and training too hard to cope with. If you want to be a soldier why not join the regular British Army?'

The gentleman was very fatherly in his approach. He was very tactful and caring, and in no way did he try to pressurize Sam into changing his mind, but he replaced the glamour of Sam's proposed mission with shrewd reality.

Sam told the gentleman that he had heard worse things said about the Legion, but he was prepared to have a go. Realizing that Sam was unswerving in his quest, the gentleman shook his hand and bade him best wishes. After the gentleman left, I proceeded to give Sam his last acupuncture treatment; he was leaving for France early the following day.

Feeling extremely concerned I inquired whether his relations were aware of his elected vocation. He told me that a few knew, but he had deliberately withheld the information from his maternal grandfather, because he felt that the news would have killed him.

Realizing that he made no mention of his mother whom he had spoken of with great concern during his previous appointments, I inquired of her reaction to his proposed journey to France. 'Oh Jac,' he replied, 'I'd forgotten to tell you that she died suddenly last year. I had to travel back home to bury her.'

I felt numb after receiving that devastating news. Suddenly my mind started to unravel the reason for his intended 'escape' to France.

Sam was his mother's only child. He told me that he did not know his father. He had always spoken about his mother whom he described as academically gifted, but he told me that instead of using her talent, she had wasted it.

Several years ago when I first treated him, he revealed a lot about his mother to me. Since childhood he remembered his mother with a dependency problem, which resulted in her death. He continually spoke with some sadness about her condition, but due to his constant referral to me, I was of the opinion that he saw me as a paradigm of what his mother should have been.

On several occasions when he spoke of his mother he would say, 'I am so angry how she has wasted her life; an intelligent woman, completely wasted.' On one occasion after a mouthful of the 'wasted' proverbial, with tears in his eyes he blinked a few times, then he said, 'Well, look at you, Jac, she too could have had a very good profession.' At that point I interjected by asking him not to make comparisons of people. This is a preoccupation which many of us are guilty of.

I told him that it was understandable that he was concerned for his mother, but instead of ridiculing and expressing anger and frustration at her predicament, he should continue to assist her in overcoming her problem.

In defence of Sam's mother. '*Great spirit grant that I may not criticize my neighbour until I have walked a mile in his moccasins.*' (Anon).

The picture of an intelligent but psychologically tormented young woman, raising a child on her own, is in itself a heroic feat. I am astounded at the number of people in the West who were either abandoned or adopted at birth for varying reasons. Nonetheless, this lady decided to raise her child rather than give him up for adoption. She must have influenced his life with a reasonable number of positive qualities, because he attended University and achieved a degree.

Why would a caring young mother let herself be swept away in the torrential stream of self-destruction? The fact, as related by Sam, indicates that this unfortunate woman may have been a victim of abandoned love, which she never overcame.

Trying my utmost not to be too speculative, I gently brought Sam's attention to the fact that his mother could have been a jilted lover. He responded by stating that he would not rule out my assumption, but he felt that if that was the case she should have been more sensible and pulled herself together.

Relations and close acquaintances tend to be some of the chief advocates for this 'pull yourself together' formula in overcoming problems. I am sure that intentions are genuinely well meaning, but that phrase is often used inappropriately when applied to mental and psychological problems.

Those who are badgered by others to 'pull themselves together', may find professional counselling useful, whereby they can have the opportunity of speaking freely to a complete stranger. There are some people who may be good at shrugging off problems unaided, but others may be in need of external assistance after trying unsuccessfully on their own.

The first time Sam had acupuncture I inquired of his reasons for not taking his mother to see a professional counsellor for support. He told me that he had tried several methods of assisting her, but nothing seemed to work and at that time he felt it was too late for her to be helped, because she was at a very advanced stage of her illness. When he told me of her demise, he said that he was surprised that she lived so long.

Several months after burying his mother, it appears that Sam also wanted to leave the life that he perceived was unkind to him. He told me that a young academic had become very fond of him, but he was not interested in any romantic involvement because he was afraid of getting hurt. He further stated that the lady in question wanted to correspond with him by writing whilst he was away. Then to my surprise, Sam turned to me and with a confused look he asked, 'Jac, what do you think, should I write to her?'

I told him that in a professional context, I felt that he should make that decision for himself after much thoughtful consideration. However, on a personal level, I felt that it would be a good idea if he found time for some personal assessment to find out who he really is. It is only when we know who we really are that we can address our personal needs. I explained to Sam that when he found out who he truly was, perhaps he would stop running and dodging, and face up to reality.

I continued, 'Your mother would have been very proud of you if she had any indication that you were destined to be a winner' (i.e. finding yourself and facing up to the challenges of life to the very best of your ability). Winning to me does not necessarily mean mastery of a particular achievement. It is the act of performing to the best of one's ability. If with such dedicated effort, one is not successful, then neither is one a loser. There is an old proverb that states: 'When man does his best, the angels can do no more.' This statement is a sensibly worded truism.

The embarrassment in losing

There are instances when sportspersons are not acknowledged unless their performances are consistently meritorious. I can remember (with a degree of annoyance), when I resided in Guyana, there were instances when young children competing in athletics were booed if they finished last.

An acquaintance once told me that her niece, who was a competent athlete in the West Indies, was beaten in an important race. The poor child was booed so badly that she cried. Although she was a promising athlete, the child refused to participate in any further race.

Yet, it is often observed that some of those who deliberately instigate that nature of contemptuous behaviour at the performance of contestants are incompetent in coordinating their legs for a brisk walk, much less competing in a sprint.

There needs to be a radical change in attitudes towards people who try hard at what they set out to achieve. People must be appreciated and encouraged for their effort, not ridiculed and humiliated. All levels of competition (including personal achievements) should be seen as acts of bravery and accomplishments.

Living in England during the last three decades, I have observed that as a sign of encouragement, those who finish behind seem to be given equal applause and on some occasions even more than those finishing before. When announcing the order in which contestants finish, sports commentators do not adopt the habit of stating 'last' when referring to the final competitor to complete the discipline; instead they state the position such as eighth, if eight people competed. This is a mark of respect, admiration and appreciation for their determination in completing the race. This is a psychological booster for those contestants.

Continuing my conversation with Sam I said, 'Please win, Sam; if you win, you will be winning for your mother as well, she was too ill to do it. Although you did your best for her, you were not successful in assisting her whilst she was alive, but you can now help yourself, you are an important part of her memory.'

Sam thought deeply for a few minutes, and then he made circular movements with the big toe of his left foot before bidding me farewell. I silently prayed that God would deprogram and reprogram Sam, thus enabling him to find peace in his troubled life.

As he left my clinic I watched him as he walked with his typical muscled-up gait. Every conceivable muscle in his body appeared to be inflated, his trapezius muscles (in his shoulders) seemed like massive shoulder pads under his flimsy T-shirt, as he disappeared down the slope on his way to the bus stop.

As he was about to cross the road, he glanced back at me and waved. Then he said, 'Bye Jac, thank you for all the help you have given me.' As he ended that statement, his voice appeared to change as if suddenly a lump had appeared in his throat.

That was a very poignant moment for me. It seemed as if I was seeing Sam off, as parents waved good-bye to their sons as they left home to go to war. That could have been my son or any other living woman's son. He too had had a mother like most young men of his age. Now he was on his own, so he had decided to venture out into what to him seemed like a cruel world, to fight a hell of a battle to appease his pain. All I could do was pray that God would furnish him with the appropriate weapon so that he could win his battle, no matter what form it took.

Part 2

Although I have not walked that mile in Sam's moccasins, I can mentally visualize that torturous journey, because two of the most important and influential men in my life were themselves participants in that agonizing mile.

My father and my husband were both deprived of their father's presence from an early age. Although in my husband's case the impact was not as severe as that of my father's, nonetheless, that experience left an indelible mark on both men. Those two men realized the hurt they had experienced by the action of their fathers, and yet despite their experience, both have demonstrated commendable paternal qualities.

This is why (without being judgmental), I find it difficult to understand the rationalization of cycles of intense abuse, whether in the form of mental, physical, emotional or sexual presentations. Children are not responsible for the actions of adults, therefore how can rational minded adults subject innocent children to similar pain to that which they themselves had experienced as children? However, I can understand the victim's frustration in coping with that problem.

Daddy's Story

My father was the eldest of four children. His father was apparently a financially stable business merchant who operated between his native country, the former British Guiana (now known as Guyana) and Surinam (formerly known as Dutch Guiana).

During one of his visits to Surinam, my grandfather met another woman and decided to leave my grandmother and her children in order to be with his newfound love.

Unable to cope financially, my paternal grandmother decided to take my father out of school at the age of eleven and place him with his father's brother to work in order to support the family. Therefore at the tender age of eleven, my father became the breadwinner of his family.

Some of my father's classmates told me that he was an outstandingly brilliant student. One told me that he remembered my father as a young student attending school with one of his first cousins, the late Cleveland Hamilton, who later became a prominent Guyanese lawyer. The gentleman stated that had my father's education not been disrupted he too was destined to become an accomplished academic.

Whilst my father worked in the field tending his uncle's cattle, his first cousins (his uncle's children) all attended and completed their schooling. One even went to university in the USA.

I am grateful to my great-uncle for assisting my father's family by providing my father with employment. However, I cannot come to terms with the fact that instead of depriving a talented child of his education, other avenues of assisting the family were not explored.

Some older family members told me that my father was adopted by his uncle. To my mind the use of the word 'adopted' in this sense is a misnomer, because my dictionary describes 'adopt' thus: *'To receive the child of another and treat it as one's own; to select and accept as one's own.'*

My father's emotional state was indented with GAPS (Grief, Anger, Pain and Sorrow). He was a very private but much misunderstood man. He never drank alcohol nor did he smoke, but he consumed large quantities of coffee, an underestimated stimulant, even at nights and he was one of the worse insomniacs I have ever known. I never observed him sleeping soundly. He merely had intermittent brief naps. I have inherited that trait of limited sleep. I could not understand why people felt the need to go to bed before 1 a.m., because I could not. Even when I manage to crawl into bed owing to sheer tiredness, I would gently elbow my sleeping (at times snoring) husband, to ask whether he was awake, just to engage in futile conversation until my tired body surrendered to merciful slumber.

I am grateful to my paternal great-uncle for his presence in my father's life. I understand that he had children of his own and they were his main priority. Despite his efforts, the love he gave my father could never have compensated for that which he must have relished from his biological father. The situation would have been different if my father had been much younger and had not established a relationship or bonded with his father.

Many people lead a normal life with only one or, in many cases, no biological parent, but when parents establish a relationship with children, then disappear without even saying goodbye the effects can be devastating. Up to the time of my father's death in 1992, he had not spoken of his childhood nor of his father to his children.

He was very protective of his family. I can remember one of his aunts named Ester, who was financially comfortable, asking to adopt me. During my childhood, many seniors were attracted to me. My father told my aunt that his children were not puppies to be selected by people. He continued his objection to the adoption by stating that he did not approved of the idea of some of his children eating steak, whilst the others had to be content with a meal of salted fish (cod fish). He concluded his brilliant defence for the preservation of the family unit by saying, 'I would be happier if we all ate salted fish together today and awaited a better meal of steak tomorrow.'

So protective was my father of his family, that when I decided to pursue nursing in the UK during the late 60s, he tried desperately to deter me from leaving home.

Although I was very fond of my great-aunt Ester, that day I felt exceptionally proud of my father. Even to this day when I remember that episode I am consumed with emotion. I feel very special with the love, care and sense of belonging that he bravely and publicly demonstrated on that day and throughout my childhood.

My Reaction. The aftermath of some people's actions can inadvertently influence the lives of generations of their innocent descendants. It is unfortunate that some people do not consider the consequence of their behaviour before contemplating acts of selfishness.

As a child I was very fond of both my parents, but I was slightly inclined to be closer to my father. I have inherited many of his mental and physical characteristics including his glowing dark complexion. However, there was a difference in our spiritual outlook.

Although my father believed in the existence of God, he was reluctant to embrace religion *per se*. I was of the opinion that he had reservations in publicly demonstrating attachment to any belief (including religion), or any one, except his family, for fear of rejection or disappointment.

Whenever I attempted to discuss the topic of religion with him, he expressed dissatisfaction with some leading proponents of this doctrine, because of their double standard lifestyles. In his words, 'They preach what they deliberately intend not to practise.'

The bond between my father and me was so strong that I often visualized his emotional pain and rightly so. Being his child, I was also a victim in the cycle of abandonment, in the sense that I was denied the opportunity of ever seeing or knowing my paternal grandfather.

After passing my primary school examination at the age of eleven, my name along with other successful candidates was published in the national newspaper. At that age, that was the most important day for me in my eleven years of life. My father was away from home working in the goldmines in the interior of Guyana, but his uncle, whom he had lived with, happened to pass by our home. I called out to him excitedly and told him the good news regarding my exam success. He immediately stopped in and gave me a congratulatory hug.

As my great-uncle hugged me, I felt very proud and happy, but that feeling was suddenly replaced by sadness. Later, as I sat on our stairs in the glowing sunshine, I suddenly thought, 'I wish my real grandad would read of my success in Surinam, then return in a posh car to see me just this once, but I hope that he does not bring that horrible woman with him.' Then I thought: 'Perhaps she was old and may have died by now, therefore he may well drag himself back alone.'

A few weeks prior, there had been a story circulating about some people in Surinam who supposedly died from drinking poisoned alcohol. Suddenly remembering that story I thought, 'Oh yes, perhaps she is one of those people poisoned by that batch of bad rum. Well, perhaps she is one of those who are now lying stiff in the mortuary in Surinam.'

I assured myself that my Grandpa would not die as a result of alcohol poisoning, because neither his brother (who adopted my father) nor my father drank, therefore he too would abstain from it.

The boil was being lanced (my imagination was becoming more vivid). I sat on those stairs with both my hands propping my rounded face whilst I proceeded mentally to concoct the entire burial of that poor woman. On reflection, I believe that I have been gifted with the knack of visualization from an early age, although it was childish and negative in those days. I have now transformed this natural ability, through reasoning and positive affirmation, into a dynamic survival kit.

After imagining the death of my grandpa's concubine, I proceeded to visualize entire burial scenario. I assumed that no decent preacher would agree to conduct her funeral service and pray for her soul. This was because she ran off with my grandmother's husband, and also because she supposedly consumed alcohol that led to her death, therefore she was evil and was going straight to hell.

I visualized six enraged pallbearers lowering her so angrily and clumsily into her grave that her head banged hard on impact. At that point I sighed heavily, then I blurted out 'Bitch, serves her right!'

Although my mother and my great-uncle were conversing and laughing aloud, my mother heard my outburst and rushed out to caution me on my 'bitching'.

Later, after my great-uncle left, my mother inquired the reason for my appalling outburst. I too was also taken aback by my audible outburst. I apologized to my mother, and then I divulged the reason for my explosion to her.

'Bitch' was a forbidden but somewhat frequently used (curse) word, by angry children during my young days, My mother rebuked me by stating that I was a child, therefore I had no right to be involved in adult issues.

Rationale. If a tree is infected, is there not a possibility that the branches and fruits would likewise be affected? Therefore, being the offspring of my father, am I not also likely to be troubled by his problems?

As readers will observe, I deliberately included that incident, because I feel that instead of white-washing my account with lies and pleasantries, it is imperative for me to be truthful in revealing my feelings as a child at that time.

Even if I was six instead of eleven, I was still a person with feelings and emotions. To this day I still find it somewhat difficult to come to terms with disappointments, no matter if it is in what some perceive as an insignificant form. However if we let the unsavoury attitudes of others permeate our minds, we would be victims of a traumatic existence in life.

Adults sometimes seem oblivious to the fact that parental issues are liable to effect and traumatise children. Children experience pain when parents separate or when there are problems within a marriage. If problems are not fittingly addressed, these unfortunate children or young adults may internalize them, then they may be affected later in life with emotional and psychological problems.

I have listened to religious devotees stating that if people truly believed in God, then they would not have mental or emotional problems. To my way of thinking, that assumption is utter nonsense.

Firstly, religion does not automatically provide us immunity from the ravages of disease. Like physical illnesses, we are all susceptible to mental or emotional problems. However, religion is helpful in lessening the impact of our illnesses. It can motivate us into accepting and coping with our problems and this may result in overcoming those problems.

Frequenting a place of worship (in some instances, twice on the holy day) would not necessarily guarantee us freedom from dilemmas. Even with the most charismatic prayer and enchantingly melodious singing of songs asking God to 'Roll my burden away' there still lies the possibility of residual emotional distress, although there are occasions in which some people testify to receiving instantaneous healing in churches.

Miracles do occur, but we must not always expect God to demonstrate his power in full glare of the public by casting away every illness from us. As indicated in the Bible, we must not put God to the test. The fact that some people appear to be suffering does not necessarily mean that they do not communicate with God, or that He has forsaken them because of their sins. God is a mysterious Being; therefore at times it is difficult for us (mere mortals) to comprehend His ways.

Mark Twain fittingly remarked: *'Habit is habit and not to be flung out of the window, but coaxed downstairs one step at a time.'* Therefore at times, problems need to be gradually drained out of the system. It is only after the internal damage has been taken care of that the burden can be realistically rolled away, because one is then freed from the central source of the agony. Therefore one can feel and enjoy the therapeutic experiences of religion. It is only then that one can sing freely with genuine sincerity.

Secondly, if someone had a traumatic childhood which later affected him or her emotionally or mentally, how can it be assumed that the condition is a result of his or her disbelief in God? When some people are afflicted by mental or emotional illnesses, they sometimes find it difficult to distinguish the difference between night and day. This may be due to the severity of their condition or a reaction to the prescribed medication. How can they be held responsible for their predicament? These people need compassion and guidance, not condemnation. It is unreasonable to blame them.

No one should make judgmental statements such as, 'If you were religious you would not have had those problems.' This is a false and insensitive conjecture. It is also a harmful statement that is liable to cause more anguish to the sufferer. People do not have to be bad or non-religious to have emotional problems. Therefore, it should not be a sign of weakness to let others know of our problems or of our frustrations in coping with those problems.

As the Christ was being crucified, did he not call out to God in pain, saying, 'Father, why have you forsaken me?' Christians recognize Jesus as the greatest and purest person ever to live on earth. He undauntedly carried out the work ordained by God his father, in a manner that is unparalleled by the action of the most obedient human. Would Christians dare suggest that he could not have had a meaningful relationship with God because he experienced human suffering and publicly cried out in pain?

My psychological profiling of Jesus, the man, reveals him as a very mentally and spiritually strong and disciplined character. He placed God's will at the forefront of every aspect of his life, from childhood to the hour of his death. He was aware that his work on earth as ordained by God was finished; therefore he was not intent on resisting death. However he was also human, so it is understandable that in his hour of need, dazed with agonizing pain, he would call out to the most influential being in his life (God) to assist him in coping with his ordeal. I also believe that it was God's intention to reveal the human side of His son to the world.

Jesus understands our emotional pain. He knows what it feels like to be rejected by a friend. His trusted disciple Simon Peter denied knowledge of him when he was arrested to be crucified. He knows what it feels like to be mocked and made fun of by gangs – he was a victim of ridicule by the arresting Roman soldiers.

Nowadays it seems trendy for some young people to bully others in the most dastardly and cruel manner. This sometimes leads to the innocent victims resorting to desperate measures including suicide in order to escape from that hurt.

Children who are ridiculed and bullied must realize that the perpetrators are often frightened and insecure people. The bullies often see their victims as youngsters who stand out like a shining star, people who are symbolic of what the bullies themselves would really like to be (decent, respectable and admirable people). Therefore, they become resentful and cruel.

Children who are harassed by bullies must not be intimidated. Tell someone. It appears that the only way some unhappy people believe they can appease internal turmoil is by channelling negative emotions such as anger and maliciousness towards those whom they perceive to be different, or who appear to be physically weaker than themselves. If only those unfortunate sad people could be positively reprogrammed, we would all enjoy a better life.

CHAPTER 12

Discussing the Welfare of the Young

Growth in Grace
Lord, 'tis a pleasant thing to stand,
in gardens planted by thy hand.
Let me within thy courts be seen,
like a young cedar fresh and green.
There grow thy saints in faith and love,
blest with thine influence from above.
Not Lebanon with all its trees,
yields such a comely sight live
(Nature decays, but grace must thrive).
Time, that doth all things else impair,
still makes them as these.
The plants of grace
shall ever flourish strong and fair.
(Watts, Ps. 92, p11).

Some time in 1997, my two daughters were engaged in an argument over television. I was so touched by both sides of the argument that, like most matters of significance, I recorded the incident in my diary.

Soon after commencing nursing, I developed the habit of documenting any detail of importance. This tendency is the result of recording vital details pertaining to patients, which was customary during my period in nursing. This practice is an important method of acquiring information regarding patients and it can also be helpful in deciding the nursing management and medical treatment for patients.

The argument between my daughters occurred because the 16-year-old wanted to watch an American chat show about uncontrollable teenagers, whilst her 13-year-old sister, who at that age disliked chat shows, wanted to watch children's television. The 13-year-old questioned her sister about the benefits of watching problematic children.

The 16-year-old replied, 'It is all educational, it helps other teenagers to learn from the mistakes of others.' The younger child raised her eyebrows and said,

'Why would you want to learn from other people's mistakes. Did God not give you a brain to think and judge between right and wrong for yourself?'

Although my older daughter was justified in her argument, I was astounded by the witty retort of the younger child.

'This know also that in the last days perilous times shall come.' (2 Timothy 3:1).

Like many adults, I am greatly concerned about the welfare of today's younger generation. There are so many unwholesome influences on young people nowadays that we must be vigilant or our children may easily become victims of this dangerous age as foretold by Timothy. Living today is synonymous with walking in an open minefield; one has to be cautious with each step for fear of activating a mine.

Young people today are the adults of tomorrow. They are our future; therefore they are of significant importance to the family structure, society and the world. It is imperative for adults to play a vital part in preparing our successors for their future role in life. As adults, we must endeavour to enlighten their path.

Although a considerably large number of the young are decent exemplary people, there are those who, for various reasons, are not representative of a commendable and promising lifestyle. Poverty, psychological problems, peer pressure, adult influence, self-opinionatedness and parental errors are some of the contributing factors towards inappropriate behaviour in children. Nonetheless, like the rest of society, these children are also God's property. They are as precious to Him as the unblemished child; therefore we must assist them as best we can.

Adolescence

During puberty there are biological, social and intellectual changes. At the time of these transformations the adolescent (part child and part adult) becomes curious about his/her identity. They are therefore inclined to ask questions including, 'Who am I? What is happening to my body?' Incidentally, this is the period when some adolescents believe that they are gay, though those feelings are primarily due to biological changes, including hormonal activities.

Common knowledge and tangible evidence isolates cultural pressures as one of the causes of stress in adolescents in industrialized societies. It is a well-known fact that children in developing countries are not as exposed to high levels of pressure as experienced by children of industrialized nations. They live by conforming to discipline as dictated by parents, elders and other members of the extended family.

Pressures of the industrialized nations have wide-reaching implications on the young people living in those countries, but there is a lesser impact on those of some developing nations. This observation is substantiated by revelations concerning children from Monserrat by the British news media.

Following the 1997 volcanic eruptions in the British dependency of Monserrat in the Eastern Caribbean, several of the inhabitants were transported to Britain. Despite abandoning their possessions and leaving their country, these brave people ventured into Britain, capturing the hearts of several people because of their resilience and pleasant disposition.

It has been reported by the media that not only were the Monserratian children in England more disciplined and attentive than their English classmates, most were also bright. The children were also surprised to observe how disrespectful some children in England were to teachers and they stated that they had never experienced such behaviour in their country.

Parental Protection

'Train up a child in the way he should go: and when he is old, he will not depart from it.' (Proverbs 22:6)

As parents and concerned members of society, we must devise a counteractive scheme to save our children from the impact of this decadent way of life that has infected humanity.

Governments and organizations cannot be wholly depended upon for the implementation of changes destined to remodel society in a positive manner. How can they when some are themselves unwitting architects of the present calamitous situation?

Anyway, as is well observed world-wide, when things go wrong in governments the responsible individuals sometimes resign (either voluntarily or forcibly) or in some cases the entire government may decide to relinquish power. How can that action be appeasing to the victims when the damage has already been done?

Let this be a lesson to young people. Governments will change, friendships may discontinue, teenage magazines offering advice may cease to exist, but parental influence is indelible. The positive manner in which your parents have devotedly groomed you will continually illuminate your lives even after their death. You will also pass on that positive trait to your children.

I am usually bewildered by the advice given by intellectuals regarding the management of difficult children. The message parents and carers are receiving from experts is somewhat encouraging to the children to have their own way, though when they have messed up, parents are then expected to be there to help them. Many children capitalize on this situation.

Children fail to realize that some suggestions put forward by establishments are not necessarily formulated to resolve problems affecting the family. Although some professionals are uncomfortable with the way they are supposed to delegate their duty, they are powerless to operate differently from the way they have been programmed to act. This is because generally speaking, people are dependent on a financial upkeep for themselves and their family by holding on to their jobs.

If employable adults decided not to work because of dissatisfaction with their work description, unemployment would rocket. Therefore, although some of us may not be in agreement with the tactics of some professionals, we must try to understand their position.

Corporal Punishment

'Foolishness is bound in the heart of a child; but the rod of correction shall drive it far from him.' (Proverbs 22:15).

'Withhold not correction from the child: for if thou beatest him with the rod, he shall not die. Thou shalt beat him with the rod, and shalt deliver his soul from hell.' (Proverbs 23:13–14).

Although it is not illegal to chastise children some parents have to be cautious when demonstrating 'reasonable chastisement' for fear of they themselves being punished by the law. This is that the very law responsible for the punishment of undisciplined children who progress to become wayward adults. It is also the very legal system which now threatens to take parents of problematic children to court for deeds committed by the children.

Nowadays parents are in a state of perpetual confusion concerning how to raise their children. They are continuously criticized for getting it wrong. And yet, those intellectuals who are entrusted with the task of advising us how to be parents seem to be failing to produce positive results.

The wife of a solicitor once told me that 'the law is an ass', and since then I have heard that expression on numerous occasions. Never mind, it seems that so far, the law has not done too badly, because during my childhood there was a popular saying that 'a jackass is sillier than an ass'. Let us hope that the law does not deteriorate in common sense, thus causing its colloquial definition to be downgraded.

In November 1998, I read of a case in a local Sunday newspaper, where a children's home in England was under investigation for mismanagement. This was the result of inappropriate behaviour by children.

A former resident of the children's home told how staff were powerless as they watched children run rings around them. The young lady, now in her early 20s, said, 'I would agree with smacking, it would have done me some good at the time.' She went on to say that the only way staff could have been in control was by using corporal punishment.

It is unfortunate that children often realize the folly of their actions towards parents and those who are truly concerned for their welfare when it is too late.

The young lady backed up claims that children ran riot in the home, but she stressed that it was not the fault of the staff, but of the law, which meant that staff could not lay a finger on the youngsters.

As a child, I was disciplined with corporal punishment and likewise my children were also beaten when they were deserving of that form of punishment. Although on a few occasions, I collapsed giggling, as the children dashed away from me like nimble young hares, whilst I unrelentingly gave chase after them. They also laughed at times as I pursued them. I sometimes wondered what was the point of it all. One positive result is that we all had a good physical workout with all that running up and down the stairs. However, there were times when I seriously dispensed some stinging lashes on them.

One day as I chased one of my children up the stairs to give her a few lashes, the child locked herself in the bathroom. 'Mom,' she shouted, 'you'd better be careful, because if I phone the police to report that you are chasing after me to beat me, you are going to be locked up and it would serve you right.'

I pounded hard on the bathroom door with my fist, as I beseeched the child to get out and receive her beating immediately so that the police could quickly take me away in handcuffs. I also told her that they might also sample the whip if they dared interfere with my parental obligation.

Shortly after that incident, that very child was involved in a road traffic accident as she made her way to school. Mercifully she was not physically injured. As I was transported to the hospital by two traffic police to join my daughter, they engaged me in various light-hearted conversations, probably with the intention of taking my mind off the problem. Then we touched on the subject of indiscipline in today's generation.

The female officer, who appeared to be the same age as me, stated that when she was a young teenager, she dared not disrespect her elders or she would have had a good hiding from her parents. The male officer said that young people would be better controlled if parents had beaten them as they did in the past.

I thought to myself, 'This may be the best opportunity to defend corporal punishment, therefore I must represent the cause this very minute.'

I immediately leaned forward to make myself audible, and then speaking softly and distinctly I said, 'How can parents beat their children when the law has given you coppers the authority to arrest those who dare?'

The male officer told me that law was misunderstood, because responsible parents would not get into trouble for disciplining their children in 'an approved manner'. He continued the conversation by stating that it was the people who brutalized children in frustration that the law was targeting.

I was somewhat relieved to find that I was not the terrible mother that my children were making me out to be for chastising them whenever I felt that it was justifiable. However, I hoped that the law would rightly differentiate between beating and brutalizing.

I informed the officers of the incident when I told my daughter that if the police dared intervene when I was beating my children, I was going to let them have a few cracks of the whip. The two officers looked at each other, then laughed heartily for a while.

After taking me to the hospital, they took turns in shaking my hand and as they were about to depart, the female officer patted me on my shoulder and said, 'Carry on beating, if you feel the need to do it, love.'

Improper Influences

The young generation of today is very knowledgeable; they are not as innocent as some may have us believe. They are aware of the difference between right and wrong. However, some choose to abandon good principles and adopt bad ones, just to be in with the crowd.

The New Age Syndrome

During the 60s some young people believed (or were led to believe) that a lot of sex was good fun. That flower power era heralded some eccentric cults, the introduction of music with a difference, a combination of recreational drugs and the sexual explosion. Today we are now faced with a legacy of injurious consequences of that fun-packed era.

Some of those who submitted to that tide of excitingly cascading but murky waters are sadly paying the price today. Sexually transmitted diseases have escalated since that period. Although it is unfair to suggest that everyone with sexually related problems is responsible for their condition, some people placed themselves in situations which consequently predisposed them to those conditions.

Sexual precociousness

From a young age I was concerned about people becoming sexually involved before adulthood. Sensing that it could not be right for children and young teenagers to indulge in sex, I conducted an experiment on mangoes grown on my maternal grandparents' property, soon after my fourteenth birthday.

I squeezed a young mango on one of the trees, and then rubbed it to incur slight bruising. I then proceeded to do the same with a larger mango, which was slightly ripened on the same tree. Several days later I returned to inspect my research. The younger mango fell off the tree; its colour was changed from a vibrant green to an unhealthy pale yellowish colour and its skin appeared wrinkled. However, the only visible change in the older sturdier mango was the indentation where I had applied pressure. It later fell off the tree when was fully ripened.

To my mind, that experimentation validates the assumption that young females engaging in early sex are more likely to be exposed to such conditions as infertility, frequent miscarriages (spontaneous abortion) and other gynaecological diseases, including cancer of the womb at an early age.

In recent years, children as young as 12 years are becoming pregnant. This is a sad observation. Children should behave and conduct themselves in a manner befitting their stage in life. Although some argue that they are physically and mentally matured, they are not emotionally prepared to deal with adulthood.

Mother or child mothering a child?

One teenager, who is the same age as one of my daughters, now has several physical ailments resulting from psychological and emotional distress.

Not only was that child the mother of a young infant at the age of 14, but the father of her baby was horrifically killed in a motoring accident. Understandably, the young teenager felt very remorseful because the last time she saw her baby's father they had argued over childish issues. This is understandable because they were both children.

There was also a fair amount of bitterness, resentment and blame between the girl's family and the family of the deceased. Several months after the occurrence, I met the teenager and her aunt. When the aunt related the event to me, the child started weeping in an uncontrollable childlike manner. Her aunt told me that at times she cried for no apparent reason.

As a human and the mother of two teenage daughters, the tears of that beautiful child burnt deep into the core of my heart and there was secondary pain in my mind. I asked myself, 'How can a mere child be expected to cope with this extremely painful situation, when many adults collapse under the pressure of less traumatic situations?'

Inappropriate behaviour by some young people today must be blamed (to a certain degree) on some celebrities, such as pop stars and actors, whom the children idolize. Innocent youngsters adapt behaviour patterns portrayed by these people.

Need we be surprised that young people are getting into relationships for the wrong reasons nowadays and because of this, the rate of teenage pregnancies and separation is constantly escalating? Teenagers understandably lack the fundamental ingredients in life. Mental, emotional and spiritual harmony are essential constituents within a meaningful relationship. Instead, some opt for sexual gratification, which is perceived by them as enjoyment.

Some of today's young generation can be forgiven for thinking that it is fashionable to have sex with anyone minutes after meeting them. The message relayed by this morally impoverished society is that sex is a portrayal of love.

'Anything that is too stupid to be spoken is sung.' (Voltaire).

Many find it deeply disturbing that some modern pop singers resort to lyrics littered with profanity and sex, in order to sell records. Some of these artists seemed to be very talented and yet, sadly, this is the manner they see fit to inspire people, especially the younger generation.

A few years ago I was travelling on a bus. A young woman boarded the bus with her infant son, who was approximately two and a half to three years old. After the woman seated the child alongside his pushchair, he took out a toy fire engine from his pocket. He then proceeded to run his toy up and down the side of his pushchair, whilst he mimicked the sound of a fire engine by saying nino, nino, nino; then he burst out singing 'Wind down Babylon'. He then switched back to 'nino, nino, nino'.

I smiled as I observed and listened to that jovial infant. Although 'Wind down Babylon' was all he vocalized, repeatedly, I could only assume that Babylon was likely to be totally exhausted from all that winding down as it hit the floor. However, is it not right for us to be careful what lyrics our children are exposed to, when they are as passionate about current trends of music as they are of toys?

I suppose sex is the only act in which some people believe they can demonstrate their potential purpose in life. It is only after we have learned to love and respect ourselves that we can truly give and receive genuine love. There are absolutely no other short cuts to a meaningful loving relationship.

How often have we sat down in the company of our children to view a supposedly good film, when suddenly up pops a semi-pornographic sequence, which sometimes bears no relevance to the story line?

In an interview by the *Sunday Mirror* on 23 July 2000, Diana Richardson, the daughter of John Logie Baird who invented the television, stated, 'My dad invented TV but there is so much sex and violence I can hardly bear to watch it.' Mrs Richardson continued, 'To be honest I just don't watch television any more – I don't see the point. Why watch when there is nothing you want to look at? These days, I am afraid, television just reflects society.'

Promiscuity is suffocating respectability. For the preservation of posterity, adults must be instrumental in reviving virtuous comportment. It is the passport to decency, morality and stability in life.

Adults have a choice in whatever they decide to do with their lives, but innocent children should be given the opportunity to enjoy a normal childhood. This will make it easier for them to make independent rational decisions later in life.

I have heard adults quietly stating their disapproval of certain aspects of behaviour. They then proceed to say, 'But there is nothing we can do, because this is the way the world is today.' Well, I for one believe that there is a lot we can do to rectify the situation.

When our children are young, do we not accompany them until they are old enough to walk unsupervised on the streets? Likewise, we must protect them from premature exposure to issues that are likely to cause them psychological confusion (which may well result in damage).

Adults must also be supportive of children and young adults when that support is justifiable. We must not stand idly by whilst brave children who rightly demonstrate their disapproval to certain elements of life in the world today are dismissed as being out of touch with reality.

Example: During the middle of 1998, my youngest child who was then a young teenager showed me an article in one of her teenage magazines.

The magazine in question published an article regarding a female homosexual, and a young reader e-mailed her disapproval of the promotion of homosexuality by that magazine, whose readers were young teenagers.

The disapproving teenager wrote: *'I was horrified to discover that you openly promote homosexuality in your magazine. Is it not bad enough that it goes on without you people giving it the big thumbs up in the eyes of teenagers? Lots of young people read your magazine, and may be confused already without you putting across the idea that homosexuality is now trendy and the latest thing to try.'*

That perceptive teenager was absolutely correct in her concern regarding the interpretation of the homosexual message by young people who are already confused.

In July 2004 it was reported nationally in the UK that one in nine young people here, including children as young as 11 years, are now suffering from depression caused by bullying, the break-up of parents and coping with modern living. Some resort to suicide.

The two young men responsible for that section of the magazine replied as follows:

'Just when we thought that bigotry was dead, we receive a letter like this. People like you should realize that your horribly antiquated, narrow-minded views don't reflect those of a modern society, and with a bit of luck your prehistoric ideas will go the same way as the dinosaurs.'

This insensitive reaction to the teenager's e-mail appeared to have saddened my daughter deeply.

Why are young people belittled instead of respected by those who believe that their modern way of thinking and behaviour must be approved and adopted by all? People are free to practise and promote homosexuality; likewise others must be given equal freedom in expressing their disapproval of it without being perceived as intolerant or homophobic.

How can young people develop confidence in addressing moral issues according to the dictates of their conscience, if those whom they are supposed to look up to for guidance are silencing them insensitively?

How often have we not observed that people with porous arguments desperately try to inject some quality of authenticity into them, by referring to overused rhetoric? It is also a well-known fact that those people deliberately conjure up certain quotations when it best suits their intentions. Therefore, those who question or oppose what they believe to be wrong should not be intimidated by being labelled by terms such as 'bigots'. Be rigid in defending what you believe to be right. Do not be intimidated.

When Lieutenant Colonel George Custer made his advance against the Sioux Indians at the battle of Little Big Horn River in 1876, Sitting Bull, chief of the Sioux, said to his people, 'Today is a good day to die.' He instructed the entire Sioux nation, including the squaws (women) to fight to the end to defend their territory. The Sioux obeyed their great chief and except for one Indian who managed to escape, Colonel Custer's entire army was destroyed.

Although the slaying of other humans should never be portrayed as an act of valour, the above reference serves as an example of a justifiable act of defiance on the part of victims. Likewise, now is the appointed time for us to spring into action to defend, protect and therefore assist the children of this generation in making decisions according to what they believe to be right for them.

Fate of the Dinosaurs

There are people who dispute the fact that dinosaurs ever existed. This may be due to increasing scientific involvement and numerous conjectures. However if we refer to Genesis 1:20–1, we will note that God created creatures resembling dinosaurs on the fifth day of creation, even before He created man.

There have been several hypothetical explanations for the extinction of the dinosaurs. One of the latest unofficial speculations (1990s) is that the extinction was accelerated by an outpouring of a large amount of lava in the Deccan Plateau in India about sixty five million years ago. If this conjecture, which bears some similarity to a number of previously stated accounts, linking volcanic changes with the disappearance of the dinosaurs, is factual, then the reason for their disappearance was due to hostile climatic changes beyond their control. They could not have migrated to a different environment, because they were trapped.

On the other hand, this present modern thinking generation is well aware of the dangers of its defiant attitude involving several aspects in life. We have been warned and we have witnessed the devastating consequence of trespassing on the outer borders of our boundary line. Yet, so many boldly tread on those forbidden territories. And just like the dinosaurs (who unlike humans, had no option in escaping their end), they too become 'extinct'.

NB: The inclusion of the fate of the dinosaur was for the sole purpose of addressing the statement made by the respondent(s) to the teenager's e-mail. It is not intended to add to the debate regarding their extinction.

Contentment

As parents, we must teach our children to cultivate inner contentment so that they will be appreciative of what they have. This will help them to become fulfilled adults. It is a sad reality, but some people incorrectly believe that monetary wealth would automatically bring happiness and general contentment. In the words of William Shakespeare: '*Oh! How bitter a thing it is to look into happiness through another man's eyes.*'

How often have we heard that 'money cannot buy happiness'? True happiness radiates from deep within the self; therefore no amount of money can genuinely guarantee complete personal satisfaction. However, some individuals can graciously manage monetary wealth if they have inner peace and contentment in life. We often hear of children of wealthy parents complaining that they had been sent to expensive boarding schools and showered with costly gifts, when according to them, all they really wanted was genuine parental love.

'Maslow (1954) proposes that human beings have a number of complex needs, but that not all of these needs are equally important at any one time. Instead they are arranged hierarchically, with each different level of needs resting on the assumption that the ones underneath have been satisfied. As each group of needs becomes satisfied, the next level becomes important.' (*Foundation of Psychology* by Nicky Hayes).

In *A Textbook of Pyschology*, Radford and Govier state, 'Maslow developed these ideas and argued that the highest need is for "self-actualization", which involves the development of an individual's potential for those characteristics which make us most human: love and affection, aesthetic experiences, altruism.'

We operate from different levels at different times, but some of us have a level where we are living much of the time. If our requirements at these levels are met, then we can move on to the next higher level. If our lower needs are not fulfilled, we will regress to them under stress.

Parental Responsibility

Parents must realize that children are a continuation of themselves and that they are also the future. Children mimic adult behaviour, therefore they are our reflection. Caring parents must be instrumental in motivating children in their quest for self-identification, for it is only when people are sure of who they are and can identify their individual needs, that they can confidently make impressive strides in life.

We must not waive our parental accountability until our children become fully pledged adults; we must continually guide them, but we must not control them. Some people are of the opinion that parental responsibility should cease as soon as children are of a specific age. Some suggested age points are sixteen, eighteen and twenty-one years. This is an unfair insinuation because calendar age is only a numeric evaluation of one's stage in life; it is not an accurate representation of our physical, mental or emotional growth.

Is it not a well-known fact that whilst some infants refuse to be breast fed, some do briefly, whilst others feed for as long as the mothers are prepared to let them? I am sure that there are several of us who are aware of cases where children have been breast fed for long periods, in some instances until pre-school age.

When I cultivate at my allotment (vegetable plot), I tirelessly remove the weeds so that they do not impede the development of my products. I stop the cleaning up operation when my crop reaches maturity, because I know that it is no longer in danger of being strangled by weeds.

Likewise parents should be supportive of their children for as long as they believe necessary; some parents are even prepared to assist their children throughout life. It is their choice and once that action does not impede the child's capability to operate as a normal adult, no one has the right to be judgmental.

We must therefore try to conduct ourselves in an appropriate manner so that we may instil strong virtuous qualities in our children. These positive attributes are often conspicuous as the children transcend adulthood. We must endeavour to support and instil a legacy of integrity in our children, then, if they transgress by adopting unsavoury qualities, we need not feel guilty because it would not be our fault.

Example: Soon after my second child started primary school, her school informed us that they were contemplating transferring her to a school for the educationally sub-normal because they believed that her behaviour did not constitute what they perceived as 'normal'. This was simply because the child was somewhat hyperactive. Coincidentally, at that particular period she was experiencing a distressing illness, therefore one wonders whether her problems were psychologically connected. She also had a slight hereditary impediment of speech.

I challenged the school authorities to provide me with realistic proof of my daughter's supposed 'educational subnormality'; meanwhile I consulted our family doctor, a child psychologist and a Health Visitor. Both our doctor and the Health Visitor were surprised at the school's findings and of its decision to have the child transferred to an educationally subnormal school.

The Health Visitor, who had known the child since birth, remarked that the assumption was total nonsense. She stated that the system expected every child to portray a passive behaviour, therefore if black children had a bubbly disposition, they were likely to be misunderstood and assessed as abnormal.

So persistent was I to obtain proof of my child's backwardness from the school that they soon arranged for her to be assessed by a senior paediatrician (a doctor specializing in disease and treatment of children). After spending a considerable amount of time with the child in the presence of my husband and me, the doctor turned to us and looking slightly bemused she said, 'There is absolutely nothing wrong with this child, she is a normal, bright, independent little person.'

Had the doctor confirmed that my daughter was educationally subnormal, I would have accepted the result and agreed to transfer her to a less demanding school where she would be able to cope. I would not have consented to her being taught in a school that was above her educational capability, where she might have succumbed to insurmountable stress and illness.

I accompanied my daughter back to her class after her assessment with the doctor. Just as an informed communicable health inspector would pacify a troubled community regarding its fear of an epidemic, I approached her teacher saying, 'The doctor said there is nothing wrong with the child.'

That individual, who was my daughter's first teacher, told me that she was not convinced by the conclusion of that experienced doctor, because my daughter spoke and read in an unorthodox manner.

My word! Despite the fact that that his manner of speaking was not tinted with an upper class accent, was Winston Churchill not one of the most charismatic orators and greatest Prime Ministers Britain has ever had? And yet, before becoming a famous leader, he too may have fallen foul of that nonsensical ridicule pertaining to what may have been conceived as an 'unorthodox' manner of speaking.

My husband speaks in what I perceive as a leisurely and quiet manner, hence it is obvious that our daughter had inherited her unhurried manner of speech from her father. Therefore, although I had been advised by well-meaning friends to send her to speech therapy after the teacher's comment, I frankly refused. Why should I deliberate erase a part of my husband's natural trait from our daughter? Why should I conform to the wishes of a snobbish and artificial society? Incidentally, her speech is now faster than before. (I refuse to use the term 'normal, or improved').

I also believed that, had I had consented to changing my daughter's speech in accordance to the expectations of the establishment, she could have interpreted my action as giving her the go-ahead to alter her natural looks in the future.

This snobbish tendency is one that is widespread in England. In some instances extremely clever children of working class families are refused entry to some prestigious universities. The reasons for refusal are usually incomprehensible to the rational mind.

I told the teacher that the child's speech was of no significance to her intelligence. I then appealed to her to assist my child, by being patient with her during reading. To my surprise, the teacher stared at me as she explained that she had other children in her class to teach, therefore she could not afford to devote time to a slow reader.

At the time of that incident, I was a staff nurse on a busy children's ward. I immediately made a mental comparison of the teacher's duty and mine. I thought to myself, I would not dream of ignoring a sick child in need of additional care on my ward simply because I had others to attend to. Severe as this statement may appear to some, I honestly would have preferred not to be amongst the living, than to be devoid of compassion for needy children.

Persistent in their ploy to prove that they were correct in suggesting that my child had subnormal tendencies, another teacher told my husband that the child was not capable of achieving academically therefore we must not expect much of 'the poor little thing'.

Yet, despite that depressing experience at her first school at a relatively young age, as soon as my daughter commenced high school at the age of eleven, she continually received excellent reports from her teachers. As a result of her determination and satisfactory performance in high school and college, she entered Coventry university and was successful in gaining a BA degree with Honours in the summer of 2002. In 2003 she commenced studying for a postgraduate certificate at Brunell University, graded amongst the most prestigious higher educational institutions in England.

It is high time for parents, carers and society to assert their rights as adults and be supportive of the children by assisting to cultivate them. The fact that we are likely to experience a tough battle from the opposition should not deter us. The efforts of our struggle would be compensated by the freedom of our children to develop undeterred into respectable and responsible individuals (if they so desire).

Advice: It is quite common for some of the younger generation to ignore the advice of parents and elders. This is wrong. Older people have been around longer than children, they are more experienced in the affairs of the world and therefore they are qualified to offer advice to those whom they precede in age.

Young people and dieting

An alarming number of today's young females are fashion conscious; therefore in a bid to be endowed with 'the perfect figure', and to wear the latest trend, they are slimming needlessly. Consequently as a result of inappropriate dieting, many become ill.

There was universal outcry of shock, horror and disbelief at the sight of victims of concentration camps including Belsen, yet today there are those who deliberately and contemptuously subject themselves into mimicking that emaciated (wasting) appearance of those defenceless captives.

Some women who slim in the name of fashion need to be observant of the fact that most of today's fashion is dictated by men. We are all aware that men are the dominant sex in every situation in the world today and they assume control over most of the top female professions. And yet females who dare to tread on traditionally male dominated professions are sometimes subjected to the most degrading chauvinistic humiliations, so that at times they have no alternative but resignation.

Even the Church is embroiled in a continuous unholy conflict against the ordination of women clergy. If it was God's intention that women should be kept in subordination, I wonder why He choose one to bear His son Christ?

Unrealistic – Unhealthy – Undesirable

A noticeable number of women who are engaged in the slimming craze are models, while some admit that they slim to please their partners. However it must be acknowledged that there are several who slim to be healthy.

How can anyone realistically believe that they can guarantee a genuine relationship by altering their physical appearance?

As we observe, some females in search of perfection also spend vast amounts of money on cosmetic surgery such as breast enlargement and face enhancement. To any rational thinking individual, these are acts of absolute contempt towards womanhood.

How many men with commonsense would want to choose a partner simply for her looks? If they were genuinely in love, they would scrutinize the heart for sincerity and the mind for purity and soundness in reasoning.

It is no wonder that there is such a frequent change in partnership involving people who follow this unnatural preoccupation. These people have an inner vacuum, which needs to be addressed before they can find true happiness.

It is a well-known fact that females are endowed with a remarkable measure of strength (much more than they have been credited for in a male dominated world). However, constant unnecessary dieting is likely to deplete the body of energy, thereby predisposing it to various illnesses, resulting in a weakened constitution.

I wonder whether a man who chooses a woman because of her lean and sensuous looks would be prepared to continue that relationship if she failed to maintain her looks or if she became ill? Is it not reasonable to assume that many men in this category are likely to abandon those unfortunate women because they no longer find them 'attractive'?

Therefore, young people, be aware of the pitfalls of following fashionable crazes. Like the Pied Piper, worldly tendency can lead the vulnerable astray.

A final reminder to children. Always remember – parents have a vested interest in the welfare of their children and like any hard working business person, they too want and deserve the best deal for their merchandise. Why should they be nonchalant regarding the value of their most valuable product?

CHAPTER 13

Discussing the Welfare of Seniors

'With the ancient is wisdom; and in length of days understanding.' (Job 12:1).

It would have been impossible for me to write a book without including seniors. Older people have been influential to me throughout my life and it is a well-observed fact by those who are familiar with me, that I am very fond of them. Anyone who is older than me automatically qualifies for my respect and affection.

I have been attracted to older people since early childhood and during my period in nursing I particularly enjoyed working with senior patients, because it gave me an immense feeling of job satisfaction. This feeling of happiness often inspired me to amuse the patients.

I once nursed on a ward where a retired blind opera singer was one of the patients. One day I felt quite mischievous, therefore I decided to pretend to be a soprano. As I approached her, I took a deep breath, and then I blasted out my rendition of a song, which I screeched out of imaginary notes. On hearing the singing, the lady in question, who was slouching in her chair, gracefully pulled herself into the upright position. Then leaning her head in the direction of the sound of my music, she listened enthusiastically. After I had finished singing, I curtsied and the entire ward applauded rapturously.

The blind patient had the most admirable smile on her face as I approached her. The look of happiness on that lady's face was indescribable and it is one memory I will always treasure. To me that moment is similar to a photographer taking a unique picture of a momentous occasion.

I later approached her and inquired the reason for her cheerful demeanour. She told me that there was a concert on the ward. However she added, 'Had the soprano practised her breathing technique she would have been much better. Her words were forced out from her throat.' I replied, 'Yes, I know, that is why my throat is stinging me as if it is on fire. I must get a drink of milk or water quickly before I lose my voice.'

The lady laughed, and then exclaimed, 'My dear, I did not realize it was you singing. What is the name of that song?'

I replied, 'It hasn't got a name, I made it all up.'

Everyone present started laughing whilst I quickly disappeared into the kitchen to soak my burning throat in water.

Ancestral influence

I believe that I have identified the reason for my fascination with older people and like most patterns of behaviour, mine is a result of early mind conditioning.

As far back as I can remember, several elders were fond of me. My earliest recognition of love and affection from people apart from my parents was experienced whilst associating with some of my senior relations and other senior people in my community. I am somewhat inclined to believe that my fascination with this group is a result of their influence on me during my youth.

By associating with older people during my youth, I received love, guidance and protection. There was no rivalry, no deception and no malice. I was happy and I felt safe. This also explains my reason for being attracted to older people and subsequently marrying someone older than me, although his favourable attributes were a contributory factor for my decision.

My senior relations seemed to relish my presence. I have been told on several occasions that they were attracted to me because of my jovial personality and my resemblance to a paternal ancestor. Perhaps my joviality was a result of their affection towards me. It would be difficult for any child not to be positively influenced by genuine love and affection.

My father's relations made the most fuss of me. Three of his aunts and one of his sisters were foremost in lavishing me with fondness. My father's aunts were of the opinion that I bore a striking resemblance to their mother (my great-grandmother). Two in particular, Aunt Eldeca and Aunt Jessica, often cried when I was in their presence, because they claimed that I reminded them of their mother.

Aunt Eldeca would often send messages requesting that my brother and I visit her and although I was happy to go, she would often weep softly as she spoke about her mother, which made me feel somewhat uncomfortable. Nonetheless, she fed and fussed over me whilst she dried the tears from her eyes with her neatly pressed apron. She was always smartly dressed and her ankle length dresses and beautiful aprons gave her the typical appearance of a slave, as seen in books. I loved her and her sister Jessica dearly.

My maternal relations were also loving and caring people, though they were somewhat reserved in dispensing affection. Although my mother's parents were the only grandparents I have known, I cannot ever recall receiving a hug or a cuddle from them. This is not a fault on their part; it was merely their mannerism. We are all aware of people of similar disposition who are genuine caring individuals.

However, I was a child who cherished affection, therefore (without any prejudice towards my maternal lineage) it is natural that I would have been a trifle more attracted to those who gave me the most affection.

My paternal relations were not wealthy. The majority of them like my father were rice and cattle farmers, but they were unselfish, loving and benevolent. It is therefore a fitting and understanding gesture that I am beholden to my ancestors and other seniors.

'Remove not the ancient landmark which thy fathers have set.' (Proverbs 22:28).

Neglect or rejection of seniors is a distressing observation that needs to be seriously addressed. Seniors are the backbone of society; if we dishonour or disregard their presence and influence in the world, there is a possibility of structural collapse. Older people are experienced, therefore they should be respected for their valuable contribution to mankind.

Age of retirement?

During the Second World War, Bismarck, the German Chancellor, was told by his adviser that life expectancy was 66 years. He therefore decided that the age of retirement should be 65 years. (Perhaps that is why the mortality rate seems to be so high immediately after retirement. People become psychologically conditioned to die.)

Calendar age is not a general indication of people's competence to function satisfactorily in life. If that were truly the case, then why is it that some younger people cannot contend with the mental and physical stamina of some seniors?

There seems to be a thriving tendency in Britain, where employers are of the opinion that once one reaches the age of 40, one is then too old for re-employment. At the age of 60, it is not uncommon to hear of stories in which the medical infrastructure has insinuated that one is too old to receive treatment under the National Health for certain conditions, then at the age of 80, they seem to be of the opinion that one should quietly disappear to some wretched rubbish tip and await one's final fate – to be discarded forever.

MAY THE GOD OF METHUSELAH HAVE MERCY ON THE OVER FORTIES IN THESE BRITISH ISLES. (According to the book of Genesis, Methuselah was the oldest living person recorded in the Bible; he was nine hundred and sixty nine years old when he died.)

The media are also indirectly responsible for the social prejudice directed towards seniors. Taking into consideration that a large proportion of retired people watch television in Britain, there is only a very small percentage of them featured in the actual programmes.

I suppose one of the reasons for their exclusion is the fact that older people would not have the gumption to spice up the action by cursing, stripping and leaping beneath the sheets like some of the present younger actors. Thank heavens for this inhibition on the part of the seniors. Yet when we look at old-time films where there were no vulgarities included in order to boost ratings, we are truly appreciative of that old-fashioned classic acting.

Treatment of seniors

When our pets become old, we love and cherish them even more, because we realize that their presence with us is approaching the end. We reflect on precious moments spent with them and we do our utmost to make the remainder of their life as happy and comfortable as possible.

Why can't we express our gratitude and appreciation for humans, who are much more important than pets? Those people who are responsible for our birth and for rearing us to the best of their ability (despite grave difficulties at times), need to be acknowledged, treated with respect, cared for and loved.

Is it not a fact that the more wine matures the better it tastes and the costlier it becomes? Are antiques not expensive commodities? This is because the value or price of important merchandise increases with time. Yet we choose to depreciate the value of humans – an important and invaluable gift from God – by our uncaring attitude towards them.

The problem of neglect of seniors has eaten away considerably at the fabric of some factions of the white British society and it is now gradually gnawing at the hemline of the Afro-Caribbean society. I am hesitant in attributing this problem to the entire minority population. This is due to the fact that people of Asian descent tend to be more caring towards the welfare of their senior citizens.

Senior members of the Asian community are, by tradition, head of their household. Their role is advisory for as long as they are mentally and physically capable of maintaining that position. They are often revered by their people and admired by others. Every senior person should be encouraged to be engaged in responsible roles for as long as they are capable.

Victims of the ageing process are so conditioned that they themselves often make excuses for society and their children. It is not unusual to hear some say, 'I do not want to be a nuisance by asking for government aid,' or 'I do not want to be a burden to my sons or daughters because they have their children to care for.'

Some people, who are in the position of assisting their parents, cite irrational excuses in the plot to avoid caring for their indefensible senior parents. The reasons are often littered with weak defences, such as difficulty due to work or inconvenience due to commitment to spouse and young children.

Some factions of society are of the opinion that children should not have their personal space intruded on by seniors. It is no wonder that so many of our young people today are so dismally spoilt; they have had too much space to themselves.

Children of extended families (especially including grandparents), tend to become more adjusted. They cope better with arduous situations than those who are less fortunate or limited in interacting with close family members.

Working on the geriatric wards has been a source of enlightenment for me regarding the neglect meted out to some senior citizens in England. I personally found it very distressing.

Once, when I was involved in supplementary nursing employment (working with a private nursing agency), I was requested to work at a geriatric hospital. There in a room was a frail solitary looking senior female patient. She looked so sad that I could not stop myself from entering her room to speak briefly with her.

After returning to the office, the ward sister enquired whether I knew the patient whom I had just visited. I told her that I did not know the patient. The sister told me that that solitary woman was the mother of a distinguished consultant in my hospital. She added that from the time of that patient's admission to hospital weeks ago, the consultant had never once visited her nor phoned to inquire of her condition. I find it very difficult to comprehend abandonment of this magnitude.

I often try to visualize what it must feel like to be neglected in later life by one's own family. It must be a very depressing situation. Several senior people have experienced grave hardships during the wars. Some are widows who worked desperately hard to raise their children singlehandedly after losing husbands in combat. Then at the twilight of their lives, when they are alone and often fearful of the future, some are neglected. It would be a good psychological boost if children could return a percentage of the love, care and affection given to them by parents.

I have listened to stories from senior British people who looked after their parents. This substantiates my reasoning that the British were once a very caring society. Today, it is assumed that Britain tops the list of countries failing to address the needs of its senior citizens adequately.

The Ageing Process

As we get older, several naturally occurring bodily changes take place. Some changes are compensatory to the diminished demands of our systems, therefore changes due to ageing are not necessarily indicative of dysfunction. I have observed that some seniors seem to possess more mental agility than some younger people.

The loss of brain stimulation is minimal in people who are mentally active through exercise, crossword puzzles, group quizzes, playing dominoes, cards or chess. This is due to the fact that apart from disease, mental inactivity is one of the foremost causes of symptoms associated with the ageing process, such as forgetfulness and inability in concentration.

The MacArthur Foundation Study on successful ageing states: 'About half of all mental loss in ageing can be attributed to inherited genes. The other half is related to lifestyle and environment. In other words there is a lot a person can do to keep their minds sharp with age.'

A wealth of knowledge can be extracted from the mentally alert senior. I have had the privilege of witnessing the dynamics of the human mind at its best through my association with several senior people.

One of our closest friends was James, a senior gentleman. Although James was not what society would classify as an expert or a professional, owing to the fact that he has not attained academic eminence, I have never met anyone who can parallel his sound knowledge of almost any topic conceivable to humanity. His knowledge of the Bible was phenomenal. If he were asked about any biblical matter, without pausing to think, he would quote the exact citation, chapter and verse in the Bible. Furthermore, in some instances, to save time, he would proceed to quote the page. I have never experienced any other human with such a prodigious attribute. I often refer to James as the 'Living Biblical Concordance'.

Sadly, James died suddenly in October 2003 at the grand age of 90.

Reasons for neglecting seniors

I cannot imagine that other nations are more capable of loving and caring than the British, but I believe that a combination of the impact of bureaucracy upon a number of too-dependent people, along with materialism and selfishness, are some of the influential factors for the dismantling of the traditional family role, including caring for seniors. These contributing factors are inevitably a sign of the times we are now living in.

According to my analysis of this situation, the downward spiral of family caring for seniors in the United Kingdom became noticeable after the birth of the National Health Service, established in July 1948 by the well meaning Labour Minister of Health, Aneurin (Nye) Bevan. The primary purpose of this establishment was that medical attention should be made accessible to all people within the British Isles.

In his book *Hope and Glory – Britain 1900–1990*, Professor Peter Clarke wrote: 'For women, for dependent children, for the elderly, the NHS established a right to a quality of medical service which had previously been a narrow privilege, hedged by costs which cast a shadow over   eholds.'

Professor Clark continues, 'What Bevan did was to transfe . the NHS. from a pipe dream into an enduring British institution.'

The concluding part of that statement by Professor Clarke substantiates my theory that the family's caring attitude towards seniors decreased since the birth of the NHS. Some people view the NHS as the surrogate keeper/provider of society, therefore they are prepared to leave all or most of the caring of seniors to that dependable system. This selfish behaviour (although not deliberate in some instances) deprives seniors of the love and attention of the family during and after hospitalization, which are generally anxious and fearful times. Simple hospital visits would be perceived as a caring gesture.

That enduring British institution which Nye Bevan conceived is now perceived to be gradually failing several seniors, because the promise of a free for all service has been undermined by the implementation of anti-ageist policies. There are numerous reported instances where treatment for seniors is either delayed or cancelled. In some cases the reason given is that the required treatments were believed to be too costly to be carried out on old people. NHS spending is therefore perceived to be focused on younger people.

It is morally wrong to refuse medical treatment to anyone; therefore I feel it is grossly unreasonable to discriminate in sickness on the grounds of age, race, religion or sexual orientation. Anyone entitled should have equal access to medical and social assistance, therefore seniors must not be denied.

Financial limitation is the obvious reason for the squeeze on care for seniors. Is it not ironic that substantial numbers of senior citizens, who contributed towards NHS insurance until their retirement, are now forced to relinquish their rights to medical treatment?

Yet, some of the younger generation who are given priority over the old with medical treatment are so spoilt by the system that they have never had the need to do a decent and honest day's work, because doting 'Big Papa State' has spoilt them rotten, by churning out numerous state benefits to them. And like pampered children, they beguile and manipulate their credulous benefactor. However there are repercussions to this act.

There are people who for genuine reasons are unable to work. However, those who deliberately refrain from employment because of laziness or the belief that there is help if they do not work are creating a stick for their own chastisement.

If we do not use a limb for a while, we tend to impede its functions. When the brain sends messages to that limb, it would be incapable of interpreting the message correctly, therefore it is not likely to react appropriately to the command. Similarly, if the brain is inactive because we choose not to use it in a positive manner, we are deliberately jeopardizing a vital function of our very existence and it reacts by becomes sluggish.

People are living longer therefore the management of seniors must be re-assessed accordingly because there is understandably a strenuous demand on budgeting. The family must strive to take more responsibility for its senior citizens. Today the pressure on the NHS is insurmountable and whilst it is understandable that seniors should receive adequate care, families must be prepared to assist in whatever ways they can.

There are, however, people who are genuinely willing to participate in caring for their senior relations, but are unable to do so because of financial constraint. It would therefore be in the interest of the government to create a system whereby financial aid is allocated to carers, thereby relieving the state of some of its mounting pressures of caring for senior citizens.

The greatest gift we humans can bequeath to one another is the gift of love. Love transcends all adversaries. I believe that if we should care, respect and love one another, we would each contribute to a vast pool of contentment throughout life.

Love does not need to be demonstrated by materialistic tokens or by verbal affirmation (these may well be empty gestures, as many of us may have experienced). Love can take the form of a multiplicity of well-intended symbols. The popular adage: 'Actions speak louder than words,' is proof that our physical deeds are more important than our vocal expressions.

I have on occasions listened to relations and friends of deceased people speaking of their guilt, because they had never told the deceased that they loved them whilst they were alive. If love was given or showed to someone during his or her life, then it is likely to be acknowledged and appreciated. Why the remorse after the person's death?

There are some people who harbour no guilt after the loss of close ones. Instead of languishing in remorse, they usually reminisce about the good times, which should outnumber the bad ones.

Prejudice against senior citizens

I often wonder whether it is the actual fear of the ageing process that causes some people to be indifferent towards seniors. Do younger people mirror their own existence later in life when they glimpse at older people? Can it be that when they look at the seniors, they interpret them as pitiful people, or are they tarnished by a tinge of guilt because of their attitude towards their senior relations?

A senior health worker once told me that he disliked senior people. Believing that he might have used the word 'dislike' inappropriately, I inquired whether he really meant that. He looked me straight in the eyes and slowly answered, 'Yes, I mean I cannot stand them.' He did not give me the impression that he was joking.

He looked about 50 years of age. I was both astonished and annoyed that someone of his professional status and age could harbour such unprovoked resentment towards seniors. I angrily retorted 'Well, mate, you have not got long to wait before your feet fit comfortably into their moccasins.'

'Not if I have my way,' he replied.

I muttered under my breath, 'You sad man.'

Preparation

Fear sometimes results from uncertainty and uncertainty is a result of lack of preparation.

I view our existence on earth as a continuous examination. We are assessed by our actions and the contents of our character and we receive feedback information on our performance.

Those who are unprepared for exams may not perform satisfactorily; they are often petrified when they face the exams and again when results are due. We must prepare ourselves for every event in life including old age.

In 1997 I visited a senior English friend, whom I had not seen for several years. She was very concerned about her future. It is customary for senior people to worry about the future, but that anxiety can be somewhat worsened because of some of the disheartening revelations concerning the fate of seniors, such as selling their homes to pay for their care and many other distressing probabilities. However sometimes seniors worry unnecessarily, therefore they need reassurance.

My friend Elsie maintained a healthy mental faculty. I reassured her that her family or the state would take her care of her. I spent a couple of days with her and on the morning of my departure, her anxiety intensified and I felt quite concerned for her.

The friendship between Elsie and me dates back to the late 70s when I was a nurse. I was one of the nurses who cared for her only sister, who was terminally ill, and Elsie developed a friendship with me whilst visiting her sister in hospital. She was like a senior relation to me and I was quite fond of her.

Twenty years later as I was about to leave her home after my short stay with her, she turned to me anxiously and said, 'If only you were living nearby, you would have cared for me like you did for my dear sister.' I felt terribly sad and helpless listening to that worried Christian lady. It was then that I read her a part of the scriptures and without realizing what I was about to do, I requested leave of her and entered her guest room.

I gently closed my eyes, and then I mentally focused on the kind lady who cared for both of her parents until their death. Elsie also cared for her husband, who died a few years earlier of Alzheimer's disease. Those who are aware of the symptoms of this distressing condition will verify that it can be an arduous task looking after patients who are afflicted with it. She nursed him at home until his death because it was his wish.

Elsie also raised a daughter and she is the proud grandmother of three. As I sat quietly, I mentally focused on her entire life from the time of her birth, taking into account what she as a Christian might have asked of God. I visualized a very caring and loving lady approaching the end, then I set about to write something to reassure her.

Although I had never attempted to write a poem before, after a few minutes, I sketched one and later I adjusted some of the words to make it sound more meaningful. I feel it was not entirely my work, I believe that I was merely used as a channel to offer consolation to a good person. The poem/prayer has been included in an anthology published in England.

Elsie's Prayer – My Journey Through Life

BIRTH

> Lord, thank you for creating me
> A servant and a child for thee
> Oh may I execute favourably
> The task that is in store for me.

CHILDHOOD

> Heavenly Father always kind
> Enrich me with thy love divine
> Help me live my childhood days
> Always attracting your approving gaze.

ADULTHOOD

> Grant me Lord thy choice of a mate
> To assist to accomplish and incorporate
> The continuum of thy creation trait
> Ensuring a blessed generation – That will be great.

PARENTHOOD

> Help me Saviour to transpire
> Bountiful care by you inspire
> Loving care through your dictate
> Is guaranteed to reciprocate.

OLD AGE

Should hope of care for me be denied
Heavenly Father, always ever mine
Let not this faithful servant fear
The homeward journey to my father dear.

J. W. Blackett

Elsie continued to live in her own home and she managed as best she could. After complaining of feeling unwell one day in June 2000, she died peacefully in her home the following day at the grand age of 90. A worthy end for a truly remarkable lady.

NB: How strange that both of my senior chums mentioned in this chapter were deceased at the age of 90.

If we endeavour to do our best in life, then we need not fear when it is time for our departure from this world. It is a natural tendency to be worried or anxious, but those are negative emotions and they are likely to cloud our thoughts, thereby sinking us into a deeper state of anxiety.

Since the dawn of our lives, we were nurtured and loved by parents (biological and adoptive) and other caring people. Let us therefore show our appreciation and gratitude by repaying them with kind deeds, even more so as they enter the sunset of their lives.

Some seniors are not easy to cope with, but as children, some of us were very difficult to control and raise. Yet we did not experienced rejection of this magnitude, as some of our seniors are subjected to nowadays.

CHAPTER 14

Self-Identification (Who am I)?

The statement: 'Man, Know Thyself', first inscribed on the temples of the Ancient Egyptians and later duplicated by the Greek philosopher Socrates, is a realistic recommendation for humanity. Without relevant information pertaining to our past, our present is likely to be obscured and our future is destined to be uncertain.

How often have we not heard of adopted people searching for their biological parents? This is not simply a case of curiosity, it is part of a personal and important fact-finding mission. Those adopted people are interested to know their parents and also to learn of their genealogy, including the medical history of the family and their patterns of behaviour.

When people know enough about themselves through information pertaining to their lineage, not only do they become more knowledgeable about their personal history, they are also likely to become more confident, understanding, respectful and tolerant of others.

If we remain in ignorance of our past, we are destined to wander randomly like blind mice because we have no control of our direction in life. If we roam aimlessly, we stand the chance of being lost and therefore harmed.

In the nursery rhyme 'Three Blind Mice', the unfortunate blind mice who unwittingly ran after the farmer's wife had their tails cut off with a carving knife. It is obvious that if they had clarity of vision, they would have run away from impending danger because that is exactly what mice do. They do not run after people, they run away to a place of safety.

Similarly, those whose identities are unknown are liable to follow the wrong course in life. They are also likely to develop distressing psychological conditions including an inferiority complex, which are likely to progress to general illnesses.

I have lived in the United Kingdom for most of my life and I have socially and professionally interacted with people of several racial groups and ethnicities. However, I have never met any people who seem to be as uncomfortable with themselves as some factions of the black race.

I have listened in amazement as some black people seemed over enthusiastic in announcing that their ancestors were descendants of English, Portuguese,

Arab or Red Indian. The manner in which they state their racial blending seems to insinuate that they should be recognized as the others (not black).

Everyone should be proud of his or her ancestry, but these people in question seem to flaunt the fact that they are not predominantly black. Never mind the fact that rape of defenceless black women, including terrified young teenagers, was an obvious factor in the majority of mixed or bi-racial people during slavery and the colonial era. These people seem to be dependent on biological blending with other races to undermine and erase the black aspect of their existence in the hope that this seemingly 'mind over skin' transformation would provide them with a sense of self-importance and general recognition and therefore a cushy existence throughout life.

This attitude is symptomatic of 'Post Traumatic Slavery Syndrome'. Past events, such as the traumas suffered by our foreparents, and present discriminatory occurrences, have contributed to a state of mental apathy for some black people. It is therefore understandable that there are so many different patterns of negative behaviour portrayed by black people.

In order for the descendents of slaves to think rationally and lead meaningful lives, there needs to be a genuine attempt to unfasten the mental shackles and ease the chronic pain and suffering initiated during the African holocaust in which people were captured like wild animals and sold into slavery.

Post Traumatic Slavery Syndrome may also be responsible for the lack of self-awareness and self-confidence in black people. This crisis of black people lacking in self-identity can also be attributed to a combination of issues. The most likely ones are:

Lack of identity owing to ignorance of ancestral history
'Let the past serve the present.' (Mao Tse- Tung).

During a brief holiday in the 1990s in a beautiful part of the English West country, I met a black couple. One day we became engaged in a conversation about the importance of knowledge of one's ancestral history. The gentleman, who was in his late thirties, told me that as a child he heard people speaking about slavery, but he had not paid much attention to them because he was of the opinion that it was a mythical tale.

One day an African American teacher (of Caribbean descent) who was employed at the school in London which the gentleman attended, asked the pupils in his class questions pertaining to slavery. The gentleman told me that the whole class seemed ignorant about that particular topic. He stated that he had never experienced such angry reaction from a teacher before. The teacher stormed out of the classroom and out of the school building. He later returned with a number of books pertaining to slavery.

The teacher distributed the books to his stunned teenage pupils and then he instructed them to take the books home and read them. The gentleman told me that he was of the opinion that the teacher bought the books with his own money.

The person who made that disturbing revelation was of Afro-Caribbean descent. One would be somewhat inclined to be more understanding had he been white English, Chinese, Indian or even African. How can one be reconciled to the fact that a descendant of slaves knows nothing about slavery?

After listening to him, my mind raced back to the events of slavery. I visualized slaves who were even younger than he was when the event occurred in his school, rebelling and sacrificing their lives to end slavery and to bring hope in the future to generations of black people.

In order to free posterity from an abysmal existence, those brave slaves were prepared to die fighting that oppressive subsistence and yet some say it is time to forget; some behave as though they have no connection to slavery. Some black people simply do not know anything about their own history, whilst others do not give two hoots about the tribulations of our ancestors.

It is also imperative that we remember and respect the memory of the admirable white people who fought for the abolition of slavery because if they had remained silent, the slaves might not have had their day when it did arrive.

Among those courageous white brothers were Thomas Clarkson, William Wilberforce, Grenville Sharp, John Brown and John Smith, a white missionary who was convicted for aiding a slave revolt in Guyana in 1823. Rev Smith later died in prison.

However we must not blame the children, who were undoubtedly the innocent little victims of ignorance of slavery. Much blame cannot be placed on the teachers, because they could not have taught subjects that they were not instructed to teach by the education authority. The education authority must be blamed, but only to a certain degree, for the understandable reason that it will not include certain topics in the curriculum unless there is enough evidence of vested interest shown in particular topics.

During the 1950s and 1960s black people and other ethnic minorities could not have expected the education system in Britain to teach about the history of every individual race in schools here. As colonists it was not in their interest to enlighten black people about black history.

It was most definitely up to the parents to make representations to the authorities on behalf of the children's education. And even more importantly, it is up to every caring parent to ensure that their child knows something about its ancestral history. Do not be too dependent on others to deliver this information to your child.

It is as much a personal duty as breastfeeding, in the sense that breast feeding prepares the child for a healthy start in life. Similarly black history provides self-awareness in life for black children.

So disturbed was I after listening to the gentleman who said that he thought slavery was unreal, that on my return from my holidays I questioned my children about the history lessons taught to them in school. Although reasonable actions are being made to incorporate black history into the school curriculum, I had a strong compulsion to do something that would emphasize the real impact of slavery. I therefore went to the local library and ordered three volumes of the film *Roots* and on their arrival, I instructed my children to watch them on three consecutive days.

The children were understandably upset, but I told them to make a mental note of the story. I also told them that the film was a mere smokescreen of the actual tribulation of the slaves.

A Hindu friend once remarked that she strongly believe that I am a re-incarnated slave because of my racial consciousness and my incessant passion and devotion to my ancestral connection. I believe that it is because I am so genuinely concerned for the well being of all people that I instinctively experience pain when anyone is physically, emotionally, mentally or socially abused. This is why I am indignant, not so much about the naïve-minded perpetrators, but of the immoral system that encourages people to belittle their fellow men.

The insignia of the abolitionists was *'Am I not a man and a brother?'* This statement denounces the slave trade as an outrage against humanity. However, evil knows no colour. It is a harmful entity that permeates the soul of any depraved human.

Self Denial
'The human mind cannot bear reality.' (T. S. Elliot).

There are some black people who are of the opinion that slavery has been long abolished, therefore it is time to forget and move on. Like the ostrich, these people are prepared to hide their heads in the sand, no matter if it leads to suffocation. Perhaps they do not want to face reality because they believe that it may be upsetting to white people, especially those to whom they are connected.

I have often observed that at times, white British people are more generously predisposed to issues pertaining to black people than black people themselves. One striking example to substantiate this claim is the response to the

'Respectable Trade March', in Bristol, England, on Sunday 12 September 1999. This march was organized by the Commission for Racial Equality in remembrance of the slave trade in Bristol. Bristol was one of the principal docks used by Britain in the transportation of slaves from Africa. Liverpool was the other main dock used for this purpose.

A white woman wrote a book defending slavery as 'A Respectable Trade', hence that name was adapted for the march. A close friend of my husband who resides in Bristol was one of the participants in the march. He told me that over 90 per cent of the marchers were white people. I was in disbelief but I was not surprised at the response of the black population to that historic event. This is why no one should be predisposed to generalizing the attitude of other races.

In an interview with *The Voice*, a black newspaper in England, in September 1999, veteran singer and composer Eddy Grant stated, 'We must take pride in ourselves and our history and have an awareness of our culture and ask ourselves, what is our contribution to our group? We should not let negative interpretation of our history become truth, and not be brainwashed into assuming this truth.'

The legacy of racial degradation

In an article published in one of the black newspapers in England, it was stated: 'An astonishing 90% of black men, at the age of 20, in domestic relationships, are with non-black women, a recent study revealed.'

The article further stated: 'Statistics show that England now has the highest number of mixed race partnerships of any European country, despite the increase of racial attacks on mixed couples. (*New Nation*, 17 April 2000).

It has been assumed that this trend is giving rise to a feeling of resentment by some black females. Although no one has the right to question the choice of partner of any individual, many people of colour and those of other nationalities are asking questions relating to this occurrence.

One of my male friends whose parents originated from Asia once told me that Afro-Caribbean men were seeking white partners, because they suffered from an extreme form of low-self esteem.

I told my friend that although the matter in question was highlighted in people of Afro-Caribbean descendant, it is also endemic in several other black cultures. I further informed my friend that some people of Asian origin were noted for their dislike of and discomfort with anyone darker or of a lower caste. We only have to examine the plight of the Untouchables and others of a low caste in India and we can grasp an insight into the depth of this matter in question. This is a continuing situation which was openly opposed by Gandhi.

I have seen newspaper advertisements where Asian men seeking wives particularly requested fair skinned women. In my ignorance of this shocking occurrence, I presumed that this custom was inter-connected with the socio-psychological effects of illiteracy. Sadly, to my surprise when I visited Sri Lanka, I saw several examples of advertisements of this nature in the newspapers.

Sri-Lanka is unquestionably home to some of the most pleasant and respectable people that I have had the pleasure of meeting. It is also home to some of the most brilliant academics in Asia.

As a self-styled humanist, I found this custom very disturbing. It must be somewhat disparaging to the extremely beautiful and intelligent females who happen to be of a dark complexion. However those admirable ladies, some of whom I am familiar with, seemed to cope in a manner that is customary of the challenge women of today's society – they get on with life. Today some are foremost in professional fields both in Sri Lanka and other countries.

Statement From A Black Woman To The 'Brothers'

You are perfectly entitled to dislike me because of my stature or my conduct.
You may also dislike me because of my acquaintances, or even my nationality
But how dare you cite my colour as the reason for your aversion to me?
God the Omnipotent created this beautiful me in His own image and likeness.
Therefore my brothers (and some sisters too), when I look in the mirror,
I see the personification of God – the infinite perfectionist.
By the way, you with such strong a dislike for your black sisters,
Do tell me, what reflection do you see in the mirror that haunts you so
That you try to hide behind a veil of 'whiteness' to mirage yourself?
Hebbel remarked –
'That Man, who flees the truth, should have invented the mirror, is the greatest of miracles,'
A black rock chicken cannot be transformed into a white leghorn bird.
Thanks to the Almighty that this is so.

J. W. Blackett

There should be no condemnation of any relationships if they are the result of sound and unbiased construct of love. Some of the obvious requirements of meaningful and respectable relationships are:

- Genuine love; compatibility of mind, spirit and emotional feelings.

- An inclination to similarity in interests.

- Understanding and tolerance of each other's culture and tradition.

- Honesty and respect for each other.

However it appears that, as far as some black men are concerned, any woman paler than themselves automatically qualifies as a partner. One cannot help noticing that the black man holds the world record for marrying outside of his race. And it appears the more prosperous the black man, the more desperate he becomes to get a partner who does not reflect his skin colour or his race.

How often have we observed the exhibition of black sportsmen and black academics returning to their countries after their accomplishment? These 'heroes' try to impress others with what seems to them to be symbolic of an exceptional accomplishment. They valiantly return to their countries with 'the ultimate trophy for meritorious achievement', a wife who is not black. Never mind the fact that they sometimes had a faithful girlfriend for a long period at home (in some cases, they also have children by the abandoned girlfriends). How many men of other racial origins conduct themselves likewise?

The frightening fact about this practice is that it dates back to immediately after slavery. Yet today instead of declining, it appears to have increased dramatically. Only the Almighty knows how much further it is likely to affect potential victims just as a virulent endemic disease attacks and at times destroys (or wipes out) several of its victims.

A well known story bearing startling similarity to the attitude of some black men today is that of Sir Conrad Reeves (1821–1902), one of the most brilliant West Indians in history.

Recognizing his exceptional potential, friends in his native Barbados raised enough money to send him to study law at the Middle Temple in London and he was reputed to be the most brilliant student in its history.

After his successful admission to the bar in 1863, Sir Conrad returned to his native Barbados and soon became his country's leading lawyer and a leading politician. He soon became Attorney General and later, the first Black Chief Justice of Barbados and it has been reported that his contribution to his country was impressive. Queen Victoria knighted him in 1881.

The astonishingly sad thing about this great black man who was the son of a slave woman and a Negro doctor (according to some people, a shoe maker), is the fact that not only is he remembered for his distinguished achievements, but equally, he is also remembered for his haughtiness, which was reported to be 'that of the typical British aristocrat of his times'.

The fact that it was reported that he refused to let his daughter marry a senior doctor in Barbados because the gentleman was too dark, bears startling revelation of a black man with a white mentality in those days. The daughter in question later married two white men.

It has been reported that in an address at Harrison College, Barbados, in the presence of the island's white governor, Sir Conrad said, 'Here I am on Olympus looking down on you ordinary mortals.' (*World's Great Men of Colour* by J. A. Rogers).

On a few occasions I have heard Barbadians stating that it was rumoured that Sir Conrad also stated, 'I have reached the top of the ladder and I have kicked it down thus preventing others from following in my footsteps.' Although that suggestion is mere conjecture, those who are aware of his snobbery may be somewhat persuaded into believing that he made the remark.

At times, education can pave the way to immense opportunities, which may be fulfilling to one's ambitious aspiration. But, equally so, it can be a destructive device to the soul, in the sense that it causes people to think and behave in an egotistic and preposterous manner towards their fellow human.

It is this open display of black on black degradation which is contributory to the continuous disrespect of black people by others, and consequently to the confusion sometimes observed in younger black people. This confusion is sometimes manifested in psychological and personality-related disorders.

Meanwhile some black conscious people, desperate to preserve the dignity of their race, understandably set out to discourage negative behaviour by trying to educate people in self-awareness, self-respect, self-love, traditional virtues and universal love. I doubt that these radical black educators are racists as is often hinted by some aspects of society. This is a typical reaction. There are several instances when black people are mistrusted and unjustifiably accused even by factions of the black community itself, simply because they try to assist in the elevation of their people.

The following references are some examples:

- Marcus Garvey, a brilliant politician who, after his ordeal and subsequent deportation from the USA to his native country of Jamaica, lacked political support. Despondent in the reaction of his people towards his efforts to organize them, he came to England, where he resided until his death.

- C. L. R James, the acclaimed West Indian philosopher, historian and writer was forced to live in England because he was perceived as a threat in his native Trinidad.

- Walter Rodney, one of the most brilliant historians to emerge from the Caribbean, was another black educator who was perceived as a threat by black people. This accomplished Guyanese academic was declared persona non grata by the Jamaican government after he was caught lecturing to the poor working class people in Jamaica about their African heritage. Rodney was killed when a bomb blew up his car in 1980 in his native Guyana.

In 1996 I read an article in *The Voice* newspaper, in which a white woman in a mixed relationship was replying to a letter regarding the number of black men who choose white women, whilst black women found it difficult to find black partners.

The woman said that the blame should be placed on the mothers of the black men instead of on white women. She went on to state that the situation must be attributed to the fact that black mothers predominantly adorn their homes with pictures depicting a white imagery of Jesus, angels and other icons; therefore the children were mentally influenced by that environment.

I have always held the belief that the situation in question was psychologically induced by parental nurturing and environmental stimulation. I therefore believe that it is absurd for blame to be attributed to white women.

First impressions

'The only things that become real to us are the things we recognize to be real.' These poignant words are excerpts from a tape sent to me during the 1970s by the late Brother Mandus, founder member of the World Healing Crusade in Blackpool, England. To me this proverb summarizes reality.

From an early age infants learn by observation. This is therefore a potentially powerful way of familiarization with the environment around them. Parents and carers play a prominent role in children's lives; therefore they are responsible for providing some necessities such as spiritual awareness, physical growth, mental stimulation and social interaction, which are essential for human development. Parents and carers are instrumental in establishing an important attachment with their children, who in turn look up to them for guidance.

It is logical to assume that parents and carers are the earliest and most influential role models and educators in their children's lives. Even though children may be problematic, they imitate or mimic the attitudes and behaviour of parents. This is partly due to nurture or nature (the way they are reared or biological tendencies).

Whitewashed Media Hypnotism

The media are another possible cause for the negative conditioning of the minds of black people. Many people are unwitting victims of media brainwashing. How many times have we become totally emotionally carried away as we watched a fictitious film? We drift into a world of total fantasy as we become helplessly captivated by the seemingly ingenious presentation of man's adroit technological skilfulness.

Although Britain is supposedly a multicultural society, the proportion of black representation in the media is minimal. Television is bombarded with white female presenters, the majority of whom seem to be natural or artificial blondes. Is it not therefore likely that some young black men would mentally internalize blondes as portrayed on the television as an indication of beauty, success and accomplishment? Therefore in their mind's eyes, the ideal woman to aim for in order to be fulfilled in life would bear a resemblance to those portrayed by the media. Is it therefore surprising that blondes are a popular choice for the majority of black men?

We blame religious cults for covertly controlling the minds of gullible people, but the media are also guilty to some extent of usurping the minds of its audience. Due to the powerful influence of television, newspapers and magazines, people become beguiled. Instead of using their influence or power to unify the races, these industries tend to saturate our minds with a web of discriminating illusion to suit their own ends.

Bequeathed inferiority complex

For hundreds of years, an inferiority complex has been forced upon black people. The myth that black people are inferior to other races has been propagated by some for social, economical and political gratification.

A diverse society should be cohesive, tolerant and understanding of the characteristics of other nationalities. But it appears that some people are expected to ignore their natural (biological) and cultural customs and adopt or conform to a universal code of behaviour. This is a dangerous idealism, the consequences of which can be docility within the system, depravity of one's culture or an inclination to rebelliousness towards authority.

It is often assumed that the principal reason why some Afro-Caribbean males under-achieve is because they are stereotyped and targeted in all walks of life, including school and the workplace. They in turn later react rebelliously by abandoning their aspirations. This behaviour, like adding fuel to fire, is counter-productive of a rational solution. It would not quell the problem, but it is likely to inflame it. The solution in addressing this problem lies in positive contemplated motivation by the victims and more open-minded tolerance and understanding of individuals by society in general.

If there is ignorance or misinterpretation of personality, incorrect analysis is likely to be made. It is impossible to know the characteristics of people simply by looking at them. That is why interviews are arranged to determine the suitability of prospective candidates seeking employment after meeting and analysing them.

Likewise, it is absurd to infer that a black male is likely to portray an assumed negative pattern of behaviour, before getting to know him, simply because he happens to be different from mainstream society. This form of unwitting stereotypical prejudice is commonplace in the West. For the benefit of posterity it is up to society and those affected to curtail its prevalence.

Black people's contribution to the continuous war against black skin

The psychological impact of slavery and colonialism is so contagious and destructive that a form of prejudice exists within some factions of black people, wherein some black people themselves believe they are justified in the continuity of derision on their own race.

As a young pupil in school in Guyana, we were taught that it was incorrect to address black females as ladies. They were to be addressed as women. However, we were to refer courteously to white females as ladies. It is this form of preposterous mental conditioning filtered through generations which is also contributory to the low self-worth so unwittingly exhibited by some black people.

How often have some of us experienced the phenomenon whereby the vessels in our necks pump excessively to the point of rupturing, when we are subjected to listen to some people? Examples of this occurrence are experienced by some people who are greatly incensed by certain situations such as the irritating mentality of some proud black mothers as they describe their sons' female partners in words to this effect: 'My son's girlfriend is a pretty brown skinned lady.' Alternatively, we may hear, 'She is a good looking *dougla* girl' (a word used in Guyana to describe an Afro-Indian mixture). This manner of discourse is mostly prevalent in parts of the Caribbean, and although it may be watered down to an extent, it is also common in the West.

I am often bewildered when I am subjected to listening to this nice skin or nice hair nonsense. All skin and hair are nice because God (an obvious 'nice' being) is the architect of man. It is only through disease or the use of chemicals when they are neglected that these exterior parts of the body seem to lose their niceness.

'*It has always been a mystery to me how men can feel honoured by the humiliation of their fellow beings.*' (Gandhi).

My husband, a friend and I once overheard a black middle-aged couple stating that all their children would 'end up marrying white people' because there were no goodlooking black people in the part of Britain where they lived. I was astounded at the foolishness of that statement. My friend gazed at the couple after overhearing the remark. She shook her head negatively and then to my embarrassment, she erupted into uncontrollable laughter.

Shortly after that annoying experience, I watched a televised US chat show in which a male member of the Ku Klux Klan remarked that black men wanted white partners because black women were ugly.

I shook my head sadly as I verbalized, 'Mister, you are not the only one with that concept, some of them black folks over here in Britain sure do share your views. Yes sir!'

Yet during the late 1970s, Anna, a very close white friend who was employed as a domestic in one of the hospitals where I nursed in Surrey, was very upset about a similar situation to the one above in which the black couple made that preposterous statement.

Anna originated from Saint Martin (French) or Sint Maarten (Dutch), a small island in the Caribbean. Her partner was a black man from the same island and they had one daughter who married a black man in the USA. Anna's daughter had several daughters and the eldest one was engaged to a black man.

Anna was an exceptionally good dressmaker and as we were very close friends, she offered to make my wedding gown. One day I visited her for a fitting only to find her very distressed. She told me that her second granddaughter had telephoned her to complain that her mother had forbidden her to go out with her white boyfriend.

Anna was near to tears as she explained that her oldest granddaughter had a black boyfriend. Then she turned to me and asked, 'If my daughter keeps on encouraging all the children to have black partners what would become of my race, would it not eventually disappear?' Instead of having a fitting for my gown, I spent that evening comforting Anna. I told her that I understood her reasoning and I whole-heartedly agreed with it.

That incident was a learning experience for me. Anna grew up amongst black people in the Caribbean and she told me that her boyfriends were all black men. She had a genuine affinity towards black people and she often spoke out on their behalf. She told me that owing to the fact that she was white, white British people would sometimes make comments about black foreigners to her and they were often quite taken aback when they heard her accent as she ridiculed their behaviour. She spoke with a deep Caribbean accent and people often questioned whether she was Jamaican. Poor Jamaica is often mentioned (sometimes unjustly) in issues pertaining to the West Indies.

Despite the fact that she had grown up amongst black people, Anna maintained a deep sense of loyalty and respect for her race, and I greatly admired her for her stance.

How can black people contribute effectively in curbing this stench of racial degradation when they themselves are actively involved in its proliferation? It is unfair to shift all the blame on white people.

This particular symptom of racism within the black race is likened to a feedback system, whereby, because of the attitude of some black people towards their kindred, people of other races evaluate them negatively. Some observers are likely to use that information as ammunition to discredit, disrespect and depreciate black people in general.

The Bible informs us that a house divided among itself cannot stand, therefore if people sensibly unite, they would stand firmly, thereby receiving their due respect. But if they are foolishly divided, then they would feebly fall and racist vultures are likely to descend upon them mercilessly.

As mentioned above, in England it tends to be more fashionable for the sons of black women to choose white partners (to the absolute delight of the mothers). It appears that the focal intention of these people is supposedly 'beautiful skin colour' which to them takes predominance over all other requisites of an acceptable partner for their sons.

And yet, from the behaviour of those very mothers in question, one can easily predict that if some were to be confronted with daughters-in-law of dark complexion like themselves, all hell would break loose, or the daughters-in-law would be cold-shouldered. Because, although they may seem to be in denial, their behaviour startlingly reveals their trend of mind conditioning, which is often subconsciously exposed.

Example: In 2000, an acquaintance who has a fair skinned son and a dark skinned younger daughter told me that her mother-in-law often takes her son out with her. One day as she left with the boy, her daughter, who was about three years old, became very distressed. The little girl burst into tears and said to her mother, 'Mommy, Granny don't like me.'

The lady told me that she was very disturbed by her daughter's announcement, because although she was aware of the fact that her mother-in-law greatly favoured the boy, she did not expect her infant daughter to be conscious of it at her age. She told me that her mother-in-law always seemed fascinated by her son's complexion.

On her mother-in-law's return, both the lady and her husband informed her that she was forbidden to take out their son again, unless his sister went along also. This is one of the most distressing illustrations of inferiority complex on the part of black people and it is frightening to know that it is prevalent in the twenty-first century.

We must never underestimate the power of the mind; whatsoever we programme into it could be accepted and kept in store for use later. However, we can cancel erroneous information by deprogramming the mind through the power of reasoning, if we so desire.

Parental Conditioning

Parents are influential in their children's choice of partners. Despite some degree of rebelliousness on the part of some young people, many will choose partners who are in accordance with parental expectations and black youngsters are no different.

By observation and awareness of parental preferences, children can easily sense the sort of partner that their parents prefer them to choose, and because they are parents (the most important people in the children's lives), the children are likely to mentally adapt and socially imitate the parents' trend of thinking and actions, thereby subconsciously fulfiling parental expectations.

It is therefore logical that when these children become adults they will seek to find a partner who they believe would be approved by their parents. This occurs more frequently than we care to admit.

Despite some degree of controversy, is it not customary for some people of Asian descent to marry partners approved and chosen by their parents?

Black parents need to ensure that their children have a broader knowledge and understanding of their history and culture. Watching soap operas, chat shows and other trivialities on television may be a learning experience or recreation for some, but I doubt whether those topics would provide pertinent information regarding black history. Black history may not be perceived as exciting or mentally stimulating enough for some, nonetheless it is an importance mental 'structural support' in self-knowledge and self-respect.

In recent years, there have been a variety of good books on black history. I therefore strongly recommend that those seeking knowledge and identification should read these books. The knowledge extracted from reading would liberate and exhilarate the minds of those who seem to abide in a state of perpetual confusion concerning their racial identity.

Some parents unconsciously encourage and indoctrinate children with a complex. One black woman claimed that her mother did not allow her to play with black dolls, because she claimed that black images were symbolic of evil.

The person also said that her mother often rebuked her children if they were caught speaking in their parents' Caribbean accent. Yet, we often overhear several foreigners, for example, Asians and Europeans, conversing quite happily in public with their English born children in the language of the parents' country of origin.

One black parent proudly informed me that her teenager interrupted the tutor when he described Africans as black people. The youngster instructed the teacher that Africans were coloured people, not black. This incident occurred during the late 80s. The manner in which that mother clapped her hands as she laughed heartily, one would have thought that the youngster had been declared

'Brain of Britain' for his ingenious interpretation of racial categorization.

That teenager of yesterday who was either in denial, confused or ignorant (through lack of appropriate education), is an adult of today with a white partner. If black parents are ignorant of their identity, how can their bi-racial children be expected to recognize black people as a part of their ancestry?

By the 1990s, I felt that people understood that the term 'coloured people' was a euphemism (a term used to avoid offending them). I cannot understand why people are comfortable to be categorized under that misnomer.

White people use it because they do not want to be perceived as offensive towards black people. In other words, they are being courteous and I fully understand their reason for that polite endearment. It is simply because some black people made them feel that they were being disrespectful by alluding to them as black.

Some black people who describe themselves as coloured or brown seem to be making a statement that they do not want to be perceived as 'black'. Their dislike of the term 'black' does not appear to be a defiant stance based on the grounds that the word 'black' was a derogatory term bestowed upon them by the early Europeans who ventured into Africa, naming it 'The Dark Continent'.

It appears that the obvious reason for these people's opposition to be described as black is simply because they feel uncomfortable with that categorization. They harbour a dislike for 'black', hence they opt for the 'coloured' identification. Anything colourful is perceived to be attractive and therefore acceptable, isn't it? In fact, some of those people actually feel that they are different from others who are darker than them. Believe you me, I have met a few.

A poignant example regarding the issue of inter-racial categorization and attitude is the conduct of the Cape Coloured in South Africa. In April 1994, during the first democratic elections in South Africa, Asians and a considerable number of white people voted along with the indigenous black people to end white domination and apartheid. However the majority of 'coloured' people in Cape Town refused to vote in support of Nelson Mandela's African National Congress; they voted instead for the apartheid regime. The reasons given were not political. Those people were prepared to remain under the white apartheid regime rather than to be ruled by black people.

In her book *Message to the White Man & Woman in America*, Dorothy Blake Fardan PhD, a white sociologist and anthropologist, referred to the continuous efforts still made to separate Egypt from black Africa.

One incident mentioned on page 56 of the book: 'surrounded a statement made by the cultural attaché at the Egyptian Embassy in Washington, Mr Abdel-Latif Aboul-Ela. Mr Aboul-Ela claimed that Egyptians are not related to the original "black Africans". His remark was published in the *Washington Post*, March 23, 1989.' Doctor Blake Fardan commented, 'White supremacy has overtaken even non-European minds.'

Parental example in self–discipline

Some black people are of the opinion that it is acceptable for men to assert their masculinity by fathering several children by different women, thereby increasing the suffering of black women. It is also hinted that black men have taken over from the slave masters by impregnating black women and leaving them to get on with caring for the children.

The slaves were raped. They had no voice whereby they could have physically or legally fought against that violation. However today's liberated women have the prerogative to use moral judgment or to assert their legal rights if they are violated. It is therefore erroneous to compare the situation of the women of today with the defenceless slaves.

The instruction given by God in Genesis can be interpreted nowadays as 'Increase [or multiply] in wisdom and commonsense.' I doubt that today God would be leaning over His pearly gates in Heaven, sternly gazing down on earth, and with gesticulating index finger demanding that mankind procreate abundantly. That is not the profile of a loving and caring creator who is fully aware of the hell-like state (including war, poverty, inequity and injustice) which his cherished world has eroded into.

'Oh, what a tangled web we weave, when first we practise to deceive.' (Sir Walter Scott).

Throughout this selfish adult game, it seems that the innocent lives involved are given little or no consideration. It cannot be easy for children to cope with the knowledge that the man living down the road with his wife/partner and children is also their daddy, although he is not involved in their lives to the extent that he is with those with whom he lives. Neither is it always an act of reassurance that the father chooses to share the same home with one set of his brood.

It is not unusual to find that children in these situations are often sympathetic to the injured parent, who in the majority of cases is the mother. Some children even become antagonistic towards the offender, whilst others silently internalize the agony. These children sometimes experience emotional and psychological problems and some later become bitter and resentful towards people in general. However, mercifully there are some who appear to be unaffected by the situation and they go through life unscathed.

In this present society where it is sometimes arduous for both parents to control children, is it not reasonable to assume that it is much more difficult for a single woman to effectively raise children especially here in the West? This situation can inevitably result in an army of maladjusted, uncontrollable children with no respect for God, parents, society or themselves.

It is therefore wrong for the parents concerned to declare (which they often do, perhaps because of guilt): 'It is my business how I choose to conduct my life,' when the consequence of their behaviour affects the innocent children, who in turn filter the symptoms onto society.

On reaching adulthood, these children make up a fair proportion of unreliable people, because they observe and learn the behaviour pattern from their parents. To their conditioned minds, that is the only way they know how to behave. Not knowing any better, they would be inclined to set out to continue the cycle of behaviour handed down from parents.

However, it must be added that there are people from seemingly well-adjusted family backgrounds who are also maladjusted.

How can children have any desire to know, far less care about, who they are when they exist in a state of confusion that has been psychologically instilled inadvertently by their parents?

Society is often critical of these children, and experts delve into science such as psychology and psychiatry in search of the cause and treatment of their indifferent behaviour. But is the most obvious cause for their disturbed behaviour not patently obvious to us, as we cast our eyes far above their easily noticeable little heads? As Bevan said, 'No need to look into the crystal, when you can read the book.'

It needs to be stated that, although not uncommon, this situation is not as serious in developing countries as it is in the West. There is a tight knit nuclear family structure in developing countries, in which the entire family (including members of the community) are often involved in raising children, so the social and psychological impact is not as severe on these children as it is on children in the West. Nonetheless, times are changing, and behaviour patterns fashionable in the West today will inevitably be the trend in other parts of the world tomorrow.

Conclusion

In order to understand who we are, we need appropriate education and guidance. However with all the relevant self-knowledge and guidance, if we are devoid of self-love, we cannot operate positively within the boundaries of our natural characteristics.

Certain elements of society are primarily contributory to the fact that some people have a tendency to dislike themselves. This constant dictatorial portrayal of the qualities of beauty (by those whose primary attribute seems to be simple-mindedness) tends to affect people who are not fortified within themselves.

There is no doubt that love is an innate quality in some people. Considering that God's intention was for us to be created out of love between man and woman, it is natural to assume that some people are born with an overabundance, which appears to illuminate their presence like a beacon. However, for varying reasons, there seem to be some people who appear to be devoid of love or who simply do not demonstrate that vital quality of life appropriately.

If we lack love, the vacuum within is liable to be occupied by another energy, which might be destructive. If we do not love ourselves, then it is impossible for us to truly love others. We are therefore likely to pretend that we are capable of loving and we may then set out to mimic love in a manner that is similar to the dictates of society. What better way to seek recognition and admiration than to feign what is expected of us? What a charade!

Self-love is the key to our identification. The Bible instructs us to 'love thy neighbour as thyself'. But it is only after we have perfected the art of learning to love ourselves that we can likewise love our neighbours.

During my acupuncture training, I regularly practised needling myself in my quest to seek perfection in that art and also to experience the subjective effect of acupuncture (*deqi*) that patients/ clients are expected to feel. This sensation could be slight numbness, heaviness, soreness, a feeling of euphoria or a combination of all. It was only after I was skilful in my needling technique and I had experienced *deqi*, that I confidently practised my skill to enhance the lives of others. Had I treated people, knowing that I was inexperienced, I would have falsely experimented on the bodies and possibly impaired the health of those unsuspecting patients. Similarly, we must know how to love, in order to give love.

I believe that despite our limitations, if we evaluate our lives and adopt a positive mental and spiritual attitude, we are all capable of accessing love from within ourselves. It is then that we would be truly enriched, much more so than with material evaluation of wealth.

'Though I speak with the tongues of men and angels, and have not love, I am become as sounding brass, or a tinkling cymbal.

And though I have the gift of prophecy, and understand all mysteries, and all knowledge; and though I have all faith, so that I could remove mountains, and have not love, I am nothing.

And though I bestow all my goods to feed the poor, and though I give my body to be burned, and have not love, It profiteth me nothing.' (1 Corinthians 1–3).

CHAPTER 15

The Contribution of Religion in Enhancing Health

'The exercise of prayer, in those who habitually exert it, must be regarded by us doctors as the most adequate and normal of all the pacifiers of the mind and calmers of the nerves.' (William James, adapted from *Secrets of Peace*).

'Beloved, I wish above all things that thou mayest prosper and be in health, even as thy soul prospereth' (John 3:2).

Several years ago I met Dorothy, one of my former nursing colleagues whom I had not seen for several years. After we greeted each other she remarked that I appeared to have peace of mind, because she thought that I looked young for my calendar age.

At that time I did not connect one's physical appearance with peace of mind. I can now state that an integral link connecting mental and spiritual harmony is often manifested in our physical appearance, unless we are unfortunately besieged by disease.

Wholeness in body, mind and spirit is essential for peace. Peace is therefore indicative of freedom from torment and anxiety. It is also a state of harmony between people. It can therefore be described as being in the right relationship not only with people, but also with God.

'But they that wait upon the Lord shall renew their strength; they shall mount up with wings as eagles; they shall run and not be weary; and they shall walk, and not faint.' (Isaiah 40:31).

Religion is an unquestionable medium for the enhancement of health. I am of the opinion that relationship with God, as demonstrated in genuine spirituality/religion, helps people to manage difficult situations much better. Religion also helps us to contain ourselves within the perimeter of health.

'Pray for my soul. More things are wrought by prayer than this world dreams of.' (Alfred, Lord Tennyson).

It is a well observed fact that sick people who are religious or spiritual tend to recover or come to terms with illness faster than others.

Speaking at the Festival of Science held at the University of Salford, England, on 10 September 2003, on the subject of patients helped by prayer, Dr Fenwick, a neuropsychiatrist from the Institute of Psychiatry said: '... the fact that science seems to confirm the ability of prayer or directed intention to heal other people, raises the question that the mind may influence other people directly.'

Dr Fenwick continued, 'It has got to the point now where the question has been raised in one of the major American cardiology journals, from the perspective of whether patients are getting the right sort of treatment if there are not prayer groups in the hospital. There has been a huge change in people's views and it is being driven by scientific data.' (*Daily Mail*, 11 September 2003).

Personal comment: Nonetheless, although it is a refreshingly inspiring revelation, the notion that prayer works should not be totally accredited to the contribution of scientific research. Religious and spiritual devotees have vigorously demonstrated, validated and maintained this truism from the dawn of religion. However, impotent in their ability to bamboozle us any longer with their age-old rhetoric, that 'God does not exist,' these scholastics are now changing the tune of their lyrics, by presenting a somewhat more tangible philosophical answer, to which they can be accredited for the discovery of the 'miraculous phenomenon' to answered prayers.

As observed, scientists have not cited the spiritual entity of our being as a possible (and most logical cause) for answered prayers. It is the spirit that influences our minds. Let us remind ourselves of the commonsensical statement made by Selwyn Hugh: 'When we bring our spirits into subjection to God, our minds are filled with the word of God, then our thoughts which are harnessed to God, can become positive and powerful.'

Documented evidence from the USA has also proven that the rate of recovery from illness was higher in cases where physicians had prayed either alone or with patients before treating them. This does not mean that those involved are better than others or that God favours them more. The primary cause for this is their unswerving faith in God; they are spiritually and mentally in control, therefore they seem to be accepting of their destiny, because they believe that whatever the outcome, it is dictated by God.

In an article released in May 2000 by *Readers Digest*, under the caption *Faith Is Powerful Medicine*, Phyllis McIntosh stated: 'Compelling Evidence – Just how powerful is the evidence linking faith and health? More than 30 studies have found a connection between spiritual or religious commitment and longer life. Among the most compelling findings a survey of 5,286 Californians found that church members have lower death rates than non-church members, regardless of risk factors such as smoking, drinking, obesity and inactivity.' I hope this statement does not send out a message that it is OK to clutch the Bible in one hand whilst holding a glass of liquor or a cigarette in the other. It is not a healthy practice. As in traditional medicine, what may be conductive to one person's idea of enjoyment and relaxation may contribute to another person's ill health.

Spiritual Enlightenment

During the latter part of 1972, someone gave me the address of the World Healing Crusade in Blackpool, England. I immediately began to communicate regularly with this group of Christian friends, whose mission is dedicated to counselling and praying for the sick and needy. To this day, we often communicate as close friends by letter or telephone.

What is the World Healing Crusade?

The World Healing Crusade is reputed to be the largest prayer group in the world. Its circulation of *The Crusader* and *Power Lines* magazines of Divine Healing reaches people in 150 countries worldwide. It is a ministry of divine healing, uniting people of different religious denominations in prayer through faith in God's love.

Thousands of people send letters to the sanctuary requesting that they be placed on the blessed altar. The letters are never opened (if so requested by senders); it is a personal communication between the sender and God and many claim to have experienced miraculous results. The World Healing Crusade is a charitable organization.

My healing experience. During the spring of 2001, I visited my friends at the World Healing Crusade in Blackpool for the first time. I received a very warm welcome from each member of the organization. They appeared very pleased to meet me in person.

I find it difficult to describe my experience in the sanctuary. The closest I can get to explaining it is that I felt a deep and peaceful feeling of tranquillity. I felt so good that I kept singing songs of praise. It's no wonder Irish men, intoxicated to the point of feeling good, suddenly burst out singing melodious tunes such as 'When Irish Eyes Are Smiling' or 'O Danny Boy'.

Early in the afternoon I purchased a small roasted chicken from a restaurant, but it was not until the evening that I reheated it and proceeded to eat it. Hours later I started to experience intermittent bouts of abdominal pain and although I administered acupuncture to myself, the pain worsened. I felt as if my abdomen was being pierced with a knife.

**The late Brother Mandus, founder of
the WHC.**

About four or five hours later, during the early hours of the morning, I decided get dressed and call an ambulance to transport me to hospital. I believed that I was suffering from food poisoning, because of eating a part of the chicken that was not reheated properly. As I was in the process of dressing for my envisaged trip to the local hospital, I suddenly remembered that I had some healing cards, which I had obtained the previous day from the sanctuary of the World Healing Crusade. I immediately placed one card on the area of the pain. As I anticipated the return of the next painful spasm, which was somewhat similar in nature to the painful contraction of the womb experienced during childbirth, to my surprise and relief, there was an instant relaxed feeling in my tensed abdomen and I felt no further pain.

Always a difficult person to conceal exciting secrets, it was impossible to contain that particular one. I simply could not cancel my jubilation. The following day I informed Andrew, my friend at the World Healing Crusade, my family and immediate friends, of my healing experience. I even told a complete stranger who happened to strike up a conversation with me in the shopping centre in Blackpool.

I honestly believe that my experience was miraculous. As a qualified nurse and an acupuncture practitioner, I know that painkillers do not act immediately. Whether administered by injection, by tablets, or in the form of acupuncture, it takes several minutes, and in some cases, over one hour before the pain disappears or decreases in intensity. Therefore, for me to experience instantaneous relief of my pain falls outside the boundaries of scientific medical explanation. This experience was not surprising to members of the WHC or to me, because I have read of more extreme miraculous occurrences involving people with the WHC.

Releasing the mind from bondage

I have been told that one effective way of addressing personal problems, is to write them down on a piece of paper, then destroy and dispose of the paper. This is believe to have a psychological affect in minimizing personal problems.

Unfortunately, that particular technique has never worked for me. Perhaps failure was due to the fact that I often retrieved the pieces of paper, assembled them and deliberately read it over and over again in a bid to induce self-pity. This act is enough to submerge anyone into a worse state of despair. However, like many others, addressing my problems to God was one of the satisfying ways of decreasing the impact of my troubles.

The psalmist David advises us thus, *'Cast thy burden upon the Lord, and he shall sustain thee.'* (Psalm 55:22). God increases our stamina (including our spiritual strength) when we make supplications to him. He increases our spiritual strength. Yet, there are a growing number of people who constantly seek guidance from other supernatural avenues. I am not prepared to discredit the practices of anyone in a malicious manner, but I find it somewhat baffling to understand why people are prepared to give others the power of addressing their innermost spiritual needs. Can they therefore truly direct our path the same way as God can?

'And when they shall say unto you, seek unto them that have familiar spirits and unto wizards that peep and that mutter: should not a people seek onto their God? for the living to the dead?' (Isaiah 8:19).

Case History

A young female academic consulted me for acupuncture treatment regarding a psychological problem. Before consulting me she had several consultations with a psychic, who told her that her father had sexually abused her during infancy. The young woman was also romantically involved with a married man who had a young family.

From the information I gathered from the young woman, I was of the opinion that she belonged to a decent, hardworking and loving family.

Although sexual abuse does occur in respectable families, I felt strongly that it was unlikely to have taken place in her case and I expressed my reservation about the medium's assumption to the young lady.

The young woman visited me regularly for acupuncture treatment and her condition soon showed signs of improvement. As time progressed we became friends and she visited me at my home. It was during one of those home visits that she once again brought up the subject of her married lover.

Feeling concerned about the situation, I questioned the moral and practical implications of such a relationship. The young woman suddenly became angry, which was in direct contrast to her placid personality. She told me that she did not care what anyone perceived of the situation, because she knew that the man loved her and that they were destined to be together forever.

A few months later she telephoned me to announce that she was dating a young bachelor. She sounded very relaxed and happy; it seemed as though she was relieved of a huge burden.

During the course of our conversation, she told me that the psychic (to whom she made several paid visits to consult) was an evil person who 'messed up her head'. On each visit, she was told that her married lover was going to leave his wife and children to be with her. The young woman also stated that she later realized that the sexual abuse could not have occurred. In her words, 'It was a wicked and preposterous lie.' I thanked God for that friend's awakening and newfound happiness.

I often wonder whether those professing to be adept in the supernatural ever consider the extent of psychological damage they are likely to inflict on vulnerable clients. There have been reported cases where people who have had such encounters have had to receive psychiatric therapy.

Some people seem to want a quick fix to a happy life so they set about visiting those professing to be gifted in the paranormal. However, it is questionable whether any man or woman can genuinely possess the power to concoct that special magical formula of peace and contentment for the souls of others. Some of those 'experts' involved in the paranormal are themselves no happier than the people they are supposedly helping (except financially, through the benevolence of vulnerable clients).

There is a vacuum in the lives of those unfortunate people who continuously seek supernatural guidance through man. Many of us experience desperate times at some stage in our lives, therefore we all have the need to hear encouraging statements from others. However, some people prefer to resort to different methods to solve their problems.

Practitioners of the paranormal often claim that they work in accordance with God, but would a loving God condone the actions of those who wilfully set out to con vulnerable people, sometimes leaving them psychologically damaged?

It must not be readily assumed that all practitioners of the paranormal deliberately set out to deceive people. There are some people who are gifted with supernatural powers, who genuinely assist others to find closure to their problems. Nonetheless, people must be made aware of some of the possible outcomes of visiting some of these practitioners.

Discussing religion

With an estimated 10 main religions and approximately 10,000 sects, it is impossible to fathom the teachings of the majority of creeds. Some observers of religion may be inclined to question whether some of these religious bodies are embracing monotheism (the doctrine of believing in one God). This is due to the numerous disparities and interpretations of the Bible, with each unit of this religious archipelago insisting that it is 'the true and only way to salvation'.

To avert the possibility of being engulfed in this torrid sea of theological contention, we must apply ourselves sensibly in our quest for spiritual guidance. After we have unravelled the truth, we must abide in the counsel of the prophet Micah: 'For all the people will walk everyone in the name of his God, and we will walk in the name of the Lord our God forever and ever.' (Micah 4:5).

The differing in biblical interpretation and conformity are somewhat responsible for the decline in religion today. In the same way that political parties are formed to promote their personal philosophies, religion too is a man-made invention and just as people who pay allegiance to some political parties are disillusioned, people are also sometimes disheartened by some religions.

During childhood we have parents/carers to guide and nurture us. At school we are guided by teachers who prepare and groom us for our future. When we commence employment, we have senior co-workers or leaders of departments to supervise and advise us. Therefore, throughout life there are people responsible for guiding and preparing us for our future. We are therefore somewhat accountable to them for our behaviour and our performance. Similarly, but most importantly, we are accountable to God our creator to live our lives in the manner instructed through His son Jesus Christ and the prophets. Nonetheless, although religion is an inspirational and gratifying concept, no one should be forced into compliance. It is a highly personal decision for individuals to carefully consider.

Can it be that, in his desperate fight for power on earth, man cannot bear to envisage a force greater than himself to whom he must be accountable? We must remind ourselves of the words of Lord Acton: 'Power corrupts, but absolute power corrupts absolutely.'

Those people who claim that 'if there was a God, He would have prevented wrongdoing on earth,' must realize that man is responsible for the consequence of his actions.

The very system of men in grey suits who (at times) formulate preposterous legislation responsible for the decay in morality are now suggesting that people are becoming too immoral and rebellious. They believe that in order to preserve traditional family values we must return to basics by instituting stricter and more sensible legislation.

There are numerous reasons why some people are not compliant with religion and although most are understandable, it is important to discuss some of the presenting causes for nonparticipation.

Why Non-Compliance with Religious Ideology?

'A little philosophy inclineth man's mind to atheism, but depth of philosophy bringeth men's mind about religion.' (Francis Bacon).

I) **Atheism.** Belief in the non-existence of God is common amongst a staggering number of people. Some of these people contend that evolution was the basic formula for life on earth. Lay people as well as the scientific fraternity hold this belief.

Evolution: Organic evolution is the theory that (independent of God's intervention), the first living organism was developed from lifeless matter. Then as it reproduced, it changed into different kinds of living things, producing all forms of plant and animal life. Charles Darwin was one of the leading proponents of this doctrine.

My disagreement with the notion of evolution is primarily based on the following reasoning: Looking at the universe, we observe that everything, including Man-Woman, Day-Night, Summer-Winter, East and West balance meticulously. This is a continuous pattern on earth. What is the source of that energy responsible for this so-called evolution? Some form of super intelligent force *must* be accountable for this perfect matching of opposite yet complementary ingredients, which collectively are of vital importance to the creation of the world, living and reproduction.

To the rational mind, the only possible imaginable originator of the universe must be God, the absolute perfectionist.

'To whom then will ye liken me, or shall I be equal? saith the Holy One. Lift up your eyes on high, and behold who hath created these things, that bringeth their host by number: he calleth them all by names by the greatness of his might, for that he is strong in power; not one faileth.' (Isaiah 40: 25–6)

The atheist requires evidence of the existence of God. Rosenstock-Huey wrote: 'Speculations over God and the World are always idle, the thoughts of idlers, spectators of the theatre of life. "Is there a God?" "Has man a soul?" "Why must we die?" "How many hairs has the Devil's Grandmother?" "When is the day of Judgement?" All these are idle questions, and one fool can ask more of them than a hundred wise men can answer. Nevertheless, teachers, parents and bishops must give answers to such questions, because otherwise, the idlers will spread their corruption.' (Adapted from *The Faber Book of Aphorisms* by W. H. Auden and Louis Kronenbergen).

It is a well observed fact that some of those very people who constantly ballyhoo about their atheist stance also ask for God's intervention at times when they are seriously in need of divine intervention. I have observed this occurrence on a few occasions, therefore I do not pay seriously attention to the arguments of nonbelievers. However, I believe that this is a commendable act, because it cannot be easy for sceptics to muster up the courage to embrace an idea that is out of bounds to their way of thinking.

We breathe air to survive and yet we cannot visibly see air, though we can detect the physiological effects of its presence as the chest walls expand and recoil. We cannot see the wind, but the evidence of its presence can be observed by the swaying of trees and we also feel its effects as it blows on us. Like other forms of energy, electricity is invisible, but we can see the effects of its action after we turn on the switch. We can verify its presence when we feel the dispersion from an electrical heater, or we can observe light after turning on the relevant switch.

Similarly, God cannot be seen, but those who communicate with Him and are aware of his presence in their lives can form a mental image of what He looks like.

My husband once took me to meet one of his close colleagues. As soon as Pat, the gentleman in question, saw me he said, 'My word, do you know you look exactly as I visualized you?' Whenever Pat conversed with my husband on the phone he would insist on speaking with me. He told us that through regular communication with me, he imagined a face to match my personality.

Some people are very adept in persuading others, and they would soon conjure up convincing excuses to justify religious abstinence. Behind the facade, it simply boils down to them wanting autonomy from God. They simply would like to carry on with their conditioned lifestyles without any conformity or guilt. That is fair enough, we all have a choice. However there is concern when these people begin to infiltrate and influence vulnerable elements of society with illogical rebelliousness against God.

In December 1999, I read an article in a British national newspaper under this heading: 'FAITH IN GOD LOST IN SPACE'. The article stated that a survey revealed that more young people in Britain believe in aliens and ghosts than in God. More than 60 per cent said spirits and extraterrestrials existed, but only 39 per cent had some faith in Christianity. (*The Mirror*, 18 December 1999).

It does not need a psychologist to probe into the minds of those young people to ascertain the reason for this trend of thought. It is undoubtedly the result of systematic conditioning by factions of the adult community. It is no wonder that so many of our innocent children appear dismally confused and lost.

Several years ago it was reported that a religious university student was preaching in the streets in Britain. The police soon arrested the young man. This was because passers-by reported that he seemed to be a weird individual (because he dared to try to bring about positive changes to our world).

Yet, there are those who interrupt events including cricket and football matches by stripping off their clothing and running onto the pitch. These people receive rapturous applause; some even have their pictures put in the papers, thus becoming instant celebrities for being 'amusing'.

2) **Inherited disassociation with religion.** Some people have never embraced religion. This is mainly due to familiar customs. It is therefore difficult for them to adapt easily to a custom with which they are unacquainted. They are also reluctant to abandon their traditional lifestyle for what they may perceive as too rigid a way of life. However religion and spirituality have nothing to do with that overbearing severity sometimes portrayed by some followers.

We should be able to stroll leisurely in the path of righteousness; this is a demonstration of confidence in our spiritual fortitude. If we walk stiffly, this can well be interpreted as protecting ourselves from avoiding a tumble because we are nervously pacing a dimly lit and uncertain trail.

3) **Confusion in understanding religion.** As I have stated earlier in this chapter, there are thousands of different religious organizations. It is therefore likely that there are several differing religious interpretations.

There are codes of practice in some churches that are difficult for outsiders to understand. I have been informed that some of the practices forbidden by some religions are laughter and eating pepper – a herb known for its culinary and medicinal purposes.

I believe that one crucial point people seeking religion must bear in mind is to prepare themselves spiritually so that they may be guided by God and their intuition to the right religion. In this way they are less likely to find themselves experiencing a spiral of denominational changes in order to find the right church.

To me God is representative of a larger than life character of a loving, approachable, understanding, but strict father, not the austere figure who is likely to punish me for the smallest of transgressions, as portrayed by some religious devotees. I would not let anyone impose his or her interpretation of religious correctness on me, if it meant compromising my lifelong very personal and workable relationship with the God whom I have learned to understand.

4) **Financial Constraints.** There are some religious organizations requesting members to donate a specified amount, such as ten per cent of their salary, to the church. It is generally claimed that these subscriptions are primarily to assist in the upkeep of the church, and for other charitable reasons.

However, I like many others find this practice questionable. It is a well-known fact that the majority of people attending churches are not wealthy; they are some of the families experiencing financial difficulty. How can it be morally correct for a powerful and wealthy organization like the church to dictate the donation that financially impoverished people should contribute? Would it not be more fitting to the spirit of religion, for people to be given the option of donating what is affordable to them? By the way, how much does God charge for His continuous services to humanity?

Those who feel pressurized to give exorbitant sums of donation may be better off financially and spiritually by worshipping at home because God abides in our homes as much as He does in the church.

How can people be expected to be spiritually uplifted at a religious gathering when their minds are preoccupied with the sight of their much needed cash perched high in the collection plate on the altar facing them? That display of their contribution is enough to induce heavy-hearted sighs by some who are financially destitute, never mind the promissory declaration by the minister that the more one gives, the more one receives.

5) **Insipid ministry.** Many young people and some mature Christians have stated that they have lost interest in their church because they found them boring.

One senior English friend, who had worshipped in the same church since she was a child, told me that she had not attended church for a long time. She told me that she feels the need for a more uplifting worship, like the cheerful services in black churches where people clap their hands and sway their bodies as they sing soulfully.

We change our physicians if we are dissatisfied with them. We rid ourselves of our friends if we cannot get along with them. We change our spouses or partners (sometimes too easily), when there is conflict within the relationship. Then why don't we discuss our spiritual needs with our minister and if the result is not to our satisfaction, change religion in a bid to seek adequate spiritual enlightenment to suit our personal needs?

My perception of religion is that it should be representative of an inner light that shines through us to illuminate our path in life. That light is subjected to dimness unless we recharge it through prayer, meditation or by simply being good people. That light can also be charged by external stimuli such as religious gatherings or positive gestures from others. If the inner light is not charged appropriately, its continuity will be impeded, then there is a possibility of it becoming extinguished.

6) **Racial politics in religion.** Race, politics and religion are three of the leading contributors to divisions and hostility within the human race.

Traditionally black people have always been predisposed to religion, but some are questioning the configuration of Christianity. This uneasiness has unfortunately resulted in the abandonment of religion by some young black people, whilst the older established Christians are breaking away from mainstream churches and setting up their own places of worship.

It is a well-known fact, that when Afro-Caribbean people arrived in Britain during the 1950s, they tried to maintain their Christian beliefs as indoctrinated to them in their countries by the British. However, they soon found out that they were not welcome in some churches. Several people stated that after a few visits, the ministers took them aside and told them that it would be best if they did not worship there again, because the regular white parishioners were not happy to have them participate in worshipping with them.

This insensitive reaction by some factions of so-called Christians has paved the way for the establishment of several 'black' churches in Britain, where people can freely participate in Christian Fellowship.

Black people are also displaying reactive behaviour towards other painful situations, particularly the way in which the church had ignored the sufferings of their fore-parents, slaves.

If a child constantly abuses another whilst the parents sit impassively (in some instances, even participating in the torment, be it in a minor way), the abused child would be greatly hurt. Knowing that there is no other recourse, the child may silently put up with the abuse. Nonetheless it is not likely to forget the incident. When the abused child is old enough it is likely to resent its parent for allowing its siblings to abuse it. It will also question that manner of parenting.

Other leading issues cited by some black people for their lack of interest in religion are:

- **If there really is a God, why did He not intervene during slavery and why do black people suffer more than other races?**

Leadership is not an easy task. Whenever things go wrong in an establishment, blame is usually attributed to the boss. World leaders are pressurized into resigning when there are improprieties within their governments. Coaches are sacked if their teams do not perform satisfactorily continuously. Similarly, God is often incriminated for man's wrongful doings.

Let us not forget that God's only son also suffered and died in a most cruel manner. Christ was a sacrifice for humanity's sin. There were lessons learned after his death, so much so that those who conspired to harass and crucify him acknowledged him as the Son of God after they had accomplished their dastardly deeds.

There are learning experiences unravelled in all aspects of events in our lives and slavery has revealed several important observations.

Although the slave trade was one of the most evil atrocities ever committed against humanity, there are many valuable attributes discovered about the slaves. Black people are the descendants of a dynasty of people who excelled in physical, spiritual, mental and emotional strength. This statement does not imply that other races are inferior; it simply summarizes the resilience of a people under insurmountable tribulations. Had the slaves not been God-fearing, strong-willed, courageous, enduring and defiant, there is a possibility that mass suicide would have been rife amongst them.

Some people are of the opinion that religion is a form of brain-washing or mind conditioning because it dictates conformity. Well, I am sure there are several people who would like to be disciplined in a manner that conditions them to fend off adversities in life instead of succumbing to them. Despite hardships, the slaves did not relinquish contact with God. They practised their traditional religions and they constantly sang Negro spirituals, which was very comforting and uplifting to their souls. Today some of those Negro spirituals are sung universally as encouragement, as is often observed at football matches.

John Newton, who once captained a slave ship, wrote several hymns. One of his popular songs is 'How sweet the name of Jesus sounds in a believer's ear! It soothes his sorrows, heals his wounds and drives away his fear.' Can it be that this hymn was inspired by Newton's observation of the spiritual fortitude of his God-fearing cargo?

Newton was a man reputed for his noxious persona who nonetheless became a ministering Christian proclaiming, 'Amazing grace (how sweet the sound) that saved a wretch like me.' He was also one of the instrumental figures responsible for the abolition of slavery by Parliament in 1806. Therefore can we not extricate negative thoughts and learn positive lessons from those real life symbolic examples?

- **The true origin and facts about the Bible have been distorted by white people, so why should black people participate, or accept a doctrine which has deliberately shadowed the historic valuable contribution of black people?**

'In the period between the fourth century and the Enlightenment of the seventeenth and eighteenth centuries, Europe recast the entire Bible into a saga of European people ... The result has been the creation of a world in which too many blacks themselves have become uncomfortable with images of biblical characters as blacks.' (The Original African Heritage Study Bible).

As we enter the third millennium, I find the argument regarding the colour of biblical characters rather an outdated subject of contention. Assumption that biblical characters were predominantly white is as logical as believing that a white Tarzan actually miraculously appeared in the jungle of deepest Africa.

Overwhelming evidence put forward by genealogists confirms that all humans originated from Africa. Therefore it is obvious that stories of a blond Moses with deep blue eyes leading his people, the children of Israel (who were black, according to prominent historians of various nationalities) is illogical.

If we continually fan the flames of racial supremacy in religion we lose the purpose of the real meaning of spiritual embodiment and the devil emerges as the winner. As for my part, even if historical research proves that Christ was akin to the members of the infamous KKK, I will continue to worship Him. His record substantiates the fact that He truly is the greatest.

- **Black people are cursed – what is the point of bothering with religion?**

Yes, the old mythical curse of Ham! It appears as though this biblical reference has been deliberately distorted to justify the ungodly deeds of some factions of humanity. The character cursed was deemed to become 'a servant of servants unto his brethren' – Ah! slavery springs to mind.

As a young child growing up in my native Guyana, I often listened to senior people alluding to the fact that 'Black people were cursed by God'. That assumption sent many a frightening shiver down my sturdy young spine. Then during my early years of nursing in Britain, I met black nurses from the Caribbean and Africa who told me that before coming to England, they too were told that black people were cursed. And yet, when I made inquiries pertaining to this subject from some religious white nurses, including nuns from Ireland who trained with me, they told me that they had never heard of it.

This issue troubled me so much that I kept asking everyone who had any scriptural command. I would even approach the visiting hospital chaplains and enquire: 'Is it true that black people are cursed because of Ham?' The answer was always 'Nonsense!' or 'Never heard that one.'

Reasoning. In Genesis 9:18 we read that Ham was the father of Canaan. Then again in Genesis 9:20–27 we read of the curse that befell Canaan, not his father Ham who saw his father Noah naked after Noah was drunk with wine.

The biblical characters involved in this issue were from the same race. How is it that the one cursed remained his original race, black, whilst his siblings mysteriously became another race?

As *The Original African Heritage Study Bible* points out, 'It does not make any sense to say logically or scientifically, that within the ten generations from Adam to Noah (and without the introduction of any outside factor), a genetic change took place which allowed one man (Noah) and his wife (of the same race as himself), to produce children who were racially different.'

- **Other nations have a religion synonymous to their race, origin and culture. Why is it that black people have none?**

'The institution of slavery tried to deny its victims their native cultural identity. Torn out of their own cultural milieus, they were expected to abandon their heritage and to adopt at least part of their enslavers' culture. Nonetheless, studies have shown that there were aspects of slave culture that differed from the master's culture. Some of these have been interpreted as a form of resistance to oppression, while other aspects were clearly survival of a native culture in a new society.' (*Britannica*, 299).

Black people had their original religion, but they were prevented from worshipping during slavery and brainwashed into conforming to one of Eurocentricity during colonialism. This exercise was purely in the interest of the slave owners and colonists. This action (similar to any other deed) has incurred a reaction whereby some black people are now questioning the tactics used in persuading their fore-parents into confirming to a different way of worshipping God. Some black people are therefore openly resentful of Western religions.

'Myalism was the first religious movement to appear to all ethnic groups in Jamaica, Voodoo in Haiti was the product of African culture slightly refashioned on that island, and syncretic Afro-Christian religions and rituals appeared nearly everywhere throughout the New World.' (*Britannica*, 299).

Voodoo was one of the traditional black religions. Contrary to popular belief that it is representative of evil influence, it is a means of enhancing relationship with God and nature. It seeks harmony with (not dominance over) nature. It considers the supernatural as an extension of the natural. This was one of the dominant religions of the captives during slavery. It is therefore understandable that the slaves would have stuck to it for spiritual sustenance.

The slaves may have asked themselves, 'Why must we adopt a religion recommended to us by our captors? What genuine God-fearing people would hold us captives?' However, some slave masters prohibited the practice of traditional religions, therefore to avoid punishment the slaves covertly continued with their traditional way of worship.

In 1791, the slaves in Haiti under the leadership of Toussaint L'Oveture defeated the French army in what has been described as one of the fiercest fought battles in history. It was the worst defeat the French army had suffered from an army led by slaves. The voodoo priest prayed with the slaves for victory over their captives Then he instructed them to fight fiercely and not be afraid of dying, because if they were killed their souls would be returned to Africa, their spiritual home.

Although a Christian, I understand the situation of the slaves in adhering to their tradition religion. I am also sympathetic with others who for their own spiritual fulfilment choose a religion of their preference to connect them to God.

We must also remember that early Christianity, as indoctrinated by the missionaries, was intended to stupefy black people into a state of subjugation, thus giving Europeans the ammunition to exploit several colonies.

Today, there are millions of followers of voodoo and other African religions in the Caribbean and North America. However, it must be mentioned that like any other practice (including other religions), voodoo can be used by devious people for negative and evil purposes. It was not intended to be used for evil intentions.

I believe that 'the church is one foundation'. It is not where you worship that is crucial to being in God's presence. No one should establish himself or herself in a superior position in God's favour because of race or religion. God looks much more deeply into the hearts and souls of people, therefore we are all equal in his sight.

People need to focus on the true purpose of religious embodiment, which should not be conformity to man's imposition or attendance at a particular place of worship. What is needed is a genuine established relationship with God.

'Then Peter opened his mouth and said, of a truth I perceive that God is no respecter of persons: But in every nation he that feareth Him and worketh righteousness is accepted with Him.' (Acts 10:34–5).

242 HOLISTIC GUIDE TO HEALTH AND SELF AWARENESS

Conclusion

'If God did not exist, it would be necessary to invent him' (Voltaire).

Religion and spirituality can be dynamic influences in our lives. Some of the global catastrophes, including diseases engulfing humanity, are the results of our self-imposed autonomy from God. We need to establish a personal relationship with Him in order to illuminate our lives. Whilst we are forcing sex education upon our young children in schools, we are denying them adequate spiritual and religious programming.

Perhaps if religion were more focused upon in schools, children would not be failing so abysmally in grasping the so-called 'message' relayed to them through sex education. The alarming statistics in teenage pregnancies in Britain, estimated to be the highest in Europe, and the rise in sexually transmitted diseases including HIV/AIDS and chlamydia substantiates the fact that there is a need to get our children more involved in spiritual and moral education.

Religion and spirituality are gaining impetus, but some sceptics argue that the reason for this increase in believers is not due to the fact that the doctrine is becoming popular: it is the result of nonbelievers losing popularity. My rationale is: if the truth is well recognized, then the opposition stands little chance of attracting levelheaded supporters.

Prayers

In sickness we often pray for recovery. This is a natural human reaction. Obviously, not everyone will recover. It is therefore good practice for us to first focus on praying for spiritual strength in order to cope with illness. If it is God's plan for us to recover, then we will, but if we do not recover, it does not mean that God has forsaken us.

We are so accustomed to requesting what we want from others or what we think suits us best, that we automatically try the same ploy with God. We seldom focus on our genuine needs. At times our requests to God are so lengthy that at the end of our prayers, we forget what the focal point of our conversation with Him was all about.

We must not be selfish; prayers should be minimal per session. (I always believe that there are others who are more deserving than me, therefore I ask for the minimum at each session.) When we do not get the things we request of God, we some times allude to Him and religion negatively.

No good parent would succumb to the intimidating tactics of a child crying for something that the parent perceives to be unsuitable. Why then shouldn't God, the parent of all parents, have the right to decide what is appropriate for us?

The following is a helpful guide to meaningful prayer:

LORD TEACH ME TO PRAY ...

I cannot pray *Our*, if my faith has no room for others and their need.

I cannot pray *Father*, if I do not demonstrate this relationship to God in my daily living.

I cannot pray *who art in heaven*, if all my interests and pursuits are in earthly things.

I cannot pray *hallowed be thy name*, if I am not striving, with God's help, to be holy.

I cannot pray *thy kingdom come*, if I am unwilling to accept God's rule in my life.

I cannot pray *thy will be done*, if I am unwilling or resentful of having it in my life.

I cannot pray *on earth as it is in Heaven*, unless I am truly ready to give myself to God's service here and now.

I cannot pray *give us this day our daily bread*, without expending honest effort for it, or if I would withhold from my neighbour the bread that I receive.

I cannot pray *forgive us our trespasses as we forgive those who trespass against us*, if I continue to harbour a grudge against anyone.

I cannot pray *lead us not into temptation*, if I deliberately choose to remain in a situation where I am likely to be tempted.

I cannot pray *deliver us from evil*, if I am not prepared to fight evil with my life and my prayer.

I cannot pray *thine is the kingdom*, if I am unwilling to obey the King.

I cannot pray *thine is the power and the glory*, if I am seeking power for myself and my own glory first.

I cannot pray *forever and ever*, if I am too anxious about each day's affairs.

I cannot pray *Amen*, unless I honestly say, 'Cost what it may, this is my prayer.' (Anon).

Finally

Those seeking spiritual enlightenment must be careful in their choice of religion. A vast majority of religions are genuine, but, as we are aware, there have been unfortunate incidents involving some cults. The following is one of the worse cases to date:

In 1978 James Warren Jones (Jim Jones), an American preacher, was responsible for the massacre of 913 of his fellow American cult members in the jungles of Guyana.

Guyana, the only English speaking country in South America, boasting an enviable area of 83,000 square miles, is renowned for the beauty of its vast expanse of hinterland. Amongst some of its other attractions are its waterfalls, including the magnificent Kaiteur Falls, the second highest waterfall in the world. The Angel Falls in Venezuela (which borders Guyana) is the highest waterfall in the world.

The hinterlands of Guyana seem an ideal resort for anyone seeking peace and tranquillity and as in the case of Jim Jones, privacy to take control of the minds of his unsuspecting followers.

The thought of innocent infants and children, forced to drink cyanide at Jones's command, seems unreal when I try to mentally visualize that tragedy, and yet the deafening sounds of their protesting screams (although a film version) remains indelibly in my mind. Those children did not choose to be there, they were simply unfortunate victims because of their credulous parents.

Yet, according to reports from those present, Jim Jones did not intend to die with his faithful followers. One of his closest aides gave one of his followers three suitcases containing 1.5 million US dollars and instructed that the cases be taken to the Soviet Embassy in Georgetown (the capital of Guyana). Tim Carter, the man assigned to undertake that job, abandoned the cases and escaped into the jungle. He was later rescued.

According to informed sources, Jones was one of the very last people to die from the bullet of an unknown assassin. It was speculated that he had planned to escape to Russia with the suitcases containing cash.

Coincidentally, in 1845, in that very part of Guyana, a white missionary persuaded 400 Amerindians (the original inhabitors of Guyana) to commit suicide in the belief that they would be reincarnated as white people. It is claimed that Jim Jones, 'a well-read man', was aware of that particular incident.

'For such are false apostles, deceitful workers transforming themselves into the apostles of Christ. And no marvel; for Satan himself is transformed into an angel of light. Therefore it is no great thing if his ministers also transform as the ministers of righteousness; whose end shall be according to their works.' (2 Corinthians 11:13–15).

NB: I would like to put on record, my profound gratitude to Channel 4 television in London, England, for their generosity in presenting me with a special copy of the video on the incident in Jonestown, Guyana.

CHAPTER 16

The Benefits of Having Pets

Apart from humans, one of the most profound and uninhibited displays of genuine companionship one can experience is that of pets. It is an indisputable observation by psychologists throughout the world that pet owners tend to be more adaptable to stress and overall inclined to be healthier than others are.

It is unfortunate that some people are inclined to be allergic to the fur of some animals; therefore it is understandable that they should have little or no contact with those animals.

'A faithful friend is the medicine of life.' (Ecclesiastes 6:16).

Pets can have a therapeutic effect on certain conditions. By walking them, exercise and fitness is achieved. They also have a sedative affect on people; this is beneficial in certain stress-related situations.

The following are some conditions and situations that may be improved by having a pet:

- Anger management
- High blood pressure
- Anxiety and depression
- Isolation and loneliness
- Circulatory conditions (by exercising)
- Joint problems (related to inactivity)
- Chronic illness
- Weight control (by exercising dogs)
- Convalescence

A notably large proportion of people in the United Kingdom keep dogs, cats, rabbits, hamsters and a variety of other pets. This is a result of man's need to be attached and to nurture. Pets are symbolic of babies and children.

Researchers in psychology have proven that stroking pets has a dual effect whereby there is a sedative response to both the person and the pets. There have been incidents of lowering of the blood pressure as a result of stroking pets. Touching activates a dynamic reaction in many situations. It is common knowledge that bodily contact with others in the form of a simple handshake, an embrace, holding hands, a caress or even a pat on the back, can activate the feel-good factor in participants.

There is no doubt that pets make good companions; they are often used as a substitute for children, friends and partners by filling a vacuum with their lively presence. Nonetheless, pets should not be treated as if they were humans because God created us higher in ordinance than animals. This fact must always be at the forefront of the minds of pet lovers as some tend to get carried away by treating pets as if they are children.

Some nations are particularly fond of pets. Traditionally, people in the West tend to appreciate pets more than other nations; this tendency is an integral part of their culture. This may be due to the fact that these people seem to be lonelier than those in developing countries. People in the developing countries keep dogs primarily for the purposes of guarding properties and hunting. Cats are kept to deter rats. However a noticeable proportion of people in developing countries have always been fond of pets. Today the number of pet owners/lovers in those countries has been greatly increased.

Apart from allergy to pets, financial restraint and a busy lifestyle, the other reason sometimes given for people not having pets is a dislike of animals. The first three reasons are understandable, but I would like to explore the rationale of 'dislike'. If one states that one has no interest in pets, that is reasonable, but it is somewhat prejudicial to state dislike as a reason especially when one has never owned a pet.

If people make a conscious effort to familiarize themselves with pets, the result would be tolerance and understanding, instead of bigotry and aversion towards our friends of the animal kingdom.

I developed a fondness for pets from an early age and as I advance in age and maturity, I have become totally fascinated by them. When my last child was two years old, intuitively and without any preparation I went to a local pet shop and returned with a beautiful white rabbit, which my children immediately named Fluffy. There were several other rabbits playing and snuggling together in the hutch, but I noticed that the only white one was cowering in a corner.

The salesperson told me that Fluffy was from a different litter to the others. Her sisters and brothers were multicoloured and were therefore perceived to be more attractive, so they were quickly purchased, but poor Fluffy was left behind. I immediately picked her up and purchased her.

I became very attached to Fluffy; she was our first pet and she behaved as if I was her mother. We were surprised to discover how sensible pets were as we enthusiastically observed her behaviour.

One day as I was sleeping after nursing the previous night, I heard the sound of tiny footsteps approaching up the stairs. Realizing that my youngest child was supposed to be asleep, I called out to her and demanded that she should come to my bed to sleep instead of parading up and down the stairs. Receiving no answer from the child, I thought that I must have imagined hearing her footsteps. Too tired to investigate, I dozed off.

A few minutes later I felt a tug at my bedclothes. To my amazement when I looked at the side of my bed, Fluffy was standing on her hind legs reaching up to me with her front legs. I could not believe that my rabbit had hopped up fourteen steps to find me.

I usually put her in her hutch before I left home for work in the evenings and I would let her out and feed her on my return the following mornings. On that particular morning my husband had let her out and fed her because I was later than usual arriving home. I must have forgotten to close the back door; therefore she seized the opportunity to invite herself indoors as she had done on several occasions, to be with me.

I was devastated when Fluffy suddenly died at the age of 5 years. Unable to come to terms with her death, two days later I made my way to the pet shop and returned home with a lovely jet-black rabbit, which we named Ebony.

In recent years, I have had several pets at different periods. Each seems to exhibit behaviour slightly similar to children. I believe that my association with pets is a reminder and continuation of my childhood role. Pets are representative of my substitute children.

Being the second child and eldest female of a family of eight, I was traditionally conditioned to assist my mother in caring for my brothers and sisters. Acquiring a number of pets reveals a psychological need in me to assimilate the role of my mother, whose nurturing abilities have left an indelible effect on me. Although my husband and three children are fond of the pets, I am the one who generally attends to them and as the others put it 'spoil them rotten'.

I often administer medical treatment including acupuncture or herbal remedies to them. It is therefore understandable that the bond between the pets and me would be strongest.

On several occasions, my family have told me that they have observed that our pets, including two chickens, two rabbits and Yixi, the dog, seem to sense my arrival about five to seven minutes prior to me coming home. The animals would run to the gate, and my dog, who I suppose believed that he was the Grand Vizier of my animal 'haven', would bark once in a high-pitched voice. He would then proceed to take a shoe or other personal item belonging to me and make his way towards the gate, where he would sit wagging his tail in anticipation of my arrival.

My dog

Several years ago, a nursing colleague's dog gave birth to a litter of six puppies. Five of the puppies were soon selected by people, but the youngest, which was also the smallest of the litter, was still awaiting a home. The person who was expected to take him suddenly changed her mind. I immediately decided to take the rejected beautiful golden brown Collie Labrador puppy. It is ironic that my first two pets (Fluffy and Yixi) were the last of their litters to be homed.

I named the six-week-old puppy Yixi, after an acupuncture point connected to the urinary bladder channel. Yixi, translated in traditional Chinese diction, means surprise or happy idea. That dog was like an extension of our family. I was so attached to him that once when I was on holiday I telephoned the family and after conversing with them I asked them to tease him so I could listen to him barking. I felt quite happy when I heard him barking boisterously.

At the age of five, Yixi started to bleed occasionally from his nose. He was taken to a vet on a few occasions but his condition did not improve.

When he deteriorated, I was prepared to make any necessary sacrifice to restore his health. I decided to abandon a planned holiday. I was disappointed at not being able to travel. However, I believed that I had made the right decision because I would have been unhappy on my holiday knowing that my pet was gravely ill.

The first vet consulted informed me that Yixi's condition was likely to deteriorate further and the possibility of recovery was remote. He told me that I had a choice of having him put on some powerful drugs that might temporarily relieve his condition, but he stressed that the treatment was costly. He also stated that in the near future the pet might not respond to treatment and might have to be put to sleep (euthanasia – mercy killing). I felt very distressed about the situation, but I was somewhat optimistic that there must be other avenues of relieving the dog's distressing symptoms, thereby promoting his quality of health.

Some well-meaning acquaintances, concerned about the expense that the sick dog was liable to incur on me, advised me to have him put to sleep. The very thought of that suggestion was so upsetting to me, that fearing that they might continue to distress me further, I deliberately avoided contact with them.

After I was given that bad prognosis (forecast) of my dog's condition, I retired to bed very distressed that night. I had little sleep and so did my husband as I spent most of that night discussing the situation with him.

Touched by my concern for my pet, my husband decided to consult a second vet the following day. Carl, the person consulted, proved to be not only a skilful veterinarian, but also someone whose understanding and compassion as demonstrated by his unselfish attitude, places him in the upper echelon of humanitarianism.

After conducting blood tests and x-ray examinations on the dog, Carl informed me that Yixi had contracted aspergillosis, a rare fungal disease in dogs, which had affected his right turbinate (nasal bone). He assured me that it was not contagious to humans or other animals. I told Carl that my dog was nearly as precious to me as my family; therefore I would like him to explore every available option of treatment for him.

The following day I received a telephone call from Carl saying that he had contacted a leading hospital in veterinary medicine regarding my dog. He told me that the cost of surgery for the dog's condition was very expensive, but he had taken the trouble of finding out the surgical procedure and although he had not performed that particular operation before, he was prepared to do it for me at a much-reduced cost. Better still, because of my nursing background, he suggested that if I undertook the post operative care of the dog twenty-four hours after his operation, he would reduce the bill further. I quietly asked myself whether he was a vet or a saint.

The operation appeared to be successful, but 14 months later there were signs of the disease in the left nasal bone. Again Carl successfully operated and Yixi seemed to be in reasonable health. Carl prescribed the occasional medication when he showed signs of problems. I also gave him acupuncture occasionally.

Yixi matured beautifully into a loyal friend. He accompanied me jogging several times weekly, leading and pulling me at his pace even up hills. Although he had always been protective of our property, he seemed to have developed guarding characteristics that closely mimicked that of a man. On several occasions when I took him for his evening exercise, he would run a few yards ahead of me. If people approached me, he would stand looking back alertly in my direction, with one of his front legs lifted up as if preparing to pounce in my defence if necessary. He only moved off after the people passed me.

'Love understand love; it needs no talk.' (Frances Ridley Havergal).

Animals like humans will acknowledge and reciprocate affection or love, they are ideal for emotional stimulation. I experience immense peace, which seem to progress into a state of tranquillity, when I spend time with my pets.

It is difficult for those who have never experienced this connection to envisage the dynamics of its effects. I appreciate that not everyone would tolerate pets. Nonetheless, people should not think of pets as a financial burden because their affection, dedication, companionship and therapeutic benefits outweigh the financial cost of keeping them.

It is foolhardy to equate money with happiness; there is little or in some instances no comparison. Money may access comfort, but that does not necessarily mean that one is guaranteed happiness in acquiring comfortable things. Anyway I doubt whether there are many who would cherish the idea of spending on pets whilst they themselves are starving or homeless.

A senior gentleman, who is the owner of several pets, once told me that his brother had left him a fairly large amount of money. He looked very troubled as he uttered these actual words to me: 'Now you tell me, what do I want with all that dough especially at my time of life?'

That gentleman has always lived a simple life, nonetheless he is always a remarkably pleasant and contented person, therefore his reaction to his inheritance was not surprising to me. Some of us do not need abundant financial wealth to be contented in life.

Intellectuality

I believe dogs operate instinctively as well as intellectually. Owing to the fact that they interact closely with humans, their intelligence may have developed to higher dimensions than normal. On several occasions, it has been reported that animals have saved the lives of their owners and other people. Therefore having a pet (and caring for it) often has several beneficial rewards.

Lately, it appears that some women are of the opinion that it is politically correct to publicly compare men unfavourably to dogs. Although this appears to be a light-hearted figurative expression to some, it should not be encouraged, because that statement is a damning insult to humanity.

It is understandable that those women are venting their frustration and annoyance because of betrayal by men with whom they were romantically involved. It is grossly erroneous to portray all men in that negative light. The unmanly attitude of some men does not automatically downgrade their human status to that of an animal.

That remark also reveals lack of knowledge on the part of those women, regarding the loyalty of dogs towards their owners. However, instead of presenting themselves as perpetual victims, women should take stock of themselves, be accountable for their mistakes and learn to avoid further distress from that breed of humans they set about to animalize.

Yixi with the author's daughter.

Update on Yixi

During the latter part of 1999 Yixi developed a slight swelling on the shoulder of his left leg. Our vet told us that the swelling appeared to be cancerous. The vet gave us a course of medication for the dog, but he was of the opinion that Yixi was not going to recover from his latest illness.

The reason for Yixi's terminal illness

Several years ago, he went galavanting with a young attractive bitch who often called at my gate to entice him into running off to the park with her. He would literally escape to go with her. Yixi was hit by a taxi as he returned late one evening from one of his outings with his friend. Although there were no signs of injury after an emergency vet examined him, that accident affected him years later.

Yixi was always so well 'muscled up' and very fit, that despite the severity of his condition, he showed no physical signs of the illness apart from limping. He even insisted on his daily walks, although I had to reduce the distance.

Feeling somewhat concerned that he might be feeling intense pain, I took him back to see the vet, as instructed. Although I was mentally preparing myself to have him put down, each time I made those visits I fetched my dog straight

Trixi.

back home. I just could not consent to having him killed. However on the third visit, as I discussed the fate of my precious pet with Carl, the vet who had given him an added lease of life by operating on him (as discussed earlier), we both emotionally came to the conclusion that he should be put down. However, once again I postponed the fateful event. I told Carl that I would rather wait until my daughter's Easter recess in three weeks' time from university, so that she could say goodbye to the dog. Carl was somewhat convinced that Yixi would not last that long.

All through that distressing discussion about his fate, my poor dog sat quietly looking at both Carl and me as we spoke. Silly as this statement may appear to some, I believe that he understood the conversation. It broke my heart to know that we were discussing his demise in his very presence, yet he was powerless to utter a bark in his defence.

Three weeks after our last visit to the vet, my daughter arrived home on the Saturday. My dog was very weak and breathless by then, but I gave him a painkilling drug and he showed no sign of severe discomfort.

As the car arrived with my daughter, I told the dog that she had arrived. He looked at me, and then to my astonishment, although he could hardly walk, he briskly lifted himself up from his bed and limped straight to the gate to greet her. After my daughter played with him for a while, he crawled back into his bed.

The following day was one of the best days for Yixi since he had become poorly. His condition seemed to have dramatically improved. Although I had to feed him fluid by a syringe, he ate small amounts of solid food. He even played with his toys. Then on Monday evening he became poorly. I made up my mind to have him put down the following day. Again, he seemed to read my thoughts.

He kept looking at me extremely sorrowfully as if to say, 'Please tell me what's happening to me?' I could not bear his fixed unhappy gaze on me each time I made eye contact with him. Realizing how sensible he was, I felt he was begging me to be honest with him.

Unable to bear his sorrowful gaze much longer, I knelt down by his side, hugged him and told him that he was going away to be with our two rabbits (who died). Yixi knew them both and he had often played with them, although at times I had to intervene because he terrified them by playing too roughly with them. As I called the names of the rabbits, Yixi looked around as if to see if they were there. I told him that he was a good boy and that we all loved him very much and that one day we would join him. I thanked him for his valuable contribution in enriching my life and for making me aware of God's purpose in creating everything in the universe including dogs (no matter how insignificant they may be to some people).

Within minutes of my conversation with my faithful pet, he died (late March 2000). I was devastated. I felt as though I had lost a member of my immediate family.

Some people are of the opinion that the dog was aware of the fact that I was reluctant to let the vet end his life and also, that he wanted to die in his own loving home. Whatever the explanation, I was greatly relieved that he died at home, in the presence of his loved ones.

I missed him so much that, less than a fortnight after his death, I purchased a puppy of a similar breed. My new friend is assisting me to come to terms with the loss of Yixi, but he is different in many ways.

CHAPTER 17

Nutrition

In order for the body to develop and function healthily, we require the correct balance of nutrition. To acquire nutritious food, we must eat foods that contain sufficient amounts of minerals and vitamins. Most foods are naturally or artificially adequate in nutrition, so, if a sensible dietary regimen is regularly taken, there is no need for added diet supplements. Over-use of some supplements may be harmful to the body.

There are instances, however, when the use of dietary supplements is necessary as some cannot be manufactured in the body. Disease such as iron deficiency anaemia require regular intake of iron in the form of tablets or injection in order to maintain a healthy life. In situations where there is intolerance of certain foods, it is essential to take supplements of that food. People who lead busy and stressful lifestyles may find it beneficial to take added forms of dietary supplement such as multi–vitamins; and those who are prone to frequent colds may find improvement after taking cod-liver oil or vitamin C for a period.

Some important nutrients

Vitamins A D, E and K are fat-soluble vitamins. When ingested, these are absorbed with fats from the intestine into the bloodstream and then stored into fatty tissue mainly in the liver.

Vitamins B and C are water-soluble vitamins. Apart from vitamin B12, which is stored in the liver and can last for years, only limited amounts of the remaining vitamins can be stored in the body. If greater amounts are taken than is needed by the body, as in other nutrients, the excess is excreted in the urine. Therefore a regular balanced amount of water soluble vitamins are needed to prevent shortage.

Minerals

Sources	Uses	Symptoms of Deficiency
CALCIUM. (Ca). This is the most important element in diet. The main sources are cow's milk, cheese, eggs, peas, beans, fresh vegetables and sesame seeds. Fish including salmon, sprats and sardines. Cereal grains such as wheat, oats, rice, nuts and barley are also a good source of calcium. Vitamin D, manufactured when the body is exposed to sunlight, aids the absorption of calcium.	It is essential for growth in children, strong bones and teeth (99% of bones and teeth contain calcium). The remaining 1% is needed for muscle contraction, conduction of nerve impulses to and from the brain and blood clotting.	Arthritis, eczema, nervousness, depression, muscular cramps, spasms or twitches, menstrual cramps. Calcium deficiency in children leads to tooth decay, poor bone formation (including rickets) and stunted growth. Long-standing calcium shortage increases the risk of bone related problems in old age.
CHROMIUM (Cr). Beef, chicken, liver, wholegrain cereals, pulses, mushrooms, molasses, nuts and seafood, eggs, green peppers, cornmeal.	Chromium enables insulin to control blood sugar. Chromium may also be involved in fat metabolism and in maintaining the structure of genetic materials (DNA and RNA). It also improves lifespan.	Deficiency of this mineral is said to be associated with arteriosclerosis (narrowing of the arteries), poor glucose tolerance, low blood sugar, diabetes, raised blood cholesterol, heart disease and depression.
FLUORIDE (F). Drinking water with a natural fluorine content of 1 part per million is the best way of acquiring this mineral. Other sources are seafood and seaweed.	When adequate amounts of fluoride are deposited in the enamel of children's teeth, the teeth become resistant to decay.	Deficiency leads to higher incidents of tooth decay than people whose water or diet is supplemented with fluoride.

Sources	Uses	Symptoms of Deficiency
IRON (Fe). Liver, kidney, lean beef, sardines, pilchards, lentils, dried apricots, prunes, green leafy vegetables (especially spinach), callaloo, wholemeal cereals, oatmeal and molasses.	Essential element in the formation of red blood cells, which are the agents responsible for carrying oxygen throughout the body. People generally associate anaemia with iron shortage; therefore as a prophylaxis (preventative measure) against anaemia they take iron often. This is an unwise and unsafe practice. Apart from lack of iron, anaemia can result from shortage of vitamins C, B6, B12, folic acid and zinc, and sickle cell disorder. Excessive intake of iron predisposes to a toxic condition known as Siderosis.	Poor memory, confusion, irritability, depression, tiredness, low resistance to disease, pale complexion. Iron deficiency anaemia, is believe to be the commonest form of anaemia worldwide. It results in extreme cases of deficiency. Certain foods such as rice and bread contain substances which bind iron, thereby causing it to be unabsorbable. Other causes are insufficient iron intake, or diseases associated with the stomach or the intestines.Symptoms of iron deficiency anaemia include: cracking at the corners of the mouth, sore tongue, brittle fingernails, flattening or curvature of the nails, thinning of hair and nails, eating strange things such as earth or coal.
MAGNESIUM (Mg). Egg yolk, okra, milk, shrimps, crabs, cereals, vegetables, wholegrain bread, wheatgerm, nuts and seeds, garlic, potato skin.	This is an antioxidant. The bones store the highest proportion of magnesium contained in the body. Magnesium is important for bone growth, the production of energy and muscular contraction.	Muscular weakness, prolonged diarrhoea and vomiting, stunted growth, nervousness, depression, confusion, convulsion, hallucination, inefficient nerve-muscle communication, insomnia, and restlessness. Excessive urinary loss as a result of chronic alcoholism and long continuous diuretic treatment leads to magnesium deficiency.

Sources	Uses	Symptoms of Deficiency
MANGANESE (Mn). Wholegrain foods such as bran, green leafy vegetables, okra, pineapple, grapes and strawberries.	This is a very important element in the maintenance of general health.	A wide range of diseases and health related problems result from deficiency of magnesium. Included in the list are dizziness, hypoglycaemia, infertility, miscarriages, ear problems, fits, problems involving cartilage and bones and retarded growth.
POTASSIUM (K) Fruits (especially bananas), prunes, steamed green leafy vegetables, dandelion coffee, nuts, seeds and potato, pumpkin, cabbage, molasses.	Potassium and sodium (salt) work together to maintain the balance of fluid in the body. Whilst potassium is lost from the body daily, sodium is easily stored. Daily potassium intake is therefore vital in ridding the body of excess salt, thereby assisting in the battle against hypertension (high blood pressure).	Since daily potassium is naturally lost in urine, sweat and stools, deficiency is immediately manifested. Some symptoms of shortage include feeling of exhaustion, thirst, irregular heart beat, muscle weakness. Severe depletion leads to mental confusion, abdominal swelling, polyuria (frequent urination). People who induce vomiting in order to be slim and those who frequently take laxatives are likely to become depleted in potassium.

Sources	Uses	Symptoms of Deficiency
SELENIUM (Se). Brazil nuts, seafood, seaweed, seeds, especially sesame.	Like vitamins A, C and E, manganese, zinc and copper, selenium is an antioxidant. (Antioxidants assist to prevent oxidation reactions in the body as it uses oxygen which can result in cell damage; therefore they offer protection from diseases such as heart disease and cancer.) Selenium may also be valuable in assisting male fertility. It also enhances the immune system.	Infertility, tiredness, heart related conditions such as cardiomyopathy and palpitation, male sterility, cancer associated with toxic by products of fats.
SODIUM (salt) (Na). Sea salt, vegetables, water, olives. Most of our intake of sodium chloride is included in the prepared and preserved food purchase. Examples of such food are bacon, ham, smoked fish, salted fish, kippers, cheese, bread, and canned food. This is why (apart from being a health hazard) it is unnecessary to add salt to cooking.	Along with potassium, sodium is required in minute amounts to maintain the correct balance of fluids in the body.	Deficiency of sodium is rare. This occurs in situations where there is severe loss of fluid as in extreme cases of diarrhoea, sweating (as experience in tropical countries), burns, and vomiting. Symptoms of sodium depletion include thirst, cramps and muscle weakness. Cases of excess in sodium are common. Excess can cause symptoms such as fluid retention (including swollen legs) and high blood pressure.

Sources	Uses	Symptoms of Deficiency
ZINC (Z). Shellfish including oysters, pumpkin and sunflower seeds, sweetcorn, eggs, cheese, nuts, meat, milk, milk products ginger root, split peas, green peas, wholemeal bread.	An antioxidant. Necessary for growth, development of reproductive (sexual) organs, energy, protects against disease and aids in the recovery of disease.	Congenital birth defects such as hair lip & cleft palate, diarrhoea, skin problems, alopecia, dandruff, frequent infections, delayed wound healing, impotence, infertility, white spots on fingernails, poor memory, loss of sense of smell and taste resulting in loss of appetite and loss of weight. In chronic deficiency there is stunted growth as in dwarfism and decrease in hormones secreted by the ovaries and testes.

Vitamins

VITAMIN A (Retinal) Retinal is found in milk, butter, cheese, egg yolk, liver, eel and oily fish such as herrings. Another source of Vitamin A is carotene, a substance found in dark green plants. Examples of carotene-bearing products are carrots, green leafy vegetables, squash, pumpkins, callaloo, green peas, red pepper and mangoes.	Antioxidant. Vitamin A is necessary for growth, development of teeth, the maintenance of health and protection of the skin and the mucous linings of the body especially those connected with the lungs. The body is thereby greatly aided by this vitamin to resist infection.	Retarded growth, eye problems including night blindness, low resistance to infections, acne, dry and roughened skin, bad teeth, mouth ulcers.

Sources	Uses	Symptoms of Deficiency
VITAMIN B-1 (Thiamine) Milk products, cereal, pork, liver, heart, kidney, mutton, oatmeal, yeast, green vegetables, potatoes, beef, cabbage and peanuts.	Thiamin is necessary for the release of energy from food. It is also involved in the efficient functioning of nerves, muscles and the breakdown of proteins. This vitamin is of vital importance in cases of excess use of alcohol and carbohydrates.	Symptoms of deficiency include confusion, insomnia, depression, irritability, difficulty in concentrating, lack of appetite, constipation, nerve damage, fatigue, muscle wasting and beri-beri, a disease caused by eating polished diets such as rice.
VITAMIN B-2 (Riboflavin) Green leafy vegetables, liver, kidney, Marmite, liver, yeast, cheese, milk, eggs, oily fish, crabs, peanuts and pumpkin seeds, bamboo shoots, cabbage, tomatoes.	Necessary for converting carbohydrates, fats and proteins into energy. It neutralizes acidity created during the transformation of nutrients into energy. It is also responsible for growth in children and repair of tissues of the bodily.	Stunted growth, bloodshot eyes, itchy, dull, oily hair, eczema, sore-ness and inflammation of the tongue, scaling and flaking of the skin.
VITAMIN B-3 (Niacin) Lean meat, organ meat such as liver, heart, kidney; marmite, yeast, potatoes, milk and milk products; squash and tomatoes.	Needed for burning of sugar to produce energy, a healthy gastro-intestinal tract, the proper functioning of the skin and nervous system, lowering of blood cholesterol. It also assists in getting rid of toxins from the body.	Stunted growth in children, roughened skin, sore reddened tongue, weakness, and depression. A disease known as pellagra (the disease of the 3 Ds – dermatitis, diarrhoea and dementia) may develop in extreme cases of deficiency.
VITAMIN B-5 (Pantothenic Acid) Widely distributed in foodstuff such as yeast, egg yolk, tomatoes, squash, wholewheat, cabbage, broccoli.	Necessary for the conversion of fats and protein into energy, the formation of antibodies and nerve chemicals. Also plays a vital part in the production of cortisone by the adrenal glands.	Deficiency is rare as this vitamin is found in most foods. Symptoms of deficiency include stomach problems such as nausea, vomiting and aching, burning sensation or cramp in the feet, teeth grinding, insomnia and irritability.

Sources	Uses	Symptoms of Deficiency
VITAMIN B-6 (Pyridoxine) Liver, peanuts, bananas, whole-grain cereals, fish, cabbage, potatoes, red meat, cauliflower, squash, onions, red kidney beans and peppers.	Plays a vital part in growth and health. Essential for the metabolism of proteins, amino acids, carbohydrates and fats. Produces hormones, enzymes and nerve chemicals. Helps to balance sex hormones, therefore used in PMS and the menopause.	Depression as experienced by some women on the contraceptive pill. Inflammation of nerves on the outside of the body, as in the case when Isoniazid, one of the anti-TB drugs, is taken. Other symptoms include postnatal depression, sore tongue, anaemia,, skin problems, irritability and nervousness, flaky skin.
FOLATE (FOLIC ACID) Green leafy vegatables especially spinach, callaloo, sprouts, potatoes, oranges, green beans, peas, Bovril and milk products.	Folic Acid in combination with Vitamin B–12 is vital for production of red blood cells, building proteins, improving the process of DNA and normal function of the gastrointestinal tract.	Anaemia, birth defects including spina bifida, growth retardation, insomnia, and weakness.
VITAMIN B–12 (Cyanocobalamin) Found in foods of animal extracts especially liver, milk and milk products, oysters, lamb, turkey, chicken, cheese.	Contains the mineral cobalt. It is obtained mainly from animal foodstuff. Essential for the healthy function of cells in the body.	True vegans and people with abnormalities or diseases of the gastrointestinal tract such as deficiency anaemia. Symptoms associated with B–12 deficiency include tiredness, dizziness, palpitations, frequent bouts of infection, eczema (resulting from low immunity) poor hair, gastrointestinal upset.

Sources	Uses	Symptoms of Deficiency
VITAMIN C (Ascorbic Acid) Fresh fruits such as oranges, grapefruits, limes, lemons, guavas, tangerines, green vegetables and blackcurrants It is also found in meat, milk and other fresh foods with small quantities.	Vitamin C is quickly destroyed by high temperature. Vitamin C is one of the vitamins noted for its antioxidation action on the body. This vitamin increases our resistance to diseases. This vitamin cannot be stored in the body for long periods; therefore daily intake is necessary for the maintenance of health.	Frequent colds and flu, bleeding gums, scurvy, anaemia, delayed healing of wounds, allergies, bruising, painful and swollen joints. Alcohol, cigarette smoking, the contraceptive pill and stress increase the body's need for vitamin C.
VITAMIN D This vitamin is manufactured by the body when the skin is exposed to sunlight. Sources of Vitamin D are oily fishes such as cod, sardines, kippers, herrings, pilchards, trout, salmon, and the oil produced by their liver. Milk, liver and egg yolk are also valuable sources of vitamin D.	Essential in the absorption and distribution of calcium. It is therefore of vital importance in the formation of healthy bones and teeth.	Reduction of bone growth in children, rickets (deformity of the bones in children), convulsion in infants, arthritis of the bones and the joints, osteomalacia (softening of the bones) and muscle weakness.
VITAMIN E Dark green leafy vegetables, broccoli, sweet potatoes, vegetable oils, margarine, eggs, wholegrain cereal, almonds and hazelnuts.	Antioxidant. Believed to be effective in preventing abortion and promoting fertility in some animals including rats. It is also an anti-coagulant; it is useful in healing scars. Due to its action in keeping the cells younger, it is an anti-aging agent.	Eye problems, high blood pressure, heart attack, strokes and cancer, hair loss, skin problems, fatigue, lack of sex drive.
VITAMIN K Green leafy vegetables such as spinach, cabbage, callaloo, carrots, peas, beans, liver, egg yolk, and cereals.	Essential for the formation of clotting factors in the liver. It also assists in storing glycogen, a carbo-hydrate substance found in the liver and other tissues.	Delayed clotting time resulting in prolonged bleeding, obstructive jaundice and osteoporosis.

Further reading: Food for Thought, Philip Day (Credence Publications)

CHAPTER 18

Sunlight

Hello Sunshine!

During my early years in England this informal greeting was commonly used by some white people, as a friendly gesture to their black associates.

One day I enquired the reason for that manner of greeting from a white male nursing colleague. He told me that the reason was that I, like so many other black people, always seemed to be cheerful. He assumed that our happy persona might be attributed to the fact that we were blessed with an abundance of sunlight.

Today compelling scientific data provides credence to the assumption put forward nearly three decades ago by my colleague.

There is also convincing evidence to support the claim that the dull weather can contribute to depression and other negative patterns of behaviour. According to Traditional Chinese Theorists, during yang times (including the summer months) people tend to be happier and our health is better. However during yin times (including the winter months) we become low spirited (melancholy) and we also become prone to illness including colds, influenza and bouts of depression. Several people in the West would agree with this view.

It is a noticeable fact that people from hot countries are inclined to be more cheerful than those in colder climates; this is a result of natural occurrence. The presence of sunlight on the body is physically, psychologically and therefore spiritually advantageous to everyone. When sunshine beams down on us, we immediately feel happy and uninhibited. That is why people in Britain tend to be more cheerful during the summer months.

In England, a changeable or unfriendly pattern of behaviour is often jokingly blamed on the weather; for example: 'Her mood swings like the weather.' Not only does light facilitate our vision, it is also contributory to the function of our skin and our hormonal system. When the skin, the hair and the choroid (middle coat of the eye) are exposed to sunlight, melanin, a dark pigment in the skin, thickens. The role of melanin is to protect the skin from the harmful rays of sunlight.

Direct sunlight can cause certain conditions especially those relating to the skin and eye, but these are minimal. Sunlight contains bands of ultra violet radiation. Scientists believe that two of these bands, Ultra Violet A and Ultra Violet B, can damage our skin in slightly different ways. In the short term, UVB causes sunburn, in the long term it is associated with skin cancer. The signs of this include wrinkling, sagging, dryness and blemishes.

It used to be thought that UVA was safer than UVB, but it is now believed that both can lead to the development of skin cancer. (Health Education Authority (1996), Trevelyan House, 30 Great Peter Street London).

According to the Pharmacy Healthcare Scheme in London:

'The last twenty years have seen a dramatic rise in the number of cases of skin cancer in the United Kingdom. The number of new cases has nearly doubled. We now have over 40,000 new cases each year and over 20,000 deaths each year from skin cancer. Though statistically it is the second most common form of cancer, many experts think it is probably the most common because many minor cases are not officially registered by doctors.'

Those who have the highest risk of being affected by skin cancer are people with pale freckled skin, blue eyes, and fair or red hair, who tend to burn easily.

Those at medium risk are people with darker hair and eyes, who tend to tan easily, whilst those at low risk are people with black or brown skin who according to the Pharmacy Healthcare Scheme 'virtually never burn'. This is due to *melanin*, which forms a protective barrier and the more melanin in the outer skin the better protection is given. Therefore the darker the skin, the more it is guarded against the harmful rays of the sunlight.

Caution

It is important to emphasize the danger of skin lightening products used by some black people. It is a potentially harmful practice because it alters the natural protection of the skin as it lightens it. This practice can predispose to skin disorders including cancer.

Black people originating from hot countries are born with melanin on the outer skin or epidermis; this is nature's way of providing them with protection from the harmful rays of the sun. On the other hand, white people originating from temperate countries such as Europe are born with melanin in the inner skin or dermis; this is why they are pale. It is only after exposure to sunlight that this melanin travels from within to the surface of the skin, giving white or fair skinned people a brownish appearance.

Prevention of Skin Damage from Sunlight

'A little fire keeps you warm but a large fire burns you.'
On his return from an overseas conference, a friend was informing me on the

progress of his trip. During the course of our conversation, he stated that a female member of the team used the above adage to evaluate a situation. I immediately liked the quotation. In its simplicity it could be applicable to many situations in life. For example, although sunlight is beneficial to us, too much is harmful, especially to those whose genetic make-up causes them to be susceptible to heat related skin disorders.

Those at risk of skin cancer should use a high factor sunscreen such as SPF15 or higher. It is wise to use a broad-spectrum sunscreen that would provide adequate protection from the ultra violet radiation. These can be obtained from most pharmacies and advice regarding sun screening can also be sought.

CHAPTER 19

Seasonal Affected Disorder (SAD)

This depressive disorder, which is often referred to as the 'winter blues', affects people during the winter months when there is little or no sunshine. It is estimated that about 3 per cent of people in the United Kingdom suffer from severe SAD whilst another 27 per cent suffer from milder symptoms of the disorder.

The morbidity (number of cases of disease occurring within the population) and the mortality (number of deaths from the disease) is said to be higher in Scandinavian countries such as Norway, Sweden and Denmark.

Several years ago a Norwegian nurse whom I was acquainted with told me that she intentionally visited England annually for six months during the winter months to escape the depressing weather in her country. She eventually married the North African chef who worked at the restaurant she frequented whilst she was in England.

Prior to her marriage, I jokingly asked her whether she was marrying for love, the exceptionally tasty food, which she often told me that particular chef prepared, or to seize the chance of permanently escaping *morketiden* (dismal times) in Norway during winter. She laughed as she replied, 'My decision was based on all of those factors and others.'

However although SAD is commonly linked to white people in Europe, it can also affect black residents and it has been reported that there is a gradual increase in the number of black people displaying symptoms of this disorder during the winter months. This disclosure may be due to greater awareness of the disorder. It is therefore important that this temporary, but perplexing, disorder should be highlighted.

Black people and SAD
SAD is a climatically induced condition, therefore it is understandable that black residents in cold countries are likely to be affected, even more so in some instances than white people. These people are accustomed to natural sunlight; therefore some would have a tendency to be depressed during the winter months. Again, owing to the lengthy periods of darkness experienced during the winter months, black people (like other races) are restricted from socializing; this leads to social

and psychological implications. Therefore, they find themselves in a climatically induced detention situation, which in turn leads to loneliness and depression.

Causes of SAD
'The light of the body is the eye.' (Matthew 22:7).

A well known proverb is *'The eye is the window to the soul.'* Without light, not only would we be unable to see, we would also be affected both physically and psychologically (unless we are born blind and are therefore preconditioned to darkness).

In the upper part of the mid-brain is situated a tiny reddish organ which is shaped like a cone or a pine, hence it is called the 'pineal gland'. In its description of the pineal gland, *Black's Medical Dictionary* 32nd edition states, 'A body resembling an imperfect eye is found in its position in some of the lower vertebrate animals, as in the lizard, *Hateria.'*

In natural circumstances during the evening as light fades, the pineal gland produces and releases melatonin into the blood stream; that is why we feel sleepy. As darkness progresses the amount of melatonin becomes greater, reaching its highest level at midnight when we are deeply asleep. As morning dawns the light beaming through our eyes emerges on the pineal gland and the supply of melatonin is automatically cut off. This is why we stretch, yawn and wake up as dawn heralds another day. (Although some of us would much prefer to dive for cover under the bedclothes, where we intend to stay for a few more minutes or even hours in some instances).

The tiny pine-shaped pineal gland is directly inter-connected with other endocrine organs including the pituitary glands, the most important endocrine gland in the body, situated at the base of the brain. The thyroid gland is situated at the front of the neck and the adrenal glands one on each kidney.

The function of endocrine organs or ductless glands as they are sometimes called, is to secrete hormones directly into the bloodstream whereby they are carried to different parts of the body. When melatonin is at its peak at night during sleep, it plays an active role in controlling the levels of hormones in the organs of the endocrine system. These organs in turn adjust the amount of hormones they form and distribute them into the body. Therefore melatonin is interconnected with several bodily functions including reproduction, growth and the regulation of nutrition in the body.

SAD sufferers generally lead a normal life until the onset of winter when they seem to become generally unwell. This situation lasts until spring.

The main symptoms experienced by the majority of SAD sufferers are:
Constant feelings of tiredness
Multiple aches and pains e.g. headache, stomachache and backache
Longer periods of sleep
Depression including unexplained weeping
Tendency to eat more sugar and carbohydrates
Overeating and weight gain
Other symptoms sometimes experienced by sufferers include:
Pre menstrual tension in women
Alcohol and coffee dependence
Irritability and anxiety
Phobias, especially of darkness
Feeling of desperation and hopelessness
Low libido (decreased sex drive)

Management and treatment regimen of SAD sufferers

If the condition can be reasonably managed then there would not be the need for prescribed medications, such as anti-depressants and light therapy.

- Firstly, make sure that there is adequate light in the home. Curtains should be opened during the day. If possible leave lights on continuously in areas frequently used during the day.

- Try to overcome the habit of staying away from work. It is much better to be mentally alert and to participate in physical activities than to remain at home where one is likely to become even more depressed.

- Talk to people whom you trust and who are likely to understand your problem. Explain your situation to your superior at work because they should be informed of your reason for taking time off work (if you do). They may well understand your predicament and even rearrange your work schedule to make it more manageable for you to cope.

- Eat sensibly at regular intervals. Include wholemeal carbohydrates such as pasta and rice. Take diets rich in protein such as lean meat, fish and nuts.

- Eat plenty of fresh fruits and vegetables.

- Avoid alcohol, coffee, tea, cola and pepsi, as these can contribute to depression.

Exercise for SAD sufferers:

- Take walks during the day to start your exercise regimen. If you are happy with walking, then simple cultivate this into a regular routine by increasing your pace and distance.
- Cycling is also an excellent form of exercise and relaxation.
- Jog if you feel inclined; do not let the cold weather be a hindrance. Shortly after commencing any form of exercise, there is likely to be improvement in your condition as endorphin levels increase in circulation.
- Fresh air assists the function of the body as the oxygen concentration is more abundant and purer.
- Meditate, this can clear your mind and improve the flow of positive energy in your body, therefore depression would be minimized or it would disappear.
- Get into the habit of making simple and meaningful affirmations on a regular basis; this is a good medium for self-motivation. You must make declarations that are mentally uplifting e.g. 'Today my thoughts and actions will be positive and this will contribute to the improvement of my general health.'

It has been said that people who regularly exercise seldom have the need to visit counsellors, psychologists or psychiatrists. They are so charged up with natural positive energy and endorphins that there is seldom much free space left in the mind for negative energy which can lead to ill health.

Treatment:

- Acupuncture. This branch of traditional Chinese medicine is performed by piercing the skin with very fine needles to balance the flow of the chi or vital energy of life throughout the entire body. (See chapter on acupuncture.)
- Acupressure. Finger pressure on specific acupuncture points on the body.
- Herbal treatment including Kira, 'the sunshine supplement'. This is another name for the herb Hypercium perforatum commonly known as St. John's Wort. Research has indicated that this much-used herb can help to maintain a healthy emotional balance. St John's Wort is commonally used as an anti-depressant.

- Light therapy: Light therapy is unlike the sunbed used by white people to acquire high proportions of ultra violet rays, necessary for artificial tanning. In light therapy, a specially designed box produces light for long periods. It is the duration of light that brings relief to SAD suffers, not the ultra violet rays.

Recommendation: If it is affordable, holidays should be taken to sunny countries during the winter months.

Caution! Although the mortality rate for SAD related suicide is relatively low, some suffers have mentioned that the thought sometimes occur to them. Any threat of suicide must be taken seriously. It is advisable for these patients to be seen by their doctors. It would also be helpful if we show human compassion by understanding and giving assistance whenever necessary. This would be an enormous psychological booster to the sufferer. In an ideal world no one can guarantee immunity from diseases, but, if we are supportive of those who are in need, their suffering would be substantially decreased. If we are to minimize the impact of disease, we need to offer assistance to the sick whenever necessary.

NB: There have been instances where patients complained of developing cataracts in one or both eyes after using St John's Wort in combination with light therapy or other drugs. Some medical pundits strongly question the validity of combining light therapy with a powerful natural drug.

Grace magazine, an informed and highly reliable authority on herbal medicine edited and owned by Thomas Bartram, stated in its winter 2000 edition, page 66: 'Revelation that St John's Wort reduces the pharmaceutical action of a certain drug is an indication that the body's intelligence and the immune system rise to repel the invader. It proves the drug should not have been prescribed in the first place. Some herbs have a pharmaceutical action of their very own and should not be given in combination.'

It is therefore important to consult your doctor or a medical herbalist before combining herbs with other medications or before commencing any form of herbal treatment.

CHAPTER 20

The Health Benefits of Laughter

'A merry heart doeth good like a medicine: but a broken spirit drieth the bones.'
(Proverbs 17:22).

Life is enriched for those who have mirth
A happy persona creates a pleasant atmosphere
Ugly humour is insipid and uninteresting
Generate a bright smile to illuminate your life
Humour is a natural antidote to depression
The ability to laugh is natural and healthy
Exercise your internal organs with laughter
Reminisce amusing times; this often induces happiness and spasms of laughter.

Laughter is a positive emotion; it is a form of involuntary (spontaneous) exercise, which has been scientifically proven to increase the level of endorphin within the body. Therefore due to the fact that endorphin is increased during laughter, stress is reduced and pain minimized. Humorous people are believed to be more capable of withstanding pain. This is a result of elevated endorphins.

'Laugh, and the world laughs with you'

Laughter is an instinctive behaviour that activates a mechanical reaction in the brain of those listening to its sound. This causes a spontaneous chain reaction whereby listeners also laugh.

After my arrival in the United Kingdom to pursue nursing, I was soon transformed from a jovial person to an unhappy one. However within weeks of commencing my training, I reverted back to my usual happy self by making jokes and laughing with both patients and nurses.

To my surprise, I was told that the nursing sister in charge of the ward adjacent to mine often laughed or smiled each time she heard me laughing. Within a short period we became friends.

A study on humour found that people who share the same sense of amusement are more prone to like, love and marry, because humour is indicative of values, interests, intelligence, imagination and needs (*Awake* magazine May 1994).

I firmly believe that a happy soul nurtures a healthy mind and body. 'A 1985 survey of a thousand US corporations revealed that people with a sense of humour tend to be more creative, less rigid and more willing to consider and embrace new ideas and methods.' (*Awake* magazine May 1994.) This report was not surprising to me because I have long observed that laughter in its pure form is a positive emotion.

Some other benefits of laughter are the following included in *Pink Ribbon* magazine, by Nikki Bayley, with contributions from Steve Sultanoff PhD.

'Laughter reduces serum cortical. It releases immunoglobulin A. Our tolerance to pain is increased. Heart and pulse rate increase and laughing also juggles the internal organs. Humour basically helps by replacing upsetting emotion with pleasurable ones, you can't feel depressed, scared, upset and angry and be happy at the same time.'

NB: Serum cortical is a hormone released by the body during its response to stress. Immunoglobulin A is an antibody that helps fight diseases of the gut and respiratory tract.

A simple smile is also beneficial to health. When we smile, the facial muscles become relaxed; this action sets up an automatic chain reaction, whereby other muscles of the body, including those of the internal organs, are also relaxed.

The revered King Solomon (the same deemed to be the wisest of men according to the Bible), tells us: *'There is a time to laugh and a time to cry.'* (Ecclesiastes 3:4).

Today, many people embrace the therapeutic benefits of humour and there are clinics in several countries operating as a catharsis (when people express themselves in drama or art form, thereby venting their feelings) for many psychological and emotional problems.

Negative Laughter

Even in laughter the heart is sorrowful; and the end of that mirth is heaviness. (Proverbs 14:13).

Public display of malicious or insensitive laughter at the misfortune of others is often laughter so impure one can actually scent the stench of rudeness or see the pangs of guilt in its echoes.

Why would a happy person find it appropriate to laugh maliciously at others? This is simply because some are angry and envious people who are greatly perplexed by the sheer burden of their problems, therefore they cannot bear the thought of others not suffering likewise. It is this type of behaviour that causes some to be sceptical about the benefits of laughter.

If we eat or drink too much, we vomit or we simply take some kind of remedy to alleviate the symptoms of feeling bloated. Therefore, if people are filled with negative emotions, they will seize the opportunity to rid themselves of that burdensome excess. The problem is that the only way in which some people see fit to rid themselves of their perplexities, is by being wilfully offensive to others. This is a sad reflection on humanity.

There are people who are of the opinion that laughter is not a healthy or good habit. Someone living in Victorian times is believed to have implied that 'laughter was a cruel distortion of the face that should not be practised'. It is no wonder that some of the older generation of some cultures are not too commonly predisposed to being jocular.

Laughter in its purity is unlikely to produce negative effects. In communities where mirth is common practice there is a noticeably happy medium and anxiety states are minimal. Such communities are worldwide, but unfortunately, owing to external negative influences, some of these relatively radiant communities are now changing. These changes may be attributed to the impulsive reduction of morality and poverty. If people's social and living conditions are declining, one can hardly expect them to be happy.

The reason for lack of humour may also be due to conditioning from childhood. It is therefore understandable that some people would find it difficult to abandon what has been indoctrinated in them by loving and caring parents. These people are sometimes so accustomed to a rigid persona that they are reluctant to loosen up in case they relinquish their acquired solemn appearance and therefore, their innate personality.

Abandonment of one's traditional upbringing is tantamount to rejecting one's ancestral link and one's culture, therefore to some it would incur loss of self-identification.

Misinterpretation of mirth

It must be taken into consideration that some people's tendency to be serious may be a way of guarding themselves from the unsavoury conduct of others. Those people may be cautious of demonstrating joviality because of distorted reactions by some elements of society.

There are instances when some people transform an innocent jovial discourse by individuals to sheer vulgarity. Some people can easily put the offenders in their rightful place, but others prefer to seek psychological shelter under a mask of a serious disposition.

Inherited Trait

Laughter is said to be an inherited emotion in black people. As a child, I experienced an enormous amount of humour and laughter in my small community. However some white friends of my age group have also experienced this happy medium in their small communities in the United Kingdom.

My predisposition to laugh must be attributed to natural inheritance from my mother and associating with my two godmothers, both of whom were my mother's best friends. Being indoctrinated into that 'sisterhood', my chance of escaping the laughter bug was minimal. It is no wonder that I can conjure up mirth to pacify myself at times when mental and emotional problems seem to want to get the better of me.

Laughter is a favorable formula in diluting (although not necessarily discarding) one's problems. I once told an acquaintance that I laugh at myself at times. She told me that that was a sensible formula, because if I did not, others would do it for me. She further informed me that when we laugh at ourselves, we are automatically desensitized from the impact of negative laughter from others.

I likened that scenario to training for a wrestling match, one of my favourite sports. If contenders prepare themselves, they stand the chance of avoiding getting hurt; but if they are unprepared, they are likely to receive a good thrashing from their opponents.

Despite their captivity and subsequent enslavement, the slaves are believed to have used their spare time for a little indulgence in humour to keep them in high spirits. In spite of their inhuman predicament, their spirituality, the ability to be humorous and their natural physical strength must have all greatly enhanced their chances of survival. Mirth is definitely a legacy handed down from the slaves to their descendants and they in turn inherited it from their ancestors in Africa.

However, we must be careful not to laugh at distressing events or serious issues. At times we may find ourselves laughing at what others may perceive as seriousness, but this may well be an innocent uncontrollable reaction to a serious issue.

Example: Two young women, whom I was fond of, were once engaged in a fight over a young man. At the time I was employed as an industrial nurse where the women were employed.

Soon after the incident, one of them visited me at the surgery to explain the brawl. After listening seriously to her account of the event, I told her that the fracas was a sad reflection on them both. A few hours later the other young woman involved in the altercation called to see me. She told me that someone had remarked that I was unhappy over the situation; therefore she came to relate her side of the incident to me.

I held a straight face as she spoke, but as soon as she started to describe how she chased the other woman to get a hold of her in order to give her a good thrashing, I burst into uncontrollable laughter. She was about 4 feet 10 inches tall and weighed approximated 90 pounds. Her rival was nearly 6 feet tall and weighed a hefty 170 pounds. The larger woman was very masculine in her behaviour; she even rode a Harley Davidson motorcycle.

I laughed because as the diminutive woman explained the scenario to me, I mentally conjured up a picture of a dwarf chasing a giant. The situation could not be compared to David and Goliath, because the 'giant' in question would have made mincemeat of our modern day female 'David' wannabe.

I was relieved of guilt when she joined me in laughing, although I dared not divulge the thought that prompted my giggling outburst for fear of being chased around the surgery during the early hours of the morning. At that time of daybreak, I am usually so tired that it is a struggle staying awake, let alone running away from a thrashing.

'When a man is not amused, he feels an involuntary contempt for those who are.' (Bulwer-Lyton).

It is a sad reality, but the sheer weight of psychological burden can hamper our ability to participate in lighthearted conversation, let alone laughter.

Several years ago whilst working as a staff nurse in a hospital in the south-east of England, I noticed that a middle-aged male hospital employee was always gloomy. If others in his company appeared jovial, he would demonstrate his resentment by sulking. On occasions, he would even excuse himself from their company.

One day whilst I was working in the accident and emergency department, I had to attend to the gentleman. He told me that he had slipped on the icy pavement and sprained his wrist. I noticed that he seemed to have a vast amount of knowledge pertaining to just about any subject and he spoke at great length about cricket.

He seemed to be astonished at my interest in cricket. In that particular hospital nurses from the Caribbean, especially Barbados, Guyana and Trinidad, were noted for their knowledge of cricket in those good old days of West Indies dominance in cricket. There was little other recreation for us, therefore we interested ourselves in a sport whereby we could identify with a collective team from the Caribbean and be supportive of them.

We took turns in sitting by the television in the nurses' home to prevent the other nurses from changing the channel whenever there were matches involving the West Indies.

One of the instances of my obsession with cricket was when I was nursing on a terminal ward in Mount Vernon Hospital. One day I was part of a team participating in a case conference in my unit. Case conferences involved doctors, senior nurses and other health professionals discussing patients' condition, treatment and progress. On that particular day, the West Indies and England were playing cricket and the West Indies were in a desperate situation.

I excused myself from the conference three times in the space of half an hour, supposedly to check on the patients. However, I only visited one patient whom I had a particularly friendly relationship with to ask her to watch the match on television and inform me of the score. The poor lady did not like cricket nor did she understand it, nevertheless, she gladly agreed to comply with my request by stating that it would keep her awake.

On my second visit to her room to find out the score, she gleefully announced, 'Oh nursey, I think your side is winning because the crowd was clapping and laughing loudly.' Feeling excited, I lingered on to view the replay only to realize that the excitement was the due to the fact that one of the English batsman had lambasted the ball for six runs. That ball was bowled by my side.

Unable to cope with any further frustrating misinformation, I gave her a pen and a piece of paper and told her, 'Just write down the score for me when it pops up on the screen; do not concentrate on the clapping, that could be misleading. Cricket is such a pleasant game that spectators will even clap if the pigeons defecated on the pitch.'

On my return to the conference after my third visit, Dr Dickson, the consultant in charge of the unit, smiled at me as he said, 'Well, Jacquie, how are your boys performing, what's the score now?' So engrossed was I in concentrating on cricket, that without thinking that I was not supposed to know the score, I sighed heavily and blurted out, 'Not good at all.' The good doctor told me that he thought that it was cricket that I had been dashing out so frequently to watch. Those attending the conference found the incident so amusing that there was a spontaneous outburst of laughter.

On the day that I attended to the gentleman at the Accident and Emergency Department of my hospital, England was playing Australia and the gentleman and I lamented the current onslaught on the English batsmen by the two awesome Australian fast bowlers – Dennis Lillee and Jeff Thompson (Thomo).

As we agonized at the merciless dismantling of the English wickets by the skilful Australian duo, I looked seriously at the gentleman and suggested that the umpire should keep a close check on those two bowlers because they might be cheating by tampering with the ball when he was not looking. Being a bad loser, I could not come to terms with the drastic loss of English wickets, therefore I concocted the cheating hypothesis to appease my frustration.

To my astonishment, the gentleman began laughing, which made me feel somewhat uncomfortable because I had never seen him laugh before. Perhaps it was my facial expression as I made the allegation of cheating that caused him to laugh. Within the period of one week, he visited me several times to discuss cricket and other topics.

Two weeks later, I commenced a four weeks' annual leave. On my return, I was told that the gentleman was sacked for taking too much time off work and he committed suicide. Apparently, unknown to anyone except his family, he suffered from clinical depression for a lengthy period. I was deeply saddened by that tragedy.

That sad case should be a lesson for others. We should not let ourselves be intimidated by the indifferent disposition of others. An intimidating look or a contemptuous stare, a sarcastic comment, a spinechilling silence or unbecoming laughter may well be indications of internal anguish. These negative reactions are sometimes difficult to control; they may be manifestations of psychological dysfunction.

Life would be much better for us all if those capable of helping others did so unreservedly thus aiding the anguished or unfortunate person. We can moderate our liveliness if there is unhappiness around us. However we must not completely relinquish our jovial disposition because we feel somewhat guilty about unhappy people (some of whom may have consciously contributed to their anguish). In so doing we may impede our natural personality and we too may become unhappy.

'For I mean not that other men be eased and you be burdened.' (2 Corinthians 8:13).

CHAPTER 21

Breathing and Exercise

Breathing

Breathing or respiration is the chemical breakdown of food such as glucose to release energy. During the process air is passed in and out of the lungs to allow the blood to take up oxygen and to get rid of waste products such as carbon dioxide and water. The air we breathe in is made up of approximately 21 per cent oxygen, 79 per cent nitrogen and 0.03 per cent carbon dioxide.

Respiration is a fundamental process for the survival of all living things. In humans, it is under the control of the respiratory centre situated in the medulla oblongata, which is located in the back of the brain. If we breathe incorrectly, we are likely to take in insufficient nourishment from the air.

Hyperventilation

Hyperventilation is an abnormal rapid rate of breathing during resting. One common cause for this situation is hysteria. Blood is slightly acid in reaction, but if we over breathe the blood becomes more alkaline because we are getting rid of more carbon dioxide than normal as we breathe out.

If the blood becomes too alkaline, this may lead to dizziness, fainting, profuse sweating, palpitations and a feeling of discomfort in the chest. This is a direct result of the action of the respiratory centre, which is responsible for monitoring the amount of oxygen and carbon dioxide in our body. The respiratory centre is also responsible for the action of the heart and swallowing, which is why the heart beats forcibly (palpitates) during hyperventilation.

Stress related problems are sometimes associated with faulty breathing.

Signs of symptoms that may be indicative of incorrect breathing are:

- Visible upper respiratory activity i.e. clearly noticeable movements of the throat, shoulders and upper chest.

- Holding the breath. This may also include pulling up the shoulders.

- Frequent sighing or yawning.

- Frequent swallowing or gulping. Although breathing is partly a voluntary action, the rate and depth are adjusted according to the body's demand as determined by the breathing control centre in the brain, therefore it is right to say that breathing is under both voluntary and involuntary control.

Breathing Exercises

Correct breathing technique is one of the basic contributors to health. Breathing rhythmically from the dome shaped diaphragm situated between the chest and the abdominal cavity is the secret of effective breathing. The functions of the body will be significantly enhanced if we breathe correctly. Several conditions are controlled nowadays by Breathing Therapy, whereby people are taught how to breathe correctly.

Some of the benefits of correct breathing techniques:

a) Gaseous Exchange – There should be a balance of oxygen we breathe in and carbon dioxide we breathe out. This would greatly influence:

b) General relaxation of muscles, nerve fibres, organs and blood vessels. This would promote:

c) Efficient blood circulation throughout the body.

Breathing Technique

We breathed naturally when we were infants and young children, but as we mature we develop abnormal breathing techniques.

There are an astonishing number of people who do not breathe correctly when asked to demonstrate this natural act. When some people inhale, they tend to compress their abdomen and chest. It is no wonder that at the end of breathing tests, some people are so fatigued that they gulp air and they are slightly breathless. This is not due to lung disease; it is the result of bad breathing technique.

Inspiration is similar to a balloon being filled with air. The balloon rises as it is inflated, then as the air is expelled, it recoils to its former shape. Expiration can therefore be described as elastic recoil.

The mechanism of respiration

Breathing or respiration involves inspiration, expiration and rest. The diaphragm and the intercostal muscles are the principal accessories in the process of breathing.

Inspiration – muscular effort. During rest, the dome shaped diaphragm is relaxed, then at the first stage of inspiration it contracts and becomes flatter in shape. In addition, the intercostal muscles (the muscles lying between the ribs) contract, pulling the ribs upwards. During inspiration, air passes through the nasal passage where it is warmed, moistened and freed from particles of dust. It then enters the pharynx or throat, the larynx or voicebox, the trachea or windpipe and into the lungs via the two bronchial tubes.

(*NB: Breathing in through the mouth is an improper practice, because the mouth is not anatomically constructed to prepare air for the lungs.*)

There is an increase in space within the chest cavity due to the flattening action of the diaphragm and the lifting of the rib cage. The lungs automatically expand to fill up this vacuum, thereby preventing air in the space from entering it and at the same time obtaining atmospheric air via the air passages.

Expiration– elastic recoil. During expiration, the diaphragm and external intercostal muscles relax. The rib cage drops and the diaphragm returns to its original shape. These movements decrease the space in the thorax and the lungs return to their original size. Air is then automatically squeezed out of the lungs through the air passages.

The average rate of breathing for adults is 18 times per minute. In infants and children it is faster.

Practical tips on breathing

Avoid slouching; this impedes an adequate amount of air from entering and leaving the lungs. An upright posture is important for correct breathing and it is also good for relaxation.

Start by breathing out to empty your lungs. Breathe at a constant pace and observe the rising of your abdomen as you breathe in. Fill your lungs and feel the air rising. Now hold your breath briefly and observe by looking or feeling the slightly upward expansion of the ribs and intercostal muscles.

I tend to disagree with some breathing exercises and meditation techniques where people are instructed to breathe in first before breathing out. I personally believe that it is good practice to breathe out before breathing in, thus getting rid of as much stale residual air as possible in the lungs, and creating more space for a fresh supply of oxygenated air.

How many of us would be appreciative of the idea of drinking tea made up of fresh boiling water added to a remaining quantity of stale tea each time we need a drink? Would it not be a better and a more enjoyable drink if we had a fresh cup of tea each time we required one? Likewise it is good practice to empty as much air from the lungs on effort, before breathing in, practising correct breathing technique.

Exercise

In order to exercise satisfactorily, we must cultivate the habit of breathing correctly. Any exercise undertaken correctly can be beneficial to the body. I have heard several people referring to various exercises as boring and I am truly bewildered at that attitude.

There are several exercise disciplines and some of the easily accessible ones are brisk walking, jogging, aerobics, skipping, dancing and weight training. If people are genuinely concerned about their health, they should choose a routine that they feel comfortable with and commence exercising.

One young woman whom I had successfully treated a few years ago returned to me for treatment for a problem which I believed could have been rectified by exercise (which she might not have had to pay for). She told me that the word 'exercise' instilled fear in her mind because when she was in the army she was forced to participate in too many unnecessary disciplines. She was of the opinion that most of her health problems were directly connected to the rigorous exercise regimen during her military days. I suggested to her that her problems might have resulted because she discontinued exercising.

When I initially saw her, she told me that she once had a terrifying fear of the number thirteen (triskaidekaphobia), but she said she managed to overcome that phobia to some degree with the aid of psychotherapy.

Although she is not fully cured, her condition is much improved. Instead of saying thirteen, she now says one three. I therefore suggested that she should think of, or use, the term 'keep fit' instead of 'exercise'.

Doctors are now encouraging patients to exercise instead of taking prescribed medications for early symptoms of some conditions including high blood pressure and some categories of anxiety-related problems.

Manifestation of the benefits of exercise is often observed physically but it can also be mentally, emotionally and in many ways, spiritually enhancing. Exercise can therefore promote our health holistically.

The benefit of music in aiding exercise

Let the music play, and receive its therapeutic advantages.

As stated previously, Qi is matter present in all aspects of nature. This means that it is present in our bodies, the air we breathe, sunlight and trees. Because Qi is also inorganic, it is present in elements and compounds; therefore artificial lighting such as electricity, music and many other fundamentals in life (some of which we may consider to be lesser important facets to living), are comprised of Qi.

'Without music life would be a mistake.' (Friedrich W Nietzsche).

As a fervent believer and follower of Traditional Chinese Medicine, I wholeheartedly vouch for the fact that music is an undisputable and often demonstrable component of Qi. How often have we witnessed the dynamic effects of music upon its subjects? These include:

- Miraculous recovery by comatosed patients.

- The ability to exercise for longer duration (although the endorphin principle is also involved).

- The capability to meditate more effectively, thereby reaching that point of contact with one's inner self.

- Stress or depression is replaced by calm and relaxation, thereby elevating one's levels of meaningful concentration.

Example: My husband, who is a jazz enthusiast, often played an instrumental tune by his favourite artist Miles Davis called 'Human Nature'. My second child enjoyed that music so much during her infancy that she would ask her Daddy to play it several times whilst she danced with him.

If the child was asleep whilst that music was playing, she would wake up and start dancing. At times when she cried, we would turn it on and it seemed to pacify her. When she started doing lots of homework for school, she would put that particular music and others on full blast in her room. She told us that the only way she was able to apply herself effectively to her work was by having her music on whilst studying. This modus operandi worked successfully for her.

Like a faithful friend, good music stays with us forever.

Although our daughter was between two to three years old when she first listened to Miles' 'Human Nature', I could not believe my ears as I listened to her playing Michael Jackson's vocal version of that song whilst doing her homework in January 2004, nearly twenty years later.

People who are dependent on so-called 'recreational drugs' would find that a regular exercise routine, especially accompanied by music would automatically assist in reducing drug dependency.

Manifestations of the benefits of exercise:

1. **Physical.** There will be increase in physical fitness, strength and energy. The cells and tissues of the body will be revitalized. Adults who regularly exercise are said to be as physically fit and mentally alert as younger people.

Paul Spangle, a ninety one year old American, won the men's 5,000 metres race in August 1990 at the Atlantic Congress Masters Track. (*Medical and Health – Britannica* 1991.)

2. **Mental and Emotional.** Important chemicals called endorphins are liberated from the brain when we exercise. These chemicals are our own natural morphine, hence they make us feel good and they de-stress us. If we feel happy we are less likely to worry about emotional problems. Exercise also promotes mental concentration. It has been stated that World Memory Champion Dominic O' Brian jogs four miles daily.

Recently there is concern in the UK regarding the lack of physical activities in children and I am pleased that this problem is at last attracting national concern and action. Research has shown that children who actively participate in sports have a wider mental faculty than others who are less inclined or who never participate in any form of exercise.

3. **Spiritual.** We are life forces (or spirits) functioning through the mind, which directly influences our conscious thoughts and subconscious actions. If there were physical, mental and emotional balance, not only would we have good physical, mental and emotional health, we would also experience spiritual well being. Therefore we would enjoy the benefits of holistic health.

Both physical and mental exercise promote spiritual wellbeing.

Swimming

This exercise is advantageous in keeping the body healthy. It is particularly beneficial for overweight people who must be cautious when jogging because of the risk of damaging the hips, spine and the knees as the feet make contact with hard surfaces. In swimming gravity is avoided, while muscular strength, endurance and mobility are said to be enhanced, thus the general health is boosted.

Although it is advisable for diabetics to take regular exercise, they are prone to cramps, therefore they must be aware of their limitations. A drink of bitter lemon or tonic water taken in moderation before swimming would reduce the possibility of cramp as both of these drinks contain quinine.

Important: Breaststroke is believed to exercise every muscle in the body. It is said to be particularly good for asthmatics.

Jogging

Jogging is running at a slow leisurely pace with short strides to improve the level of fitness. It is said that at a speed of over eight miles per hour, one is running, below eight miles per hour, one is jogging.

Jogging is one of the most beneficial and inexpensive forms of exercises available. It is also one of the most frequently used (including swimming) in the range of purposeful exercises; however swimming is the better of the two in the sense of accumulation of general strength.

Like many other forms of exercise, jogging can become addictive if participants do not sensibly monitor the amount of exercise they participate in sensibly. There have been reported instances when 'joggerholics' and other exercise fanatics have had to resort to medication in order to slow them down from overdoing their fitness regimen, because their gruelling workout was becoming injurious to their health.

Endorphins

The word endorphin is a combination of two Greek words translated as endogenous morphine (the morphine within us).

Jogging is a beneficial aid to slimming when combined with a good diet plan. However, we must realize that fitness is an acquired habit therefore it should be encouraged from an early age.

People who have never participated in any regular fitness regimen must have a medical examination before commencing exercise.

A word of caution!

Occasional exercise is of little benefit to the body; on the contrary it may create more harm than good. To achieve benefit, one should exercise at least three times weekly for half to one hour per session.

Precautions

1. If you are receiving medical treatment for any condition check with your doctor before commencing any exercise programme. Also be aware that some medications have a tiring effect on the body.

2. If you are suffering from epilepsy always jog in the company of others.

3. If you are severely overweight, riding a bicycle or swimming is safer than jogging.

4. Do not take stimulants such as coffee, tea, cigarettes, alcohol or hard drugs before commencing to jog as they can have an adverse reaction on the body.

5. Your pulse rate should not exceed 180 minus your age, until you become quite fit (e.g. age 30 – reach for 150 beats per minute). Learn to take your pulse.

Warning. If you experience any pain or feel unwell whilst jogging, **STOP** immediately and contact your doctor as soon as possible. Do not jog again unless your doctor gives you permission to carry on.

Some of the benefits of jogging.

1. General feeling of well being due to the release of endorphin.

2. Central nervous system – Improved concentration, mental relaxation, improved sleep.

3. Breathing becomes easier because the respiratory muscles are more relaxed.

4. Circulation becomes improved in the heart vessels and the skin.

5. Digestive problems such as acidity, constipation and peptic ulcers may improve.

6. Excretory – sweating is promoted thus the body is more capable of getting rid of waste products.

7. Weight can be reduced and controlled.

8. General strengthening – Improved stamina and toning of the body.

9. Muscles and bones – Improved muscles, bones and joints. Jogging increases the density of bones and is therefore a worthwhile exercise in the prevention of osteoporosis. Approximately five and a half million people in the UK have this disease which contrary to belief does not only affect menopausal women. It affects people of both sexes.

10. Immune enhancing – The rate and frequency of infection is lowered.

11. The general appearance is enhanced by a younger looking body.

Tips on Jogging

- Stretching is a favourable pre-exercise warm up routine; it is beneficial to bones, muscles, tendons and ligaments during exercise. Warming up before any exercise prevents physical accident and post exercise stiffness.

- Gently running on the spot for 7–10 minutes is also an important pre-exercise aid. This also gently increases the heart's demand for blood during exercise.

- Start running at a slow pace (between walking fast and running slowly); slowly increase the pace as soon as you feel confident. If you are quite satisfied with a slow pace do not feel that you have to increase it. Remember jogging is running at leisure.

- Jog for half an hour on your initial trial, then increase the time to three quarters or one hour as you become confident with your performance (if you so desire).

PART 4

CHAPTER 22

Death

Death is the conclusion of life on earth. Duality or the law of opposites has been a prominent part of nature since creation and in the same way as night follows day to complete the cycle, death is the inevitable factor for the completion of life.

Some people are uncomfortable in dealing with any aspect involving death, the phenomenon destined to end all life forces on earth.

Adverse reaction towards death is understandable to some extent. It is unreasonable to expect every one to be prepared for death with equal enthusiasm as for births and marriages, because death is not a pleasant event. It is an adversary. Death has been described as the second enemy of God (the devil being the first) and it is written, *'The last enemy that shall be destroyed is death.'* (1 Corinthians 15: 26). Meanwhile until the end of suffering and death, like brave soldiers we should armour ourselves to stave off the enemy by endeavouring to live a healthy and meaningful life.

I have experienced children speaking bravely and openly about death and although to the adult mind, children's interpretation of death may appear to be mere fantasy, their vision has spiritually enriched me to a certain degree.

One of the most indelible experiences in my nursing career involves a terminally ill child, who unfortunately witnessed the death of another child on his ward. That child narrated the whole experience to me, then to my utter surprise he told me that he was not afraid of death.

Somewhat taken aback by his statement pertaining to death, I told him that I too was not afraid of dying. Then as I caressing his curly golden blond hair, I asked him to tell me why he was not afraid of death.

Lying on his back with his feet placed high up on the wall, he flicked over and landed on the front of his body (although not as energetically as the average seven year-old would be inclined to do). Then he lifted up his head and propped it with both hands, thus appearing as if he was in great contemplation.

After a matter of seconds of what appeared to be serious contemplation far beyond the capability of a child, that little boy sat partially upright and stared me in the face, then told me that the hole in which his Grandpa had been put to rest when he died was not as big as the one in which he played in the field with his friends before he became ill. Then he sat boldly upright as if he deliberately intended to deliver a special message to me.

Staring me straight in the eyes, he told me that when he dies, he would clamber out of the hole that they put him in after he'd had enough rest.

As I pensively listened to that child's interpretation of death I was overwhelmed with admiration for his innocent bravery coupled with grief for myself at the impending loss of a dear little messenger and friend. However I was not prepared to distort that positive vision of earthly demise for my gravely ill friend. I cuddled him, then I told him that he was a very handsome, brave and clever boy.

That day as I left the ward, that simplistic contemplation of death resonated in my mind. Although it was typical of childlike innocence, yet it seemed somewhat visionary to me as though a prophet had revealed it. After retiring to the confines of my room in the nurses' home, I was overcome by grief for that adorable child. My sorrow was a natural human reaction to an impending human demise.

A few weeks later the child was transferred to a hospital which specialized in the treatment of terminal patients, and he died shortly after his admission. Although his death was inevitable, I was devastated. Although I was a young childless nurse, I felt somewhat as though I was the parent who had lost that dear adorable child.

Like me, that child was a chatterbox and as soon as we met on his initial admission to hospital, we bonded like old friends. Therefore his death had a personal effect on me.

Everyone on that ward was aware of the closeness between us and I was often requested to care for him. Even if I had been assigned to work on a later shift, my colleagues would leave his non-urgent nursing care for me to perform. This, I was told, was primarily due to his tearful insistence.

I was determined not to let the death of that child affect me in a negative way, because in his childish chatter about climbing out of the grave, I unravelled a positive side to death.

In his praise of the Lord, these words from the psalmist David were a fitting although somewhat poignant consolation for me: *'Out of the mouth of babes and sucklings hast thou ordained strength because of thy enemies that thou mightest still the enemy and the avenger.'* (Psalm 8:2).

Therefore, if in his innocence, a young child can contemplate addressing death in such a positive manner by visualizing a way of rising above it, then why should adults not be prepared to accept it with the utmost courage and dignity. They too should seek to visualize a way in which they would be triumphant in death, instead of believing negatively that it is the conqueror of mankind?

Personal observations and learning experiences

During my term in nursing, I have observed the deaths of countless patients. They could be placed in certain groups or categories.

Some who claimed to be atheists or agnostics. If one is sceptical of the existence of God, the supreme creator of all life forces, then there is every likelihood that as death approaches it may be faced with trepidation. This is simply because those individuals have no idea what lies in store for them during and after the process of dying. This does not signify that they are evil people, it is simply because they have no foresight beyond their earthly existence.

Some wealthy people. Those who are caught up in materialism may find it difficult to be spiritually prepared. It is understandable that these are some of the people who would be fearful of death, not because they are evil, but because they have not prepared for their spiritual side, the very essence of their existence.

It must not be readily assumed that all wealthy people are inclined to negative materialistic tendencies. There are several who are sincere and some are very humble people who happen to be wealthy, therefore wealth is often seen as a secondary asset to them. Some wealthy people have worked intensely to achieve their goal, therefore it is grossly unfair for others to be judgmental about them simply because they are wealthy.

The problem with wealth is that it is like an addictive drug; therefore it causes some people to be out of touch with reality. Some wealthy people seem to be psychologically conditioned into believing that money and power can bring them happiness and fulfilment, therefore they do not see the need to seek any other requisites for a meaningful life such as human compassion and spirituality.

'Then Jesus said unto his disciples, Verily I say unto you, That a rich man shall hardly enter into the kingdom of heaven. And again I say unto you, It is easier for a camel to go through the eye of a needle, than for a rich man to enter into the kingdom of God'. (Matthew 19: 23–4).

Some people with a young family.
This group of people may not necessarily be connected with the previously

mentioned groups, but fear of dying in this instance is often due to genuine parental concern regarding the future of young dependents.

No matter how religious some people may be, despite the well-meaning biblical assurance that 'God will provide', it is a natural human instinctive reaction to be concerned for the welfare of young children. Yes, God does provide for his children, but sometimes those who are in the position to deliver what God has provided for those in need, shamelessly usurp the proceeds for their own selfish ends. Therefore it is often the thought of what may or may not happen to dependents that is responsible for triggering off the anxiety mechanism in some people. It is also quite common for children to worry about leaving their parents.

As far back as I can remember I have never been fearful of natural death. (I do not believe anyone who is afraid of death would contemplate a career in nursing.)

One possible reason for my desensitized reaction to dying may be due to the numerous funerals I attended during my adolescent years. I was such a bold and inquisitive youngster that I often made my way to the front of the mourners just to be in a position to look at the deceased.

As I advanced in age, my outlook on death became more accepting. However, like several others, I would be somewhat anxious about the welfare of my children if they were of a young age at the time of my demise.

Nonetheless, despite my attitude towards death, I would not be prepared to succumb to an axe-wielding lunatic. Neither would I refuse meaningful medical intervention if it was necessary to improve the quality of my health. Also being of sound mind I would not be prepared to terminate my life, because I believe this act is contra-indicative of God's gift of life to me. However it has been assumed that in several instances of suicide the victims were not of a sound mind, therefore sympathy must be extended to those unfortunate victims and their relations.

The following reasons may also be contributory to my disposition towards death:

Spiritual. My personal relationship with God. A relationship that may not necessarily be exact in biblical meaning of a follower of the teachings of Christ, but it is unique to my interpretation of Godliness; therefore it is appropriate for my expression of spiritual fortitude.

Familial. I have been greatly influenced by positive conditioning by my parents and older relations. Some of those responsible for nurturing me and giving me love and affection have experienced death. Why then should I be afraid to undergo that phenomenon?

To my way of thinking, whether death is a good or a bad encounter, I should not be afraid to share the experience of Christ, my beloved family (including both my parents) and my friends when it is my turn. Traditionally some black people believe in the afterlife, and if there is truely an 'afterlife', the thought of being reunited spiritually with those loving wonderful people dilates my soul with joy.

Professional. Since my involvement in nursing I have developed a profession-induced attitude towards the acceptance of death. I have observed the deaths of patients of various ages and although witnessing man's transition from life to death has proved distressing for me, that experience has spiritually fortified me. I hasten to add that although I have witnessed the death of several different nationalities, the impact has always been the same for me in the sense that each death appears to be a personal loss. In my mind and my physical vision, 'death' has no colour. I perceived every death the same, another brother or sister's departure from earth.

The poet Donne wrote: *'Any man's death diminishes me, because I am involved in Mankinde.'* That statement is a truism for those who are devoted to caring for the sick.

From early childhood, I desperately wanted to be a nurse, purely for the sake of caring for the sick and the suffering. I am of the opinion that there is no other occupation that would have given me such immense professional and personal satisfaction.

Like several other health professionals and carers, I feel an immense sense of responsibility for my patients. Although we often experience the gamut of human emotions through our involvement with birth, sickness, recovery, relapse and death, we are privileged to be involved in a vocation which focuses on the health and welfare of humanity.

The saved / the dammed! It is due to the fact that I have repeatedly observed the process of dying that I can state that it is erroneous for some people to speculate the fate of others simply by observing pre-death behaviour. There are those who are of the opinion that anyone who does not have a so-called peaceful death must be evil and is therefore being punished by God before they die. This abstract concept is so ingrained in some cultures that they are devoid of logical reasoning. Since childhood I have listened to this ridiculous contention and surprisingly, this mythical concept continues even to this present day.

There are a number of factors that are responsible for pre-death behaviour; some include the physical and psychological affects of illness on the body, medication, and temperature. If a seriously ill person suddenly tries to remove his/her clothing or suddenly begins to pick at the bedclothes, this may be an indication that the person may be feeling hot even if the body feels cool on the surface. It may also be an indication that the patient is lacking in nutrition such as magnesium. It certainly is not an indication of pre-death penitence or punishment as believed by some people. Anyone, be he or she a righteous priest or a heartless convict, can be similarly affected by the symptomology of disease.

Case 1

When I was a student nurse during the late 60s in Gloucestershire, which is located in the west of England, my very first assignment after my nursing induction was on a chronic medical ward. One of the patients was a retired senior clergyman who appeared to be well liked and respected by his fellow ministers and parishioners alike. He was a model patient who got on well with the other patients and nursing staff. If we were poorly staffed, the kind minister would assist with minor duties such as distributing meals and even feeding the patients who were incapable of helping themselves.

The clergyman's condition slowly deteriorated and it did not respond to his usual treatment therefore he was prescribed stronger medication. He soon became critically ill and to our horror that pleasant, placid, gentleman of the cloth was transformed into a confused and obnoxious person.

Never before had I observed a senior swearing to that extent, let alone a minister of religion. However, the staff noticed that he did not swear at anyone in particular. He would direct his aggression to objects such as the wall, his room, his meals or even his bedclothes. Nonetheless we were all very upset to witness the repulsive change in that pleasant minister. He died shortly without regaining his original personality.

The minister's change in behaviour may have been due to either of the following reasons:

Firstly, although meant in good faith to improve his condition, the introduction of strong painkilling drugs may have proved too much for him.

Secondly, the disease may have infiltrated his brain, thereby causing uncontrollable irrational behaviour.

Case 2

I recall nursing a senior gentleman in a hospital in Berkshire. He was of a very quiet and shy disposition and he also appeared to be somewhat sad. He was a widower and he never seemed to have received any visitors. Although he must have experienced some degree of pain, he never complained, therefore he was given a limited amount of pain control medication. One evening as I commenced night shift, I was told that he had become critically ill and I was assigned to care for him during the night.

As I approached his bed, he seemed a bit fidgety, so I sat by his bedside, held his hand and then I whispered to him, 'Do not be afraid, Alfi, I'm here with you.' Acknowledging my presence by smiling at me, he proceeded to tap me gently on my hands. He later settled and appeared to fall asleep.

About one hour later he sat up and began smiling at something at the foot of his bed. Then suddenly he extended both his arms forward as if he were reaching out to greet an invisible person whom he was acquainted with. Then to my amazement, he laughed out loud and then gently settled down in his bed.

As I leant over him to straighten his sheet, I noticed that he was dead, but surprisingly he had the most amazing smile on his face. I could hardly believe what I had witnessed.

Reflection on the two examples. Can we really speculate on which of those two men mentioned was 'saved' or which one died a 'sinner'? I doubt it. They both seemed to be good people, but the situations at the end of their lives were different.

'For as the body without the spirit is dead, so faith without works is dead also.' (James 2: 26). Spirituality is the most important factor in life and it is the passport to our transition from life to death. I am of the opinion that although the physical body may experience excruciating pain, or the mind may appear irrational thus reacting in bizarre patterns of behaviour, the spirit remains intact.

Respect for the dying

We must respect the instructions of those who are dying. Some of those wishes may seem somewhat strange to us, nonetheless, we must abide by the terms implied, even if we make slight reasonable adjustments to the conditions. However, we must endeavour to ensure that the main requests are fulfilled.

'With all the scientific progress and new techniques in medicine, it is essential always to remember that patients are people.' (A General Textbook of Nursing by Evelyn Pearce).

It is imperative that the dying maintain their dignity to the very end. We must realize that although people may be dying, they are still someone's loved one and they are a unit of the family of mankind. We are therefore obligated to treat them with utter respect and dignity. We must make them feel loved by caring for them adequately, by being understanding of their needs and having consideration for their situation.

We must demonstrate fellow-feeling for the dying. This is not a difficult task. We simply need to visualize ourselves in their position, then think of how we would like to be treated. I am sure that most of us would not be appreciative of people inconsiderately blabbering volumes of nonsense at our bedside when we are trying to focus on another dimension that is far above earthly trivialities.

Some people's thoughtless remarks distract and also upset the dying. People should realize that during the process of dying the senses of sight, smell, touch and taste may be absent, but the sense of hearing for those who are not deaf is often present to the very end. Therefore, when we visit the dying, let us bid them farewell with words and actions that are likely to make their journey less cumbersome. Do not engage in negative chatter that is likely to place an added burden on them, thereby impeding that final journey.

The search for immortality

There are an alarming number of people in the West who it has been assumed have paid large sums of money to be partially or completely frozen after their death.

Through this science known as cryonics or suspended animation, these people believe that sometime in the future they can be brought back to life on earth. Some have included loved ones such as husbands, wives, children and even pets into the bargain.

The estimated cost in the late 90s for this extraordinary scientific mimicry of the miraculous resurrection of Lazarus from the dead, is a staggering £80,000 for the whole body and £40,000 for the head as reported in *The Mirror* on 27 November 1998.

Some of the people who are prepared to purchase immortality are quoted as having stated that they are afraid of dying, whilst others expressed their wishes 'to continue living life to the fullest'. If cryonics becomes a medical revolution, it is obvious that the wealthy would be the privileged immortals on earth. However, there are many who would be petrified at the mere thought of man having the power to recreate life. The mind boggles at the very suggestion.

Lazarus had the full work free of charge, because as with all of his works, Jesus proved that he was no pretender – *HE WAS THE MESSIAH.*

Fate after death

There are several conjectures regarding the fate of man after death. A popular Western insinuation is that those who die without embracing Christianity are doomed. Note that I have not mentioned the teachings of Christ, because some people tend to sail in their personally invented ship of Christianity, which seems to be constructed without a compass (symbolic of the teachings of Christ). How then can that vessel be capable of navigating its passengers to their expected destination?

The term Christian was invented in Antioch, Syria to describe the Apostle Paul and other followers of the teachings of Christ.

During the mid-eighties, I was involved in a discussion regarding this topic in question, with a senior Christian friend. My friend, who was an ex- British Army sergeant, appeared to be of the opinion that he was always right, therefore I found myself engaged in an awesome verbal battle, which I was prepared to thrash out.

He read aloud from his Bible: 'Thomas saith unto him, Lord, we know not whether though goest; and how can we know the way? John 14:5.' Then he hit the Bible with the full force of his right fist as he read slowly and deliberately aloud:

'JESUS SAITH UNTO HIM, I AM THE WAY, THE TRUTH AND THE LIFE; NO MAN COMETH UNTO THE FATHER, BUT BY ME. John 14:6.'

Staring at me, he emphatically repeated, 'No man cometh unto the father but by me.' Then looking at me in a way I perceived to be somewhat menacing, he said, 'That means no one can guarantee a place in heaven, unless he or she embraces Christianity.'

After overcoming the initial shock of him pounding on the Bible, I exhaled, then took a long deep breath. Then breathing out slowly, I composed myself for a counterattack.

I retorted, 'You are partially correct, but you, like so many people, read the Bible without applying rational commonsense.' I told my friend that Christ told his disciples to preach his doctrine so that those who received it would follow it. It was those to whom the new gospel was preached whom Jesus was referring to in John 14:6.

Like so many Christians who continuously proclaim that they are the legitimate heirs to God's kingdom, my friend was not prepared to compromise his belief, neither was I prepared to relinquish commonsense in the evaluation of that sensitive issue. Despite the fact that I am usually respectful of seniors and would not set out to offend them, I was determined not to give in to his trend of thought, even if it meant upsetting him.

I felt that he was somewhat displeased that a mere 5 feet (and a bit) much younger female dared to stand her ground, although straining her neck up to face him, a tall and stalwart man, on that sensitive debate.

We thrashed it out in a controlled manner for what seemed like eternity. At the end of our religious dispute, with his right index finger gesticulating in my face as if it were suddenly seized by a bout of uncontrollable convulsion, my friend warned me to be careful of my religious views in case I ended up a lost soul. Then he walked off looking somewhat flustered.

That day I felt that I was going to be confronted by a prejudicial judgment jury after my death. With my head tossed high in the air, in total defiance of that unjust fate and sulking like a spoilt child, I prematurely made my way home.

After trying all of one's life to walk on the straight and narrow path that leads to Heaven (at times against the odds), it is no fun to be suddenly confronted with the thought that one is destined for the fiery pits of Hell. How can one be expected to be accepting of so cruel a fate, when even a simple spark of electricity is a petrifying experience for one?

After relating the religious altercation to my husband, I felt 'saved' when he agreed with my rationalization of the disagreement. Perhaps my relief may have resulted from the fact that I felt reassured at the thought that if I were to be flung into hideous Hell after my death, the outcome would not be too unbearable for me. Because as I sizzle like a fowl in Hell's wicked everlasting fire, I would be fortunate in having the human love of my life as my accomplice in punishment for the act of religious sedition.

Rationale: If Christianity had not been preached to certain people who practised their own religion, why would a just God punish them? That would be tantamount to children in some schools with technological advantage being equally examined with those attending underprivileged schools with no such aids. When these two sets of children are tested collectively, would it be fair to pass the privileged children simply because of their scientific approach to the test, whilst failing the disadvantaged children despite the fact that some may have performed outstandingly with the aid of old-fashioned facilities?

Technology is an important advancement in the history of mankind, but there are many who have never had the privilege of accessing it; nonetheless, some are as knowledgeable as, or much more clever than those who use modern devices such as calculators and computers.

It is therefore wrong (according to my reasoning) for any particular religious group to assume that they are on course to meet God, whilst others of different religions, primeval people and those who are not religious but are morally decent, are doomed. What gives anyone the right to believe that they alone are God's chosen?

Nowadays we are focusing on the concept of diversity strategies, which offer a direct challenge to several intolerances including race and religion. The aim of diverse guidelines is to evaluate difference as equal, not as inferior. Therefore if we are to embrace the language of mixture we must rid our minds of the age-old negative attitude towards those who do not look and behave like us, but whose sole intention, similar to ours, is to live a decent life.

Lest we forget, Germany's Adolf Hitler and Italy's Benito Mussolini, two of the most sinister fascist European dictators the world has ever known, were both Christians. Even if those two departed leaders sought God's pardon and were granted it before their death, their human rights record is far from what is expected of Christians.

Some non Christians may well have a stronger foothold in heaven than some of us professing to be Christians – the so-called 'enlightened ones' – because unlike us, some primeval (ancient) people have strict religious laws and moral codes. Problems such as greed, rape, murder, worldly obsessions and corruption are minimal within their loving, caring and non-materialistic communities.

Salvation is an individual achievement; we are not automatically entitled to it simply by taking cover under the shelter of a specific religious order. We have to make conscious spiritual and moral efforts in order to achieve it.

'For not the hearers of the law are just before God, but the doers of the law shall be justified. For when the gentiles, who have not the law, do by nature the things contained in the law, these, not having the law are a law unto themselves: Which shew the work of the law written in their hearts, their conscience also bearing witness, and their thoughts the meanwhile accusing or else excusing one another.' (Romans 2: 13–15).

Final thought on death: *'We have nothing to fear, but fear itself.'* (Roosevelt). From the moment of birth we are scheduled for an appointment with death and just as we prepare for any important assignment we must be spiritually prepared for death. As we have experienced with exams and important meetings, preparation is the key factor to any satisfactory performance in life.

Consolation: Those who are fearful of death may find comfort in the words of Jesus immediately before his death:

Let not your heart be troubled: ye that believe in God, believe also in me. In my Father's house are many mansions: if it were not so, I would have told you. I go to prepare a place for you. And if I go to prepare a place for you, I will come again, and receive you unto myself; that where I am, there you may be also. (John 14, 1–3).

Those were the words of a man who knew that he was about to experience an awful death and yet he thoughtfully reassured his disciples about the positive side of his departure. That event is symbolic of a caring father leaving home to prepare the way for better living conditions for his family. As the family becomes distressed, the father consoles them by stating that he will return to take them all to the beautiful and better home which he was going to prepare for the family.

The following inspirational song by Watts can assist to appease the fear of dying:

> There is a land of pure delight
> Where saints immortal reign
> Infinite day excludes the night
> And pleasures banish pain.
>
> But timorous mortals start and shrink
> To cross that narrow sea
> And linger shivering on the brink
> And fear to launch away.
>
> O! Could we make our doubts remove
> Those gloomy doubts that rise
> And see the Canaan that we love
> With unbeclouded eyes!
>
> Could we but climb where Moses stood
> And view the landscape o'er
> Nor Jordan's stream, nor death's cold flood
> Should fright us from the shore.

CHAPTER 23

Final summarization

Initiate Health

Despite increasing health consciousness, no one is guaranteed perfect health throughout the entirety of life. However, although there are several contributory factors to disease, if we are attentive to our health, we stand the chance of avoiding or delaying the onset of serious life threatening conditions. This would consequently lead to a reasonably satisfactory quality of life.

By identifying the causes of disease we can personally address our health, thus avoiding unnecessary medical consultation and preventing simple treatable conditions from advancing to chronic and life threatening disorders.

When we help ourselves by addressing our health needs (when possible), doctors have more time to attend to patients who are more deserving of medical attention. With reduction of workload, doctors would also be less likely to suffer from insurmountable levels of stress, so commonplace lately within their profession. Doctors are much-overworked people; so if we are to get adequate attention from them, we must genuinely have compassion and consideration for them.

Euan, a friend of my husband, told us of a very disturbing occurrence when he was employed as cook in a London hospital. It concerned a hungry surgeon who had been operating on a difficult case for hours.

The tired doctor rushed into the hospital's restaurant just before the kitchen staff was about to leave. After stating his reason for being late and offering his apology, he asked whether he could at least be given a simple meal as he was late for the main course. Euan immediately agreed to prepare a light meal for him. However as he was already engaged in other business he asked his female assistant to prepare a salad for the doctor.

Euan told us that the assistant sulked and told him that her shift had ended so she was not going to stay on to prepare the requested meal. Euan was shocked and incensed at her reaction, but he immediately abandoned his chore and quickly prepared the meal.

Words fail me in my evaluation of that woman's reaction. It was very difficult for me to comprehend the motive for her attitude. Whatever the reason for that reaction, I was displeased by her insensitive behaviour.

Why is it that some people's interest and consideration lie within the boundary of satisfaction for themselves or their circle. There are situations in which we must all have feelings and compassion for one another because collectively we are the family of man?

Several years ago, when I worked in the operating theatre at Frenchey hospital in Bristol, there was a very serious case. A young man was stabbed and the knife penetrated deeply into his chest. The black handle of the knife was standing tautly very close above his left breast, which was covered in blood, and there was no sign of the blade.

The consultant surgeon, who was usually a cheerful and pleasant man, tentatively operated on that patient. There was heavy perspiration on his tense face, which was constantly being wiped away by the senior nurses in the team. Although he often engaged in light conversation during surgery the only talking he did during those crucial hours was to request the surgical instruments he required as he performed that lifesaving operation.

How can it possibly be justifiable for anyone to deny such a man a morsel of food (incidentally, which he had to pay for)? How can anyone reconcile themselves to the fact that those who battle to save lives (and in some instances, owing to insurmountable stress of trying to save others, jeopardize their own health) are denied human compassion or recognition for their effort?

Self-help guide in maintaining health

Diagnosis
We know our body better than anyone else because it is our personal property. The body is our spiritual abode; therefore at times even with the slightest manifestation of physical signs and symptom of malfunction, we intuitively know that we are unwell. We are therefore the first to be aware of an impending illness.

Just as a child immediately informs its parent of a particular discomfort, the body often sends out early signals to us when sickness is developing. We must not accelerate our illness by ignoring that information.

Procrastination
Humans are renowned for postponing attending to personal health issues. Some of us would sooner be involved with assisting others with their problems, whilst we are reluctant in helping ourselves. If we are not well, how can we effectively

take on the position of helpers, carers or healers of others? We may worsen our health or we may not be in a position to help others to the best of our ability. We must first help ourselves before others could benefit from our assistance.

Analysis of some symptoms

a) If there is stomach ache after eating a particular meal, it may well be that one of the causes of the problem is the result of an irritant which may have affected the system.

b) If normally active and healthy people suddenly find that they can no longer cope with routine activities without being breathless or they experience occasional backache after gaining weight, this is an obvious indication that the additional weight is causing extra strain on the body.

c) If there is adverse reaction such as depression, unexplained headaches, nervous tension, muscular spasms, a feeling of anger or resentment after someone or a particular event is either seen or made mention of, these symptoms may be indicative of psychosomatic reaction to unpleasant memories.

Addressing the problems:

a) Simply avoid eating any ingredient contained in the food until the cause of the stomach ache is identified. When you become aware of the ingredient responsible for your problem, avoid eating all foods containing it in the future. If it is difficult to isolate the cause of the problem, then a general exclusion of that particular meal should minimize the chances of any future occurrence of the stomach ache.

b) Decrease your activities to lessen the strain on the body. Also try to reduce the weight by following a sensibly diet regimen. After losing the required amount of weight, slowly return to routine activities. Do not be disheartened if you find it difficult to lose weight, simply explore other healthy options such as exercise; this is also favourable in increasing the lung capacity, thereby addressing the breathlessness. If a less rigorous and comfortable routine is frequently practised it generally leads to fitness and weight reduction.

c) *'You can close your eyes to reality but not to memories.'* (Lec).

Memories are our mental diaries. They are recorded events stored in the mind or written down for the purpose of recollection.

Some memories are quite pleasant whilst others are hideous. However they are our personal memorabilia, and in order to get on with our lives we must be prepared to cope with them. I fail to agree with those who claim that one should forgive and forget. We are gifted with memory for a specific purpose. They can serve as a learning experience and a protective device from harmful situations in the future.

If we bash our feet against a stone, do we leap in agony, dismiss the occurrence and then later nonchalantly walk along that particular area without looking out for the offending object? Common sense compels us to make a mental note of the incident, so that we can be vigilant for obstacles whenever we are in that particular vicinity.

Should we be forced to leave the confines of our homes and venture out into treacherous weather, do we not dress and equip ourselves appropriately? Similarly, we should try to be mentally prepared to deal with unpleasant memories because they are part of life.

Some people's memories of past events are so painful that it is not unusual to hear them angrily state: 'I hate him/her' or 'I will never forgive that person until I die.' I have often questioned that concept of reasoning, leading to the build-up of such negative destructive energy.

Although people may be reluctant to forgive, they should not be consumed in bitterness. The past has already occurred and when we hold on to it bitterly, we forfeit the compensatory rewards for our suffering. We must bear in mind that there is no gain without pain.

Why compound one's psychological torment by harbouring hate or resentment? Why not seek a formula for dealing with the hurt in order to establish peace of mind?

One way of finding inner strength to forgive is through meditation. Find a quiet moment then set about to banish the incident. The mind is a dynamic repair kit and if we use it positively, we may ease our pain, even if we cannot banish it completely.

'Vengeance is mine saith the Lord.'

It would also be consoling for the aggrieved to note that God is a just observer. He comforts the sufferers; He chastises the wilful sinners; however, He also pardons the repentant ones. Therefore it is all right to leave judgment to Him. Nonetheless, He has imparted wisdom to humans to identify and address wrongful deeds; therefore we can use that privilege whenever it is justifiable.

It is unreasonable to expect some people to easily forgive others for wrongful acts which they have been unjustly subjected to endure.

If someone wickedly covets another's belonging, then benefits from that dishonest deed whilst the legitimate owner becomes impoverished because of losing that property, how can the dispossessed person be expected to readily forgive? The fact that some people are not prepared to forgive does not necessarily mean that they are bad or vengeful. However, it is unhealthy to live with that magnitude of hurt without finding means of coping with it.

It is a reasonable assumption that we should emulate the example of Jesus in forgiving others for the wrong they have committed against us. However, it must be borne in mind that although some of us may strive to conduct our lives in a devout manner, we cannot equal the ability of the Son of God in forgiving because we are only mortals.

No one has the right to force the doctrine of forgiveness upon a victim. Each individual should be left alone to deal with injury as best as he/she possibly can before imparting absolution to the perpetrator. If we pardon as soon as we are requested, then we may falsely forge the process of forgiveness. This action may result in undermining the natural mechanism of emotional healing. Our action may also be a licence to our offenders to hurt us again, because they may believe that they would be forgiven each time.

This scenario is similar to a child misbehaving. When the child becomes aware that it is likely to be punished because of its behaviour, it becomes distressed and consequently it is let off or even given a cuddle in some instances. That child may well continue to behave inappropriately, because it is aware that it is likely to receive an embrace instead of punishment for its maladjusted behaviour. It is also extremely likely that the child may grow up behaving inappropriately, because it was not given the opportunity to correct its improper behaviour.

Forgiveness should be appropriate to the characteristics of the individual and the degree of the injury.

The practical approach to health related problems

It is understandable that some people choose to seek medical intervention as a first-line solution to health related problems. However swallowing a prescribed pill is not always the best possible manner in which the body should be encouraged to cope with all problems.

Remember that one of the primary actions of medications used in emotional conditions is to suppress symptoms for an unspecified time. They cannot banish the problem automatically, neither can they mentally condition one to deal with that problem. If used indiscriminately, these drugs may later also cause additional problems to the body.

The very pill given to someone for his or her constant weeping, which is symptomatic of depression, may also be the same one given to the next person who walks into the doctor's surgery complaining of nervous tension probably brought on through guilt and remorse, because he or she was responsible for causing the depressed person's problem in the first place.

Here we are faced with two different faces of illness. One may be representative of the victim, someone with an emotionally weak personality who is open to abuse. Then there is the perpetrator, someone with a dominant characteristic who is an abuser or a bully. Does it seem reasonable that the same drug should be used to address the psychological symptoms of both these cases? Each case needs to be assessed and treated individually.

Final Thought

At their conference in 1978, the World Health Organization agreed that 'health is not simply freedom from disease', but that it is 'a state of complete physical, mental, and social well-being.' However, it is imperative that we must also strive to attain spiritual well being, the most important factor of our being, yet so often ignored, if we are to achieve a reasonable state of sustainable holistic health.

If we do not take the basic food requirements we are likely to be deprived of nutrition; we may then over-eat and yet still feel hungry. We are also likely to become ill. We need a diet which includes a varied collection of the appropriate nourishment to enable us to function effectively.

We need to access a variety of essential factors that would be generally benefiting and enriching to us if we are to function reasonably well. This is the formula for health and contentment. If we are devoid of this fundamental recipe in holism, then we are liable to be deprived of a meaningful life on earth.

THE NEW MILLENNIUM – A TIME TO MOVE FORWARD

Let us all be prepared to inspect every aspect of our lives with positive vision as we enter this new millennium. Like the parable of the five wise virgins filling their lamps with oil in preparation for the arrival of the bridegroom (Matthew 25:1–12), we too must be positively prepared to attend to important issues in life.

Mankind is speculating diverse changes in the world during this period.

Some of these changes appear somewhat optimistic whilst others are dismally pessimistic. Like numerous people, I too would like to envisage a hopeful future for humanity. My favourite singer, the late great Otis Redding, vocalized:

'It's been too hard living. Oh man! And I'm afraid to die
I don't know what's up there beyond the clouds
It's been a long, long time còming, but I know, but I know,
Change is gadda come; Oh yes it is.'

The outlook on life in the world today forecasts a shadow of doubt on any imminent expectation of hopeful changes. According to biblical forecast as recorded in Revelation, we are destined to encounter worse times than we are presently experiencing. Nonetheless, if we strive to attain mental clarity, spiritual fortitude and physical conditioning, we will be armoured for the impact of ensuing times.

We must acknowledge and abide in the fact that despite race, skin colour, religious beliefs or financial status, **'God hath made of one blood all nations of men.'** (Acts 17:26). Therefore, since God created all people the same, it is reasonable to believe that we all fall into one important fundamental and equitable category: **the human race**. If we acknowledge and abide in this reality, we will be inclined to diffuse further symptoms of impractical categorization and segregation of humankind. We should be able to work together to make the world a universally enhancing habitation, in which **health** plays a prominent role in the happiness and well being of each of earth's inhabitants.

We must recognize the fact, that health and self-awareness are two of the foremost ingredients of successful living. This duo are the precursor to other components of life in the world today. In reality, without this fundamental partnership, nothing else can be realistically meaningful to our earthly existence, not even the popularly acclaimed monetary wealth.

An optimistic outlook for this Millennium.

1. And there shall come forth a rod out of the stem of Jesse, and a branch shall grow out of his roots:

2. And the spirit of the Lord shall rest upon him, the spirit of wisdom and understanding, the spirit of knowledge and the fear of the Lord;

6. The wolf also shall dwell with the lamb, and the leopard shall lie down with the kid; and the calf and the young lion and the fatling together; and a little child shall lead them.

12. And he shall set up an ensign for the nations, and shall assemble the

outcasts of Israel, and gather the dispersed of Judah from the four corners of the earth.

13. The envy also of Ephraim shall depart, and the adversaries of Judah shall be cut off: Ephraim shall not envy Judah, and Judah shall not vex Ephraim. *(Isaiah chapter 11).*

References

Atherton, Dr Peter, *The Essential Aloe Vera* [Ch. 7]

Auden, W.H. & Kronenbergen, Louis, *The Faber Book of Aphorisms* [Ch. 15]

Awake (Watch Tower Bible & Tract Society) [Ch. 1]

Black's Medical Dictionary (A&C Black Limited London) [Ch. 1]

Brent Sickle Cell & Thalassaemia Counselling Centre, London [Ch. 2]

Britannica Micropaedia (Encyclopaedia Britannica 1998), Vol.7 [Ch. 1 ,15]

Clarke, Peter, *Hope and Glory: Britain 1900–1990* (Penguin Books 1997) [Ch. 6, 13]

Concise Medical Dictionary (Oxford) [Ch. 7]

Daily Mail, 2003 [Ch. 15]

Davidson *Principles & Practice of Medicine* (Churchill Livingstone 1984) [Ch. 1]

Day, Phillip, *Food For Thought* (Credence Publications) [Ch. 17]

Dixon, *The Truth about AIDS* [Ch. 1]

Farden, Dorothy Blake, *Message to the White Man and Woman in America*
    (United Brothers and United Sisters, Communication Systems 1991) [Ch. 14]

Grace magazine [Ch. 18]

Hayes, Nicky, *Foundation of Psychology* [Ch. 9, 12]

Holy Bible, The, King James Version (Nelson 1976)

Hornsey-Pennell, Paul, *Aloe Vera The Natural Healer* (Wordsmith Pub. Co 1995),
    [Ch. 7]

James, Andy, *The Conscious I* (Somerville House Publishing 1992) [Ch. 8]

Jayasuriya, Anton, *Clinical Acupuncture* (9th edition. Chandrakanthi Press)
    [Ch. 4]

Kaptchuk, Ted, *Chinese Medicine - The Web that has no Weaver* (Rider 1985)
    [Ch. 6]

Lupus UK [Ch. 2]

Luton on Sunday [Ch. 1 & 12]

McLeave, Hugh, *The Damned Die Hard* (Saxon 1973) [Ch. 11]

Mandus, *Relaxit and Get Fit* (N. Fowler + Co Ltd 1982) [Ch. 8]

Medical and Health Britannica (1991) [Ch. 1]

Mirror Newspaper, [Ch. 15, 22]

New Nation Newspaper 2000, [Ch. 14]

Original African Heritage Bible, The (James C. Winston Publishing Co. 1997)

Pearce, Evelyn, *A General Textbook of Nursing* [Ch. 22]

Pink Ribbon (Breast cancer awareness magazine, 1999) [Ch. 19]

Porter, Prof. Roy, *The Cambridge Illustrated History of Medicine* (Cambridge

University Press 1998) [Ch. 4]

Radford, John & Govier, Ernest, *A Textbook of Psychology* (Sheldon Press 1986) [Ch. 12]

Rogers, A., *World's Great Men of Colour* (Macmillan 1972) [Ch. 14]

Sunday Mirror [Ch. 12]

Voice, The [Ch. 9, 14]

Thomas, *The French Foreign Legion* [Ch. 11]

Wallace, Daniel J., MD, *The Lupus Book* (Oxford University Press 2000) [Ch. 2]

Useful Contacts

Brent Sickle Cell Association
112 High Street
Harlesden
London NW10 4SP
Phone: 02089619005

Diabetes UK
10 Parkway
London NW1 7AA
Phone: 02074241000

Lupus UK
St James House
Eastern Road
Romford
Phone: 01708731251

For information on HIV/AIDS, contact
Terrence Higgins Trust
52 Grays Inn Road
London WC1X 8JU
Help line: 084512212000

The World Healing Crusade
476 Lytham Road
Blackpool FY4 1JF
Phone: 01253343701

About the Author

Jacqueline Wendy Blackett (nee Halley) was born in Guyana. She resided in Perth, Mahaicony, located on the East Coast of Demerara until she left Guyana to pursue nursing at Standish Hospital, Gloucestershire, England in 1969.

She was educated at Mahaicony Church of Scotland School in Demerara and Victoria High School in New Amsterdam Berbice, Guyana.

She successfully studied various branches of nursing, including Registered General Nursing (previously known as SRN) at Wexham Park Hospital in Slough, Berkshire and was employed at several hospitals in England.

She also pursued a career in Acupuncture and gained a Diploma at the Academy of Traditional Chinese Medicine in London in the 1980s. Shortly after qualifying as a practitioner in acupuncture, the author was so enraptured with this form of natural therapy that she was determined to expand her knowledge. She commenced her postgraduate studies at The Open University for Complementary Medicine in Sri Lanka, host to students from 170 countries in the world and subsequently qualified for the International Certificate in Acupuncture gaining first class honours. This result was recorded as the second highest in the history of the university at the time of achievement (during the 1980s). The university was established in 1962.

So impressive was her performance that she was encouraged by members of staff at the university to pursue a PhD, which she successfully completed in 1989.

She previously worked as an associate member of staff for Bedfordshire Health Promotion Agency. She is an assistant researcher in Black and Minority Ethnic Housing Needs at De Montfort University, Bedford.

In 1993, she was voted Health Professional of the year at the Luton Caribbean Heritage Award Ceremony. Mrs Blackett also worked part time as a visiting lecturer in Adult Education, teaching Acupressure at Lea Manor Community College and she is currently employed at South Luton Community College, Bedfordshire, England since 1992. In 2003 she was a national winner of the Citizens Action Millennium Award for her well structured project on health education for several groups within her local community.

Mrs Blackett is an acupuncture practitioner in Luton, Bedfordshire. She has been happily married to Victor for 25 years and the mother of one son and two daughters. She is also the owner of Trixi the dog.

In 2006 she was appointed weekly health columnist for the Voice newspaper in London.

Index